MEEGOOK

Jeanhee Kang

Meegook

Dry Bones

A True Story

At Sea of Galilee on April 27, 2017 Photo by Richard Wise

Jesus said to me,
"Why aren't you going to church?"
"Me?"
"No way…"
"You must not know of my dark past."
November, 1982

Dedication

God – *Hananim*

Acknowledgments

Oprah Winfrey

Mississippi Girlfriends

DeColores - Emmaus Walk #154

PineLake Church

Title: Meegook
Subtitle: Dry Bones

Table Of Contents

Glossary

Algo (Sigh...similar mean to...'Oh my god')
Babo (Stupid)
Banchan (Various side dishes for Korean meal)
Boogo (Funeral announcement)
Bulggogi (Korean style beef dish)
Chalga (Good bye- sister)
Chosang (Ancestor)
Choggi (Striped bass fish)
Chonmal (Really)
Chopche (Clear potato noodles with mix vegetables)
Ekku (One eye)
Emo (Aunt)
Goggitang (Beef soup)
Hananim (God)
Keewha (Clay roof)
Kef halack (How are you to Arabic man)
Kef hatick (How are you to Arabic woman)
Kimchi (Fermented Korean cabbage)
Meegook (Asians call America, Beautiful Country)
Makuly (Made from fermented wheat or rice or milky)
Mudang (Shaman Priest)
Mychutsyu (Crazy)
Myungtae (Pollack fish)
Na do dyteggo ga (Take me with you)
Na Mottssalyu (I don't want to live)
Nepalzza (My unfair life)
Nettal (My daughter)
Nyu Mychutyu (You crazy)
Ozingyu (Squid)
Sanbok (Off white funeral clothes)
Sanchae (Relish salad)
Tulbo (Hairy man)
Ummuni (Mother)
Wonbulkyo (Syncretic Buddhism)
Yi Man-won (Equivalent to $20.00 in the 70s)

Chapter 1

Purpose

I KNEW EARLY ON NOBODY was coming to rescue me out of starvation. I was born to be an extra laborer. From the time I could walk, I followed my mama into the fields, planting black beans, soybeans, corn, peas, potatoes, Napa cabbage, millet, barley, and radishes. I placed rice plants in the paddies while midnight-black leeches sucked the life blood from my thin little legs. We didn't waste even the smallest parcel of our land and grew crops on any space that would allow planting. We cherished each tiny sprout and curling vine as a promise of a future in which we might finally fill our empty bellies.

Our family was better off than other families in 180 Dochi-burak, Sinyong-dong, Ikan-gu, Jeollabuk-do, South Korea. We had a bigger rice paddy than they did. Mama always reminded us how lucky we were to have land after the Japanese lost the war to the American GIs.

"The only reason the Japanese didn't take our land is because it was too heavy to carry back with them," she told us.

Many people struggle an entire lifetime to find purpose, but I found mine when I was only five years old. As I stood mired in a muddy rice paddy with my legs covered in blood-sucking leeches, I looked up and saw a gorgeous house atop a faraway hill.

I wanted to be in that house, far above the mud and heat. Mama explained to me that the house belonged to the Dam Keeper. He controlled the water gates for the rice farmers and received a big salary from the government. He lived in that beautiful house built in the woods with real windows, and he wore clean clothes. The best part was that he never had to work in the muddy rice paddies and be chased by leeches.

"Why not?" I asked. "And why does he get to live in that beautiful house with real windows?"

"Because he got an education from a high school in the city to get that job," my mama said without stopping her planting. The moment I learned those new words, *high school,* I heard my hope knocking on my head to live for another day.

The giant mountain outcroppings looming beyond the village of Dochi-burak dwarfed me. As I stared up at the huge hunk of granite carved like the shape of a gigantic man's face looking up to the heavenly sky, I was certain it was the face of God, even though I did not know Him yet. Only He would have a hand large enough to shape a mountain to His likeness. I'm not sure if I fully realized what my thoughts meant, but I do believe that was *Hananim*, which means God in Korean. I asked God as if He could hear me, "God, please help me to run away. God! I am so hungry."

From that day on, I had a purpose. I was determined to get out of a life I hated, no matter the cost.

The year was 1962.

Chapter 2

Hunger and a Gap-Toothed Grandmother

AS A CHILD CATCHING SHRIMP in the river next to the rice paddies, I would pray, "God, I'm so hungry. Just this once, let me catch enough to fill my hungry belly."

Dochi-burak was poor—with the kind of poverty that causes eyes to sink into their sockets. I often daydreamed about my next meal, a mixture of barley, beans, small clumps of white rice, and watered-down meatless soybean soup. Those were the lucky days. On unlucky days, my siblings and I ate nothing but flour dumplings with kimchi, a fermented vegetable dish. We rarely had meat and *never* had enough food to go around, especially for me, the eldest. Only on our birthdays did my siblings and I get to eat a bowl filled with steamy white rice and watered-down chicken soup laced with seaweed.

This yummy treat was the only reason to look forward to living for another year. Mama would chase to catch the slowest chicken and wring its neck. Its legs would continue to thrash about, even after she chopped off its head. She'd dunk the kicking bird into boiling water, pull it back out, and then dunk it once more before plucking the feathers from its pocked skin. Her fingers were so calloused that the hot water didn't burn her. With a butcher knife sharpened on a river rock, she'd slice the dead bird wide open, splitting the breast in half. She'd find the liver and kidney still steaming inside the rib cage, slice them out, rinse away the blood, and dip the organs in rocky sea salt. I'd open my mouth like a baby bird waiting for her to drop the liver first and then the kidney as a reward for helping her while my siblings watched.

While my mother cooked, my siblings and I rubbed our stomachs and paced, asking when the food would be ready. If she was having a bad day, she'd shoo us outside. On good days, she'd give us a pinch of rice to quiet us down. After what felt like hours, she would garnish the chicken soup with seaweed, the savory aroma causing our mouths to water and bellies to grumble. We would devour it in seconds, all the while wishing our birthdays came more than once a year. One chicken for seven of us, by the time we finished, there was no evidence a chicken was ever there.

When fruit was in season, I was the first out of bed to see if any tasty surprises had fallen off the trees. I'd trek to the river to search for wild berries, raw corns and raw potatoes. I was like a honey badger in the wild. I would eat anything that didn't eat me. I would catch rats, birds, grass hoppers, silkworms and toss them into an open fire pit until they were chargrilled. Half the time, I didn't know what it was that I was eating. As a result, I spent many hours doubled over with stomach aches. If my mother found out, she'd grind special leaves into a potion, her famous cure-all remedy. I tried not to let her see my discomfort. I preferred having the stomach aches over the gloppy green goo. If she had known the cause of my belly aches, she would have yelled at me. I couldn't bear to tell her about my constant hunger when she only allowed herself to eat after we were fed.

One late afternoon the river water was low, and I went fishing for shrimp with my grandmother and offered up my usual prayer, asking God for hills of rice, chickens stacked as high as my house, kimchi and seaweed,

ripe fruit, and thick meaty soup. Swaying young rice shoots rippled in a sea of green that stretched to the horizon. The seven matchbox houses that made up our village shrank beneath God's stern brow. Beneath the blue sky, our tiny village sat in quiet beauty. Even so, to me it was a prison. I wanted to see what lay beyond the mountain. How I desperately longed to venture into the world beyond God's face...

Mireuk Mountain top shaped like God's face - Photo by my brother in 2012

We hadn't been fishing long when Mama called out, "Jeanhee, ya!"

The time had come for me to go home and scrub the floor. I never minded the other chores—tending the rice paddies, hauling water from my neighbor's well, feeding the pigs, chickens, and my sweet *Yellow Dog*—but I hated scrubbing that floor with a deep and unyielding resentment. The floor was dirt, and dirt would never become clean, no matter how hard I scrubbed. I was furious. I wanted to spend the afternoon with my grandmother. Her stories transported me beyond to the dazzling adventures of her youth. The hours I spent by her side passed quickly.

But I was an obedient daughter and did what my mother asked, gritting my teeth as angry tears rolled down my face. I scoured the large cast iron cooking pot and the smaller black pans that surrounded it, silently cursing my heavily pregnant mother for making me spend my time on such useless tasks. Though I could not see Him from inside the small room, I pictured my God's face looking down upon me, taking note of my misery.

While I scrubbed the floor that day, my father and cousin went down to the riverbank to chop wood in preparation for the coming winter. Only a few minutes passed before they came through the door with grim faces, this time laden down with a large bundle they had not carried when they left. What I had assumed was stacked wood soon took on a more familiar shape.

They had returned with the cold, lifeless body of my grandmother.

Her clothes were waterlogged and ripped, her face, pruned and gray. They brought her in through the sliding, rice-paper door and laid her on the floor in front of me. She had drowned shortly after my mother had called me home to scrub the floor.

As I looked at her gaping mouth, a quiet fire surged through my body. Had I been with my grandma, I could have saved her. I had been robbed of her gap-toothed smile. Her warm, scarred hands would never again smooth my tangled hair.

My mother had made me leave her for a dirt floor.

Korean funerals were lavish affairs. We sent rice paper invitations to all my relatives and busied our hands with preparations for the funeral. The busy-work was a welcomed distraction. Outside of our muddy house, we set up tents in case of rain. Neighbors brought envelopes of cash to help pay for the funeral, and our usually-empty kitchen was suddenly filled with delicacies I'd never heard of, much less tasted. Mountains of fluffy, white rice and pig's-blood-stuffed sausages rose up from lacquered plates. Next to them were sculpted rice cakes, rows of colorful popped rice, pears, apples, chestnuts, steamed spinach, bean sprouts, salted sesame-seed leaves, sting ray salad, various grilled choggi, dried myungtae, ozingyu, chopche, ssangchae, kimchi, grilled pork chops, and bulggogi.

My father used chopsticks to symbolically feed my grandmother before she departed for the afterlife. The food had been prepared soft, without too much salt or spice, as the dead do not like hot peppers. Jugs of makuly, a poor man's wheat wine, filled the prayer table. The head of a pig, slaughtered in my grandmother's honor, looked down upon the feast. We poured wine into a goblet for my dear grandmother in case she got thirsty and burned incense day and night in her honor.

The Buddhist funeral, a celebration of the transformation of death, lasted for two days and nights. Cries of *algo*, or pain, often filled the air. Men gambled while the women and children ate and gossiped. When the time came to lay my grandmother to rest, my mother washed her with a clean rag and dressed her in pristine white clothes. My father placed pennies in her mouth and upon both eyes to pay for her passage to the afterlife. His hands trembled as he touched his mother for the last time. That was the first time I'd seen him express any emotion other than anger.

Eight pallbearers carried my grandmother in a Korean-style hearse, decorated with white paper flowers. They marched her from the house, through the rippling paddies, all the way to the ancestors' mountain, located in another village. My siblings and I followed, singing funeral songs in rhythm with the director's ringing bells. I got to wear fresh, clean clothes for the funeral. Even though they were *Sangbok,* made for the family of the dead, I enjoyed the feeling of new clothes. The thin, off-white poplin felt soft against my arms and belly. Each woman and girl related to my grandmother pinned a white bow to her head, which was to be worn for a year. The bow told others of our loss and reminded our neighbors to be glad that they did not suffer as we did.

My mother and three aunts cried, "*Napalzzaya*! Our mothers are dead and gone! *Umunni, Na Do dyutggoga*!"

I never knew people could cry like that.

Even my mother, who had never gotten along with my grandmother, cried all the way to Burial Mountain. Her hair, usually tightly bound, flowed down her shoulders and back as an expression of mourning.

After they placed my grandmother into the ground, the men pressed damp earth over her coffin in the shape of a round moon. They seeded grass in the loose dirt and left behind burning incense, sliced fruit, and a cup of white wine to hold my hungry grandmother over until our next visit. As we left, our songs drifted up the mountain to the place where the ancestors lived.

We prayed they would love her as we did.

From the time of her death, my family prayed to my grandmother every Thanksgiving and on New Year's Day. We would set up an elaborate display of fruits, rice cakes, wine, meat, and fish dishes that were unaffordable any other day of the year. After my grandmother and other ancestors had enjoyed their first helpings of food, we would bow twice, circle a cup of wine two times over each stick of incense, and pray for our ancestors to give us peace and prosperity. Then we ate.

All year long, I dreamed of this meal.

My mother dreaded the holidays. Since my grandmother's death, my mama had been burdened with deep, inconsolable guilt that stemmed from her animosity toward her mother-in-law. My grandmother had blamed my father's absence from our home upon my mother's failure as a wife. Her sudden death made it impossible for my mother to reconcile with her, and she grew increasingly certain that Grandmother would come back to haunt her, cursing her with illness, sudden death, a lost limb, or ungrateful children.

Three years passed before my mother was able to save enough money to hire a *Mudang* for the *Goot Ritual*. The *Mudan* and her assistant, *a Mudang-in-training* came to our home with bamboo sticks, bundles of bamboo branches, two large swords, two sets of extra ritual costumes, and a large metal *Jing* to drum. The *Mudang* inspected both rooms of our house, then asked my mother for my grandmother's clothes and a lock of her hair.

For two days and two nights, the *Mudang* chanted, drummed the *Jing*, and mumbled nonsensical words, petitioning for the passage to open so Grandmother could cross over into the afterlife. No one, including our neighbors, could sleep with all the drum banging, but no one complained for fear of a backlash from the spirit world.

My siblings and I were bleary with exhaustion when the witch finally stiffened, threw back her head, and stretched her claw-like fingers toward the ceiling.

"Be ready. She's coming," the *Mudang* warned.

We stepped back, our eyes wide. My brother Junghee, my parents' firstborn son and the carrier of the bloodline, turned pale. He was my grandmother's favorite and was too young to fully understand what was happening. He was afraid, and so was I.

"One of you must be the medium for her to speak through," the *Mudang* commanded in a husky voice.

Our neighbor stepped forward and gripped the bamboo.

"Let her spirit enter your body," the witch crowed.

Within minutes, my neighbor started to shake. Her black eyes rolled back and she jerked about, nearly knocking the bowl off my grandmother's altar. After a few moments, her body calmed, and my grandmother's reedy voice rang through our small house.

"I am here," she said.

My mama looked as if she wanted to run, but she stood her ground and let the Mudang speak.

"Your daughter-in-law did not mean to let you down," the witch said in a soothing tone, in an attempt to appease my grandmother. "She was nine months pregnant and had grown tired. She needed Jeanhee's help. Your daughter-in-law has given you two grandsons, and now she has called you back to make peace. Let her rest easy in her life here on earth. Let her have peace. Will you please forgive your son's wife?"

As the *Mudang* spoke, the neighbor, filled with my grandmother's spirit, stroked my mama with one of the swords, running it over her arms and legs and around her stomach and neck. Mama remained stiff, and the knife never once nicked her skin.

"Please, honored ancestor," the *Mudang* said. "It's time for you to make peace. Drop the blade and your bitterness along with it. Give your daughter-in-law peace."

The *Mudang* continued her pleas, her face drawn tight with the effort.

After nearly an hour of the ritual, my grandmother—still in the body of our neighbor—finally dropped the sword.

"Let us have peace," she agreed as she left the medium's body. Our neighbor crumpled to the floor, drained and confused.

"What happened?" she asked, wiping her brow.

The *Mudang* packed her tools and trudged out the door without explanation. Inside the house, the air felt fresh and clean. Still, my mother was unhappy. Though she rested easier knowing revenge no longer lurked around the corner, her shoulders would bow beneath the invisible yoke of guilt for the rest of her life.

Something about that did not seem right to me. I was only a child, but I sensed a void within her and ached with the knowledge that I could not fill it.

Chapter 3

Rice Paddy Prison

OUR VILLAGE WAS AN ENDLESS paddy of forgotten dreams. Only twice a year did somebody on a horse or cow-drawn wagon roll through my isolated village of twenty-five people to collect our recent harvest. But as quickly as they arrived, they would disappear again, taking our crops to sell at far away market. Trucks and buses sped by, leaving only clouds of dust.

The bus never stopped in our village—no one could afford the fare. Our only regular visitors were bicycle vendors who peddled through town, pulling small carts filled with goods, stopping often to ask if anyone had any extra eggs or dogs. If we had eggs, mama sold all of it but one, always saving one for my father.

Every once in a while, when I was feeling brave, I would take an egg and hide it for days until I got a chance to run away to the next village, where my father's sister lived. In her town was a small candy store where I'd trade my egg for a piece of candy and steal a moment to enjoy the exhilarating rush of sugar. I would stay with my aunt as long as I could until my cousin ran me off or my mama showed up. She would yell at me all the way home for pulling her away from her work.

My workload grew as I got older. The oldest of five kids, I helped raise my siblings, drew water from the neighbor's well, and fed the chickens, pigs, dogs, and rabbits that we raised as meat to sell to rich people. By the time I was seven, my hands and feet were as calloused and cracked as any grown man's.

I knew that when I grew up that I did not want my mama's life of hunger, patched ill-fitting clothes, and endless farm work. The last thing I wanted was a posse of dirty kids to tie me down. Afraid I would hurt my mama's already broken spirit, I kept these dreams to myself, fantasizing about a future in which I'd wear silk clothing and live in a big, beautiful house with real windows like Dam Keeper's. A maid would pick up after me and deliver big bowls of steaming white rice to the table three times a day.

My father was rarely with us, except during harvest season. Often times he would go into the city and disappear for days, never letting mama know where he went. When the dreaded *thunk* of his bicycle would hit the side of the house telling us he was home, I would draw my brothers and sisters together for protection.

He'd burst into the house, his voice slurred, and his face red.

"Get them out," he'd scold my mother, ordering her to drag us into the freezing winter air and line us up in our thin nightclothes and bare feet on icy snow. Then with a branch from a nearby tree, he'd beat our backs, legs, and bottoms until welts rose and blood beaded through our clothing. I always positioned my body so that my drunken father would aim for the center of my buttocks, rather than my bony joints where no fat cushioned his whip. The searing pain would climax until it overwhelmed my mind and I dreamed only of killing the trees that had produced my father's weapons.

My little sisters and brother would stumble in fear, and I would quickly pull them back in line, holding them up so they wouldn't get a worse beating. The easier it was for him to beat us, the more quickly he would tire and pass out. When he finally slumped to the ground, I would pull my siblings back into the house. We would hide underneath the blankets in our room, and they would tuck themselves beneath my arms.

"Put your hands over your ears," I whispered as I pulled the covers over their heads.

I didn't want them to hear our mother cry when our father decided to punish *her*. She would yell at him to hit her instead of us.

"I brought them into this miserable life. Hit me!" she would yell. "Kill me dead. I never asked for this life. I don't want to live anymore."

Their arguments would last for hours.

"I never wanted a woman like you," my father would scream. "Ugly and useless. Look at you! Why should I come home to dirty kids and a dirty wife? Why should I take care of you?"

"I must've done something terrible in my past life to deserve you, drinking your life away and giving our money to whores," my mother would cry. "Algoya! You can live without me, but not without them. One day you'll come home, and I'll be gone. Then who will raise your children? Your whores?"

Her pleas and accusations echoed across the rice paddies. My brothers and sisters, exhausted from fear, would fall asleep, but not me. As the oldest child, I felt a duty to feel my mama's pain and take it as my own. I didn't understand this demonic presence that seemed to inhabit my father. I thought his anger, directed at my siblings and me, must be our fault. On nights like that, I felt guilty for being alive. The blissful release of sleep eluded me.

At breakfast, my father would be sober and quiet. He'd nod without meeting our eyes, his neatly combed black hair bobbing on his head. My bruised mother served him with an egg while the rest of us wished that one day we, too, could have an egg with barley mixed with beans.

My father scanned the newspaper and drank hot rice water. When he finished, he puffed a cigarette and stared into the vegetable garden outside, his calm demeanor no more than a thin veil hiding the true darkness beneath.

I don't remember exactly when I began to hate my father. But I know now that my relationship with him shaped the early direction of my life. Because of him. I swore to myself, "*I will not get married.*" And "*I will not have children.*"

My siblings and I didn't have many places of refuge, but the nearby river became our escape during the warm season. We would wade into the water once a day to bathe. When the little ones got too far from my reach, I'd dart after them, pulling them from the currents and back onto shore. After we swam, I'd pull the leeches off their bodies as gently as I could. They never complained. The small black creatures were a tiny price to pay for the freedom of the river.

Whenever my mother's cry of "Jeanhee, ya!" echoed impatiently over the paddies, I would sink as far as I could, holding my nose while snakes swam through the current above me. Only when the dam was open, releasing a torrent of water, could I truly drown out my mother's call.

In early spring, while my cousins and I were crossing the bridge, I looked down to see if the dam had been opened. Thirty feet below, the river was nearly dry—leaving nothing but marshy grassland. I stood at the edge of the bridge for a moment, a faint breeze rippling through my hair. It felt so good, so perfect. Before I knew it. I had stepped off. For a moment I was a bird, the wind rushing past my face, no ground beneath my feet, a moment without my mother or my father or the farm, a moment of complete freedom.

My feet hit the ground first. I remember crushing pain, and then pulling myself into a fetal position to offset the agony in my legs, back, and feet.

"Jeanhee is dead!" my cousins screamed as they rushed down the bank.

For a moment, I thought I *had* died, but I could still hear them in the distance. One of my cousins said, "Not yet, she ain't."

They knew I hadn't fallen… that I had jumped.

"We are in so much trouble with *Emo* because of you!" they scolded. They picked up my limp body and carried me to Mama, taking turns carrying me on their backs.

I didn't cry. I wanted to, but my body couldn't handle the effort. I was racked with pain and feared my spine had been broken. For several days, I was forced to lie flat on my back. Though I was in pain, I savored the break from my chores.

During this time my mother nursed me back to health, checking on me night and day, feeding me delicious apples and trying to force Chinese Dragon Medicine down my throat. She didn't' have to tell me how much she loved me. I felt it through her soft voice and tender touch, which carried me for the rest of my life.

No one ever asked me why I jumped off the bridge, and I never bothered to explain. The chasm in my heart was too wide.

One of three remaining bridges next to dam keeper's house

As soon as my back was healed, I was back to my daily chores. I was responsible for our water tank to be filled. I hauled water from the neighbor's well, I would overfill my two water buckets so I could cut down on the number of agonizing trips, especially during the freezing winter. With two buckets on a wooden beam on my shoulder, I had to master a balancing act down uneven icy steps to keep from sliding twenty feet to the frozen river below. Any misstep meant that I and both water buckets would slide down that twenty-foot drop and I would have crawl back on an icy hill to draw water from the well to refill my buckets and start all over again. Mama scorned me for taking so long to bring the water, I forgot to tell her of my ordeal on icy uneven steps. Instead, I took out my frustration on my siblings, by telling them there was a water bug underneath water tank in hopes they won't drink so much water.

My burdens grew as my father's presence at home dwindled. Even though I was a girl, because I was the oldest, I had to take on his job of planting the rice paddies. Villagers took turns planting each others fields. We would line up across the field and hold poles attached to each other by string. Planting rice required perfectly synchronized teamwork, and one mistake could throw off the entire row.

The pole holders were the leaders. When the pole leader yelled *uyah*, it meant that both pole holders would pull up their poles, while two *uyah-uyha* signaled that the planters should gather handfuls of rice shoots and plant them, then back to one *uyah* yell then two yell, repeat, until entire plots of paddy are planted

By the end of the day, I would find my legs covered in leeches. The small ones were easy to pull it off, but there was always one jumbo leech that required more than two fingers. I would slide a machete between the pulsating slug and my leg, careful to avoid slicing my already bleeding flesh. I hated those slimy monsters, and for their punishment, I would leave them on the dead grass to shrivel and die. The big leeches would often leave behind bloody craters as proof they had once been a part of me.

Snakes lived there as well. I hated those snakes. I'd jump over their slithering bodies and work around them, careful to avoid the poisonous types with triangular heads. Some of the braver villagers captured those poisonous snakes to sell to rich people as home remedies.

As I was finishing up my fights against leeches and snakes, the Dam Keeper went by on his fancy bicycle in his fine clothes with real shoes looking down at me where I stood in the muddy rice paddy as if he was flaunting his untouchable life to me. I raised my face and gazed upon the Dam Keeper's beautiful home on the hill, and I had a surging urge to find out his secret for success. His job was to guard the dam and release water to flood the rice fields. He never had to work in the fields like me.

It was the only house with a telephone, and it was rumored that his family ate steamed white rice and toasted seaweed for every meal. I needed to know his secrets, to look into his house and understand that there was something beyond the meager life I knew.

Next day, I couldn't wait to witness Dam Keeper's life with my own eyes. I wiped the blood from my legs, smoothed my tangled hair with my fingers, and picked my way through the paddies toward his house. I hadn't had a bath in months and hoped he wouldn't notice. I knocked on the heavy wooden door and waited for him to answer. Within moments he stood before me in his pressed pants and buttoned down shirt.

"Mister," I said, "I came to see what a telephone looks like, please."

I'd chosen to visit him at lunchtime in hopes that he would be generous enough to give me a bowl of steamy white rice.

He lifted his left eyebrow and pointed down the hallway.

"There it is," he said, indicating a shiny black box that hung on the wall. I'd never seen a telephone before and had trouble comprehending that it would allow him to communicate with people miles away. I waited for it to ring and stared in awe as he picked up the receiver and talked to an invisible colleague. I couldn't believe how quietly he spoke. I had been sure he'd need to yell to be heard from such a distance. He must have learned to use that strange machine in high school.

I watched while his family ate lunch, my eyes trained on their chopsticks, piled high with white rice and toasted seaweed. Eventually, his wife saw me staring and nudged her husband.

"Here. This is what you wanted, isn't it?" He handed me a bite of seaweed-wrapped steamy white rice and shooed me out the door. "Go on home, now."

I bowed and ran off, cramming the wrap into my mouth the second I sped through the gate. The seaweed and rice tasted like heaven. I tried to chew slowly, to savor the flavor. To this day, the taste of sea salt and toasted sesame oil still lingers on my lips.

On the way back home, my little brain was ticking overtime. I had no idea what kids did in *high school*, but I wanted what Dam Keeper had as my own when I grew up. I burst through the door of our little mud house and asked my mama to send me to school.

She responded with a look of pity. "You're only five years old. No one goes to school at five, especially girls. Wait until you're seven or even eight. They won't take you now. Besides, I need you here."

"Mama," I cried. "I want to go now. I want to go to *high school*, Mama."

"No." My mother refused to hear me. "Hush. Get out there and finish your chores."

As I walked to the neighbor's well to draw water for our dinner, I thought about how I never wanted to plant rice or pry leeches from my legs again. I had good food in my belly, and I wanted more. I stared at the God's face as if He could see me.

I asked God's face. "Please, God, help me to run away?"

Chapter 4

Teη Mile Walk

ON MARCH 1, 1963, SIX days after my sixth birthday, my mother finally agreed to walk me ten miles to *high school*. My heart nearly beat out of my chest from the excitement. Mama gave me a warm water bath in a large clay tub outside. The winter snow hadn't melted away yet, so I jumped in quickly. Mama scrubbed my face, body and hair with an expensive soap. Then she quickly dried me with my father's old t-shirt as my teeth chattered. She used a fine wooden comb in an attempt to remove lice from my long, tangled hair. I put on clean underwear and brushed my teeth using rock salt and my index finger, being extra careful not to miss the red freckles of pepper flakes from kimchi. Mama dressed me in my newest sweater, an American GI family's hand-me-down that my uncle had sent to me from Kunsan City.

The air was chilly that morning even though the sun shone down brightly, its vibrant rays full of promise. For the first time since I was born, I was venturing out of our village. I gripped Mama's hand tightly. She took long, fast steps, and although I always lagged behind, she never slowed. I walked as quickly as I could without complaint. If she had asked me to fly that day, I would have.

"Can you study like the other kids?" she asked me.

"Yes! Mama, I can do it! I can do it, Mama!" I was so worried she might change her mind on our way to high school.

The road we followed was unpaved, dusty, and filled with small stones that skittered beneath my feet. Despite my excitement, I tried to remember every landmark we passed— the twisted tree in the chicken yard, the boulder shaped like a horse's hoof, the old barn with its thatched roof half caved in, and the tilled farmland waiting for warmer weather to plant. I knew my mother wouldn't be waiting after school to walk me home.

The homes we passed looked better than the ones in our little village. The sun glinted off the brightly colored metal of their roofs, and some of the nicer houses even had glass windows. A few homes had tall metal gates, telling me they belonged to the few lucky rich families who did everything they could to keep poor visitors like me away from their doors.

The homes grew even nicer as we neared the Wonbulkyo area, with no rice paddies in sight. To the right, sat the Wonbulkyo temple and the small homes with cement roofs that housed its members, and to the left hunkered Wonkwang University, where three-story buildings with glass windows rose from behind thick stucco walls patrolled by uniformed security guards. Tall, draping trees stretched across the campus. The scholars inside had fair, beautiful skin, not tanned and swarthy like my own, and they read books on benches outside the campus while they waited for the bus.

Beyond Wonbulkyo was the town of Sin-dong, with general stores on every corner. Although none of the stores were open so early in the morning, the grocers were already out arranging their wares, and a lone dog skulked along the side of one building. I passed a town registry office, a police station, a butcher shop with dark green walls, an empty beauty shop with black-and-white photos of the newest hairstyles, and a pharmacy. Compared to Sinyong-dong, this was a thriving city.

As we passed ceramic barrels filled with fermenting wheat, my mama informed me that the Makuly Brewery was owned by distant cousins I'd never met.

"They're very rich," she said. "And they never run out of food."

At the edge of town, the red-clay road wove between the general store and a candy shop. Next to a small fruit farm sat Bukil Elementary School, where I would start my education. No mansion would ever look as beautiful to me as that school building did at that moment.

When we reached the school, I glanced down at my thin chest, sure my fluttering heart was visible through the fabric. I clutched my new possessions tightly, marveling at the pristine blank notebooks and sharp pencils Mama had managed to buy for me. So enamored was I with the school grounds, that I barely noticed when she left my side to fill out paperwork in the teacher's office.

The school just had one floor, shaped like an L, with a large dirt meeting ground in the center where the Korean flag waved. At one end sat an office for the teachers, and at the other was a small room where they took turns sleeping at night to ward off potential robbers. The classrooms were identical—six in total, one for each grade——and all were spare and austere, with windows on each side and a stove in the center. A shiny silver pipe rose from each stove and ran along the ceiling to release smoke into the sky. Dark wooden desks with cubbyholes for books lined the classroom walls, and bells chimed to mark the hours, study breaks, lunch, and release. From the moment I set foot inside the building, I determined that I would not miss a single day.

When my mother was done with her business in the office, she left me in front of my classroom.

"Don't dawdle around after school is dismissed, Jeanhee ya," she said. "The chores on the farm won't wait for you, and I can't do them alone."

Then she turned and strode away, her shoulders held straight as she headed back to the life I so desperately wanted to escape, while I turned and marched into my new classroom.

I hugged my notebook and sat at one of the desks. Eighty-three kids filled my classroom alone, with six total rooms in the school and only one teacher per grade. Unlike the upper levels of school, boys and girls attended elementary school together. I wasn't intimidated, though. I had cowed bigger boys back home than the ones here. Besides, no one could match up my mouthful of nasty cuss words. The boys faded into the background, no more of a concern than the girls.

I noticed the clothes other kids were wearing. While a very few kids wore nice clothes, others wore shirts and dresses with more holes than fabric. I was most fascinated by the wealthy girls with pale >skin color with shiny, braided hair. Not a strand was out of place, unlike my lice-filled, tangled hair.

When my teacher walked into the classroom, the boisterous chatter and chaos came to an immediate halt. All eyes followed her as she placed her books and her whipping stick on the large desk at the front of the classroom. Before she'd even called roll, Ms. Soomi lined us all against the wall and arranged us according to height in order to determine our designated seats for the year. As the youngest and shortest student in class, I was seated by the teacher's desk, eye to eye with her whipping stick.

Unfortunately, my home life interfered with my studies. I managed as best I could, but I had difficulty finding time to do my homework. Whenever I failed to complete my homework, Ms. Soomi would take her whipping switch from her desk and order me to stand against the wall with the other perpetrators. Her beatings hurt, but that was the price to pay to go to *high school*. Every afternoon when I got home from school, my daily chores were waiting on me.

At night, I studied under a small kerosene lamp that offered only a dim yellow light. I had to keep my papers directly under its flickering glow and squint in order to make out the fine print. I often awoke bent over my papers with an excruciating headache and watery eyes.

On top of my other problems, my siblings constantly vied for my time.

"Let's play ghost," my sister Sunhee would whisper, draping herself in Mama's big shirt. She'd dart in front of the kerosene lamp, laughing at the flickering, spectral shadow that chased her from the wall, moaning, "W-o-o-o... I'm coming to get you!"

The other kids whirled and tracked the shadow with big, frightened eyes. Since we didn't light the kerosene lamp often, this was their chance to play. The shadow ghosts would morph into shadow chickens and quacking ducks. Meehee cried because even the farm animals scared her. I'd lay on my belly and prop myself on my elbows, using my finger to trace the characters in my textbook, trying hard to focus while Meehee sat on my back and Sunhee tickled my ribs.

"Get off!" I yelled. "I'll get a whipping from the teacher if I don't finish. And if I do, I'm going to come home and share that whipping with you!"

Finally, I agreed to tell them a ghost story to buy a few minutes' peace.

"In the side of the mountain where we bury our dead, a tall tree has lived so long it has grown twisted and wise from all it has seen," I told them. "The tree god noticed this and turned it into a man. Its bent limbs became arms, and the hard knob on top of its trunk became its head, and vultures liked to roost there. The tree god had never turned a tree into a man before. Even so, he remembered to turn little chips of bark into toenails and fingernails, and a woodpecker's hole into a bellybutton. But the tree god forgot to give the tree man a set of teeth. So the tree man's lips sank into his face, and he grew hungrier each day.

"One day, he became so hungry, he went down to the river to get water to fill his hungry belly. There he found many children splashing each other and swimming. The tree man watched the children from behind a big rock. They looked so sweet and soft, and his hungry belly growled. When the children got out of the water and started skipping rocks, he couldn't help himself any longer. He sneaked up behind them and bit off their fingers."

I told the same story every night, and although the story line changed slightly, fingers, hands, their toes were taking turns and although they knew it well, the younger kids would sob in fear every time they heard it. Sunhee would grab Meehee's small hand and pretend to take a big bite.

"Yummy, yummy. Give me your other hand," she'd say in a deep tree-voice.

Meehee would cry in response while hiding her hands underneath her shirt.

"Tomorrow night, he might eat Junghee's hand," I'd say to Sunhee.

"You'd better keep your hands under the covers so the tree man can't find them."

Mama never did wake up hearing Meehee's cry. She was too tired at the end of the day to do anything except collapse on the floor. I don't think an earthquake could have woken her. Every once in a while, when I stayed up late studying, she would stir and say sleepily, "Have you done your study, Jeanhee ya?"

"Yes, Mama," I know why asked me the same question every night. She wasn't worried about me being tired from studying. She was more concerned about me wasting expensive kerosene inside the tiny lamp. Many nights, I was too bone tried to concentrate. Other times, I didn't understand the homework. Math and science were difficult for me, and I couldn't ask my mama for help. Because she could barely read, my questions would only frustrate and embarrass her. Despite my fear of a whipping, I often left those questions blank.

My favorite day of the school year was an annual sports competition. Class was canceled for the entire day, which meant no homework. The teachers arrived at school early that morning to hang a banner between two high poles in the center courtyard, and they would use white powder to draw boundary lines on the red-clay ground to create a makeshift sports arena. We wore special black shorts with tight elastic so our bellies wouldn't show as we participated in rock throwing, hurdles, rope pulling, and foot races. The boys would compete against the girls, and whole grades would compete against each other. We would yell taunts, calling each other weak chickens and limp-wristed ducks.

The more privileged kids—most kids other than myself—brought lunch bags with goodies for a special day, and while I would beg for nibbles of their food, I always chose a lone spot to eat. In fear the other kids might laugh at my meager lunch box with only a barley-rice mix and kimchi.

I entered the hundred-meter race. I felt confident that, despite my bare feet and the soft red clay without running shoes, I could outrun a few of the bigger girls. I knelt behind the white chalk line and waited for the whistle. When it sounded, I jumped forward with all the power I could muster. My short legs pumped up and down as I focused on the crowd waiting at the end. I forgot that the other girls were even running with me. As I crossed the finish line, an imposing figure caught my eye. It was my father. He had come to watch me race. He had never been to my school before, and I have no idea what had prompted him to come to my school that day, but he stood up straight and proud when the teacher announced that I had won.

"Kang, Jeanhee!"

I stood proudly to claim first prize—a notebook. The tall kids with long legs watched jealously as I ran to my father to show him my brand new notebook. He looked handsome in his black suit, gray tie, and shiny leather shoes. His hair was nicely greased and combed. He was proud of me and asked a photographer to take a picture of us.

I held my notebook to my chest and tried my best to look good standing next to my stylish father, but I wasn't sure how to act in front of a camera. As I stood there, my father wrapped his arm around me. It was the first photograph I had ever had taken and the first time my father had ever touched me gently.

The only photo of my childhood

Going to School wasn't always fun. I was scared to death of the teachers. Mr. Tak, my 2nd grade and 3rd grade homeroom teacher never smiled at us. His stoic face always gave all of us chills the minute he walked into the classroom. He often gave us harsh whippings, slashing at our calves with a stripped-down branch. The welts lasted for days. Mr. Tak would explain, "I am whipping you to teach you a lesson. You must do better."

His logic made no sense to me. After each beating, my legs hurt too much for me to focus on school work. When my mother saw the bruises, she would shake her head.

"Jeanhee ya! You said you finished your work. You used enough kerosene to finish two weeks' worth of work! What happened?"

Winters in South Korea were bitterly cold. Snow was often knee high, and I was on the verge of hypothermia the whole walk to school. No matter how many layers I put on, I never had enough hand-me-downs to keep warm. I never just walked to school. I made the trek a race, walking as fast as I could to generate enough body heat to keep me warm and to keep my hands from freezing. My gloves had been patched so many times they barely held together. I often walked with my hands tucked into my armpits, embracing my shivering body, doing anything I could to avoid freezing to death. Without snow boots, I had to pick my path carefully to avoid deep drifts so I didn't get my feet wet. Once I reached my classroom, over an hour would pass before my feet would thaw enough for me to feel my toes.

At night, my hands and feet would be swollen from frostbite, and I could barely bend each digit. Before I went to sleep, my mama would fill my dad's socks with soybeans and tie them to my hands and feet. The remedy worked like magic. Each morning the swelling had gone down, but my hands would carry the scars from the icy weather for the rest of my life.

As trying as the winters could be, cold wasn't the only monster that hounded me. Monsoon season followed winter, dumping torrents of rain from the sky, and thus began my battles with the buses. Every day they sped by, throwing dirty, melted snow onto my school clothes and blowing noxious exhaust into my face. No umbrella could block the onslaught of filthy water and mud. Since my book bag wasn't waterproof, I either had to leave it at school or try my best to keep it dry, standing under the eaves of strangers' roofs until the rain slowed.

When I would get close to school, I'd join a group of kids in the woods near Wonkwang University. No one had a watch to know what time it was, but we knew the pace of our walking speed by heart, so we always arrived on time. We chattered and sang, running off the road whenever the impending roar of a bus rose up behind us. I often wondered what it would be like to ride a bus to school, traveling there in half an hour rather than the two hours it took me to walk. I never asked my mother if I could try the bus because I knew her answer.

"Jeanhee ya! What are you thinking? Why would you pay to ride in a big lazy bus when you have two good legs to take you?"

One Sunday afternoon, a scrubby bicycle vendor stopped at our home. After a double count of paper money, Mama handed over her usual delivery—a batch of freshly laid eggs. She walked over to my best friend in the world, my *Yellow Dog*. She released his chain and dragged him over to the vendor. My heart sank. I cried in silence, knowing my protests would not stop my mean mama from selling my only friend. He was always hungry like me and ate every scrap I gave him in his beat-up tin-can bowl. I called him *Yellow Dog* because his hair was yellow. He was going to the butcher's shop to be slaughtered and made into a rich man's remedy, and I could do nothing to stop it.

I watched helplessly as the vendor pulled my beloved *Yellow Dog* down the long dirt road toward the city far away. My sweet *Yellow Dog* faded into the horizon, but he kept looking back, fighting against the rope tied to his neck with his saddest eyes to ask me why I wasn't coming to rescue him.

Then he was gone...

I hated my mama for that. I hated being born into such a poor home. Angry, I hid from my chores and stayed in the river as long as I could. I dipped down into the cold water near the bottom, my tangled hair floating in lazy circles around me. The water was murky and quiet, and I stayed down deep as long as my lungs held out. When I finally had to surface, I put my foot down on a jagged piece of glass. Searing pain raced up my leg, followed by a hazy cloud of blood.

I hopped back to our house, my toe throbbing. The gash was too deep for my mama to patch with her usual home remedy. She washed the wound with water and wrapped it in the cleanest piece of cloth we had. Then she nursed me, hovering around me for hours, fretting until the bleeding stopped. I was temporarily crippled and could not walk the ten miles to school and back. That meant I would get behind, and that when I returned, the teacher would whip me for my absence.

The following morning, my mama shook me gently awake and pulled me up from my pallet instead of her usual yell to wake me. I didn't know she could speak so softly to show me that she really loved me. She fed me extra white rice mixed in dreadful bean and barley bowl for breakfast. I was eating it up, wishing my hurt foot would take longer to heal. Then she told me it was time for me to go to school. I didn't question her although I wondered how I could possibly limp my way to school when I could barely walk to the end of the yard. To my surprise, she stopped at the road where buses roared by and stuck out her right arm, motioning for the bus to stop.

When the bouncing bus slowed, my mama squeezed my shoulder.

"Run up the steps when he opens the door and sit down if you can. If you can't, hold on to a seat when he takes off. Otherwise, you might fall and hurt yourself again."

"Yes, Mama." I'd never known her calloused hand had the power to bring that monstrous machine to a dead halt. And now that I knew the secret—raising my hand in the air and waving it up and down—I had the power, too.

The same mean driver who had tried to splash me with water every day of the year opened the door to let me on. Before I darted up the steps, my mother tucked the return bus fare into my hand.

"Don't lose that," she yelled as I climbed the stairs, "Or you'll have to limp home!"

Once in the bus aisle, I bent and tucked the money into my sock. Then I stood up, bumping into several men and a pregnant lady. The bus was packed like shoots in a rice paddy, everyone crammed together in a sweaty hodgepodge. The air reeked of kimchi breath. Garbled conversations overwhelmed my sense of hearing as each person talked louder than the next, fighting to be heard over the noise. Being used to open spaces and country life, I felt off-balance amidst the chaos. I was too short to reach a handrail and the other riders gathered so tightly around the poles that I couldn't squeeze through. I was terrified someone would step on my throbbing toe. The bus lurched and slowed, constantly taking on more passengers. I barely had enough room to breathe.

Despite the discomfort on the bus, riding it beat the ten mile walk. I'd have chosen to ride the bus everyday if possible, because then I would have energy for both school and my chores. I tried to remember exactly where in the river I'd cut my toe. If riding the bus was the benefit of a wounded foot, then I would go back and find that jagged glass again. I needed to do more damage quickly, before my first cut healed.

My thoughts were interrupted when a strong hand inched across the small of my back. Many people had touched me since I had been aboard the bus, but this was no accidental touch. I froze as the hand snaked around my stomach and inched toward my private area. I sucked in my stomach and looked down. The hand was covered in curling black hair and ended in dirty fingernails.

I didn't dare turn around to see who was touching me, but I was certain it was a monster. I held my breath as the fingers inched downward, grabbed the hem of my dress, and lifted it above my knees. My heart raced. I inhaled deeply and shook myself out of the trance. I moved quickly, wiggling through the sea of jutting hips and bulky packages until I reached a section of the bus that contained more women than men.

I trembled uncontrollably. My mama had told me to never let anyone touch me there. I felt so ashamed. For the rest of the bus ride, I was nauseous, worried the monster man would find me and try again to touch me in that forbidden spot.

At school that day, throughout my lessons, I plotted how to avoid the monster man's hand on the ride home. My ears rang as I tried to forget the slippery strong feeling of the snaking hand, and I didn't hear a word the teacher said.

The second my teacher dismissed us, my classmates zoomed off toward their villages. My wrapped toe throbbed as I limped on my barefoot heel, homework tucked into my armpit, bus fare in my sock. I had to hop and walk almost a mile to the bus stop in town, and as I teetered across the stepping stones over a small creek, I made a plan to wait for a less crowded bus, one where no man could shove up against me. My heart was beating on my chest as the buses passed by, one after another. Finally, a less crowded bus pulled to a halt and the door squealed open. I spotted an empty seat behind the driver and raced to it. I could see the bus driver in the rear view mirror and waited until his dark eyes made contact with mine. I nodded hello. I wanted him to know I was there—I was sure he wouldn't let anything happen to me.

I never told my mama what happened on the bus. She had enough to worry about.

Chapter 5

Smile

AS ONE OF THE INCENTIVES for going to school, we got to eat a hunk of hard-as-rock cornbread and a cup of warm milk every afternoon, both courtesy of the Red Cross. I'd never had a snack like that before. I devoured every crumb of that cornbread, and I reminded myself that I must come to school every single day, Monday to Saturday to get that delicious snack.

The girl who helped the teacher pass out lunch was one of my classmates. She was beautiful. Even her name was lovely, the syllables like sparkling mountain water.

Woojung.

She was one of the richest students in the school and was also the teacher's pet. She knew the answer to every question and always did her homework. She was courteous, friendly, and never had a bad day. Everyone loved her, and I wanted to be just like her. In class, I would daydream about her clean, silky hair, wondering how she kept it so shiny and lice free. Her teeth were straight and white, not yellow and crooked like mine. Woojung always wore clean, matching clothes that actually fit and had not come as charity from a GI base. I was dying to know her secrets.

For months, I watched her from afar. I couldn't imagine approaching her, unsure if she'd even talk to someone like me, someone so poor. One day, as she passed by, she stumbled and dropped her books. I bent and scooped them up for her.

She smiled at me. It was the prettiest smile I had ever seen. I asked if she wanted me to carry them to her desk for her.

Her smile grew wide, showing every white tooth in her mouth.

"Okay," she said. "Thank you."

I later learned she was often ill and that even the smallest tasks tired her. My friendly offer had touched her deeply. I'm sure everyone wondered why a girl like Woojung hung around with me. She sat up straight, while I slouched. She kept her hands folded neatly, and I fiddled with a pencil. Whenever she laughed, she laughed gently, her mouth a small "O" of amusement, whereas my laugh came out as a hooting shriek of joy. We couldn't have been more different, but we quickly became best friends.

The day Woojung and I first spoke, I raced home from school and tried to comb my hair into a straight black curtain like hers. When I found that impossible, I started using my dad's rock salt twice a day to whiten my teeth. Because of Woojung, I paid more attention to my style. Her dresses, always made of soft pale fabrics, fit her body perfectly, and she had more of them to wear in one week than I'd owned in my entire life. Standing next to her made me feel filthy. I started shaking the dirt off my dresses before I went to school, taking care to wear clothes with no visible holes.

Even so, I was powerless to do anything about the construction of my dresses. My mama made dresses for all three of us girls in the same A-line style, with a hole cut in the center to put our heads through. We only got new dresses when the harvest season was good, meaning that sometimes one dress had to last us a few years.

One day after school, Woojung told me her mother had instructed her to make a poor friend to play with and to fetch her assignments whenever she missed school.

"She wants me to have company. So I'm not lonely," Woojung

said. "She said you can come home with me sometime."

I had a feeling that Woojung's house would be nicer than the Dam Keeper's, and I was dying to see it. The whole walk there I pictured a gleaming stone house, with shiny glass windows, sheer curtains, and a tidy *keewha* roof. I imagined an imposing iron gate and an immaculate yard full of flowers without chickens running about.

I wasn't disappointed. Her home was close to Wonkwang University. Unlike the shoddy wooden gate that led to my mud-walled house, her gate was built with ornate, scrolling metal and opened to reveal a path of stepping stones edged by manicured trees. The path led through a beautiful flower garden to a big house bordered by smaller identical houses on either side. As we walked through that magical courtyard, I thought, *this is what I want. I have to live like this. This is why I need an education.*

A small garden filled with colorful flowers and elegant plants surrounded a water pump. No one had to haul water to Woojung's house. In fact, no one even had to walk through the mud when it rained. Little round stones were scattered through the grass in crisscrossing walkways. The roof was made of cement, not woven rice leaves like the mats that covered my home. Her family didn't have to worry about leaks during monsoon season or about replacing the roof every year. It was like a fairytale castle.

Beside the front door was a little deck, and upon it sat several pairs of nice black shoes, none of them dirty or scuffed. They looked as if they had never been worn. No dirty clothes were scattered about like inside my house, either. Everything was folded neatly and tucked away in cabinets and closets. The wooden foyer, leading into the main room, was spotless. I wondered if Woojung had ever even seen dirt.

With all the excitement, I realized that I needed to use the bathroom but hadn't seen an outhouse anywhere in the yard. When I asked Woojung about it, she giggled and took me to a little room. Inside was a sink with running water and a string hanging down from a porcelain water tank. I had never seen anything like it.

"Where is the real bathroom? This is not funny. I have to pee right now before I wet my panty, Woojung."

But it *was* the real bathroom, right inside her house. Woojung never had to venture out into the cold snow or pelting rain to go to the bathroom. She showed me how to squat on the shiny white circle and pull the string after I finished my business. A roll of clean, white toilet paper was attached to the wall next to the hole, and she assured me I could use it to wipe myself.

I walked out of the bathroom with my mouth open.

"This is how rich people live," I said with a gasp. I could have gone on about it for hours, but the serious look on Woojung's face made me stop.

"Jeanhee ya," she said, "I'm sick. The doctors say I won't live much longer unless I follow their instructions exactly. Look at my medicines."

She pulled me over to a little cabinet and showed me many different bottles of brightly colored pills. She took out a few and washed them down with a cup of water.

"Yuck!" she said.

I had never seen medicine in a bottle before. Each pill was a perfect bright circle tailored to a specific ailment, almost like magic candy. My mama's remedies were mostly cure-alls made from ground grass and leaves. They tasted horrible and rarely worked.

"Can I have one?" I asked. I couldn't imagine that those shiny little tablets could taste bad. Woojung nodded. She was right. The pill did taste funny, but I made up my mind to like it. After all, this was rich people's medicine.

I wondered if maybe Woojung's family could adopt me. I wanted to live in this big, beautiful home, wear pretty clothes, and have long shiny hair, straight teeth, and a maid to clean up after me. I decided that one would have to be pretty to deserve such wealth, and I was not pretty like her.

Woojung took me into the main living room. Hanging in the middle of the wide back wall was a photo of a man Woojung told me was their living God.

"How did you get his picture?" I asked. Besides the mountain that looked like God's face, I had never seen a depiction of God before. I didn't know what the words *a living God* even meant.

"Our religion is called WonBulgyo," Woojung explained. "We were taught to be good to each other and kind to the weak and poor. Otherwise, in our next lives, we could come back as ugly dogs or stray cats. Mean people come back as snakes."

Perhaps I had better start being nicer to my younger brothers and sisters and stop beating them up for not following my orders. I certainly didn't want to come back as an ugly dog or cat. This life was bad enough. If I came back as a snake, a poor paddy farmer would catch me and turn me into a home remedy for rich people. I wanted to come back as someone like Woojung. She must have been a saint in a past life unlike me.

"One more thing," Woojung continued. "You must smile more today than you did yesterday. People will like you and be nicer to you. You'll have more friends."

"Smile?" I would just about do anything for sweet Woojung to let me eat all the white steamy rice I could, but smile more than yesterday sounded like a lot of effort. I wanted to protest, but I decided I had better shut up and listen for my own good. More white steamy rice for more smiles seemed like a fair trade.

"Okay, but one question."

"Do I have to smile at people I don't like?" I asked, suspicious because everybody I knew fell into the category of *I don't like,* except maybe my youngest brother, who couldn't talk yet.

"Yes, you do" she said with a nod. "You must smile at everyone. All day, all the time."

I wasn't sure about this. First of all, what was there to smile about? Woojung didn't lie awake at night on a dirt floor while wrenching stomach pains made it impossible for her to sleep. But I would do anything for my beautiful friend. Maybe smiling was the secret to wealth. I stretched my lips away from my teeth in a strained grimace.

"No," she said, laughing. "You look like you just ate a piece of bad fish. Try again, and look happy."

I did so, and she laughed even harder.

"That's worse than the first one. You're not trying, Jeanhee."

"Wait a minute, I got another question. Don't I need a reason to smile?" I asked. "Why would I smile when there's nothing to be happy about?"

"If you smile, you'll feel happy," she insisted. "Stretch your lips all the way to the left and right at the same time. Then open them and show your teeth."

She smiled at me, a glamorous, glorious grin that made me want to smile back. After many attempts, my smile met Woojung's standards and she let me stop practicing. By this point, my cheeks were hurting.

I tried to think of reasons to be happy, telling myself that I would add one reason a day until I did nothing but smile, but it sure wasn't easy, I ended up day dreaming that I was rich, living in a house with real windows like Dam Keeper. Planting fields and scrubbing floors certainly didn't make me happy. Neither did my long walks to school or having to care for my obnoxious brothers and sisters. The smile trick worked for Woojung, but I wasn't sure it would ever perform the same magic for me.

I remembered that I had smiled when I used her clean indoor bathroom, wiping her soft white toilet paper across my privates, as water I didn't have to carry poured down a hole and disappeared into the ground. Thinking about the experience made my lips curl up. I peered into the broken piece of mirror in my house. I wasn't pretty. My face was ugly yet kind and soft.

The longer I peered into the mirror, the more Woojung's advice made sense. I made it a goal to smile every day and be nice to everyone so I wouldn't come back as a dog or a snake in my next life. I practiced smiling with my lips closed so no one could see my ugly teeth. My mama must have thought I was crazy, standing for so many hours in front of the mirror, but she didn't say anything.

The next time I saw my cousins, I tested my new philosophy on them. Instead of giving them an earful of cuss words whenever they made me mad, I gave them compliments.

At first, they were confused.

"Are you sick?" one of them finally asked. He put his hand on my forehead to see if I was running a fever. "What happened to Jeanhee?"

"I'm not sick," I answered.

"No way," they laughed, when I told them about Woojung and her toilet with running water and soft paper. "Why would a rich girl be your friend and let you play in her beautiful house? You're making that up."

My patience began to slip, but instead of losing my temper, I blurted out a compliment and saved myself from a future as a legless snake.

"She'd be friends with you, too, if she met you," I said.

Soon, my smile became so natural that everyone, including my classmates, started calling me "Smiley." And I soon had more friends.

When I thanked Woojung for her lesson, and she smiled and said, "I told you, Jeanhee. My mother will be so happy."

Woojung was often sick, and she missed a lot of school. On the days she was absent, I'd stop by her house after school to play. If she wasn't able to get up, I'd say hello from her bedroom doorway. Sometimes, she was lively and in good spirits, and we would romp and run from glorious room to glorious room. On other days, she was wan and lethargic, and I would worry all night until I visited her again. I didn't understand why she couldn't get better with all her expensive doctors and beautiful round pills.

Whenever I'd come to visit, Woojung's mother would say, "Jeanhee ya! I'm so glad you came over."

She said it in such a welcoming, heartwarming tone that I always believed her and felt as if I were doing Woojung and an honor, instead of the other way around.

Woojung's mother was elegant and kind and smelled faintly of flowers. Unlike my own mother, she didn't have a single line on her face, even when she smiled. She had attained the highest rank in the ladies' division of their religion and was well respected in the community. I felt like a cave girl who had crawled right out of the dirt whenever I entered their spotless house, but every time I walked through the door, she accepted me and treated me as an equal. Her kindness impressed me and made me want to be good to others.

Dinner at Woojung's house was always the highlight of my week. Often, she was too tired for me to stay and eat with them, but when she had the energy to get out of bed, I smiled so big she laughed out loud.

"No one loves food like you do, Jeanhee," she often said. "I never knew rice could make someone so happy."

I'd eat my steaming bowl of white rice so fast that Woojung would scoot hers over to me to see how much more I could hold.

"Jeanhee, where do you put all of that rice?" she asked. "How can you eat so much at once?"

I couldn't explain to her what it was like to be so hungry your stomach hurt. She'd never had to worry about where her next meal was coming from.

I asked as soon as she stopped eating, "Why aren't you eating more?"

"No, I'm on a diet this week," she said

I'd never heard the word *diet* before.

"Diet?" I asked. "What's that?"

Doctor said that I have to be careful not to eat too much. If I eat too much, I will be sick for two days.

"In my house, we never have diet. We can eat as much as we want to eat every day. Especially this steamy white rice. We get to eat steamed rice like this bowl only on my birthday and New Year's Day"

I wasn't sure she could imagine what it was like to be me.

"May I have more dried fish? And more toasted seaweed?" I was never too shy to ask for seconds.

When I absolutely could not eat any more, a maid would whisk my bowl away.

Going home always made me sad. My house looked so small after I spent time with Woojung at her big and beautiful house. Instead of joyful conversations and endless smiles, I had to listen to my mother lament about her horrible life.

I was like her sounding board. She had no one to talk to, and even if she had, she wouldn't dare to share her pitiful life in fear it would be spread like wild fire all over to the next village.

"Why did I marry your no-good father? When the matchmaker brought two men, your dad and another, the other one was wealthy and sweet, but was also a one-eyed ekku man. How could I have made such a terrible mistake? I should have chosen the one-eyed ekku man instead of choosing your father's good looks." Mama was very unhappy, and we all knew it. "I'm stuck here with five kids," she groaned, "Algo, Nepalzza! Algo!"

I knew even then that if it weren't for us, she would've run away from my worthless father and never looked back. We were the reason she was stuck in a life without hope.

One night when I was seven years old, I awoke to wrenching sobs echoing from somewhere in the house. It was my mama's painful wrenching sobs. I followed the sound of her sobs to my grandmother's old bedroom. Mama's face was pale and heavily strained, and her stomach was visibly swollen.

"Jeanhee ya!" she said. "You must run to the pharmacy as fast as you can. Tell the pharmacist I drank rat poison. Go quickly. I'll die if you don't. Go, Jeanhee ya. Run!"

I bolted out the door and ran toward Sin-dong where I went to school. I had never made the journey at night before, and the towering trees kept the moon from lighting the road. But the moon followed me all the way to protect me from the ghosts. Except for the distant yelps of dogs, the night was dead quiet. Neither a car nor a person passed me. Only thing that were moving was me and the moon. Too scared to look back, I focused on the moon over my head, hoping it would protect me from the monsters of darkness.

I finally reached Sin-dong, where all the shops were closed, their doors latched tight, and no lamps burned in any of the windows. I pounded on the pharmacy door, not caring whom I woke.

The pharmacist yanked open his door.

"Who is it? How dare you come here in the middle of night?" His angry tone faded when he saw that a small, shaking child stood before him. "What do you need, child?" he asked, adjusting his glasses in order to see me better. "Who's sick?"

"My mama. She drank rat poison. She said to tell you she'll bring money when she feels better. Please, sir, help me."

"Hush, child. Come inside. Tell me how she looked."

He lit a lamp and moved over to the shelves behind the counter, where he rummaged through various remedies and produced a few pouches of medicine. His tight, drawn lips told me I would have to run as fast as I could.

Sensing more urgency from the tone of pharmacist, I ran faster going back home although I had to stop several times to catch my breath.

When I finally got home, I rushed to my mama in Grandmother's room. I could tell my mother was still alive but had been in unbearable pain ever since I'd left. I lifted my mama's head to help her to drink the medicine. She choked down the medicine and lay back, exhausted.

"Algo, napalzza ya... I can't even kill me dead." She was telling me her destined life was so horrific that she couldn't even kill herself.

Mama stayed sick for five days, and during that time, neither of us worked. I skipped school and stayed by her side, making sure she took all of the medicine the pharmacist had given me. I never told anyone about that terrible night with my mama. Not my dad, nor my siblings.

For the first time in my young life, I saw my mama as a trapped, broken woman.

I knew my mother must have had a very bad match maker or she had committed a crime of some sort in her past life. I worked harder and stayed up later to finish *my homework.*

As the year wore on, the other children grew restless, ready for the harvest season break, but I dreaded the day when school let out. There wouldn't be any breaks in farm work for me, and I would have to wait until I returned to school to savor the delicious cornbread with warm milk.

I saw my future with astonishing clarity. The only way that I would have a better life was through education, and I must get the hell out of the rice paddy one day.

One cold, wintry night in December when I was seven years old, a neighboring boy came knocking gently.

"Hey, can you hear me?" he said. "Let's go to the Church."

"Church? What is that?" I whispered. He didn't skip a beat, ignoring my question, "I heard they give away rice cakes for coming to church tonight. They said it is a very special night, a God's baby's birthday from *Meegook.*".

"Oh yeah?" I couldn't care less about somebody's baby. The only word I heard loud and clear was rice cake. "How far is it?" I asked.

"The next town, next to the rich people's houses. You remember seeing three cows and lots of fruit trees in their yard?"

"Yeah!"

"Remember a tall white wooden building with a wooden stick on top of the roof like this? "He asked, bending his arms in the shape of a cross.

"I'll go!"

There were only six kids about my age in my village. Two kids backed out, saying the church was too far away.

The church looked warm and inviting when we arrived. It was filled with expensive candles, giving the room a peaceful glow. There were real windows and a real wooden floor with a wood-burning stove in the middle of the room.

We were greeted by people with clean, unjaded faces who spoke softly.

Someone had built what looked like a stable at the front of the church, where a plaster baby lay in a bed of straw. A man and woman knelt beside the baby while three old men in long robes carrying canes taller than they were stood smiling down on him.

An organ played a song called "Silent Night," and a man stood next to the stable telling a story about three old men following the bright light of a star to a barn where they would find a special baby named Jesus. They said the baby was the son of a God from heaven.

I don't remember much else. I was waiting to get my treat.

The man finally stopped talking about Jesus and turned to pick up a tray from a table in the corner. On the tray were sweet rice cakes to be given out as a thank you to us for coming to their special service. Our eyes lit up in anticipation. Everybody got a sweet cake—that is, everyone except me. They'd had more visiting kids than they had anticipated, and they ran out of cakes just before I got one. My heart dropped to my feet. The pastor must have seen the disappointment on my face, he quickly pulled out the yellow pencil he had used to mark his place in the book and gave it to me.

"A gift from the baby Jesus," he murmured with an uneasy smile.

But I wanted a rice cake...

Why would I want a pencil when I was so hungry?

Chapter 6

"Hershey Bar"

DURING THE EARLY SPRING, A farmer from a neighboring village brought his mule to till our fields. Just as she had said the previous years, my mama told him she couldn't pay him with paper money. Instead, she gave him her *word of honor* that he would be paid with newly harvested rice in the fall.

The task of pushing a hoe behind his tired mule took him a day and a half, but when he was finished, the rows were immaculate, long vertical lines with identical space between invisible lines for the monsoon waters to flow out.

Ever since I was old enough to walk, my mama had enlisted me as her right hand laborer. By the time I turned eight years old, I was almost as fast as she was and knew exactly what to do. I followed behind mama, covering the freshly planted beans with earth. We never talked as we worked, although sometimes, as sweat rolled off her nose, my mama would break the silence with soft cries of, "Algo! My bad decisions make my daughter suffer so much." That was a rare compliment from my mama. My heart tingled with love just hearing it.

Watching my mama day in and day out, dragging herself to live for another day because us five kids. I knew that when I grew up, I would get a good job somewhere in the big city to take care of my mama. As the oldest, it was my duty.

As we planted beans, a loud boom ending with a screech and raised voices echoed through the air. My curiosity got the best of me, and I dashed across the field to find out what had happened.

A hulking, dark-green GI truck had pulled over onto the shoulder of the road, and four Americans exited the vehicle. American GIs had saved us from the Communist North Koreans, and I couldn't believe they'd pulled over right in front of my eyes. The other village kids came racing up behind me, chattering excitedly. We had seen GI trucks pass along our road before, but none of us had ever seen American GIs up close. The black GIs had tight, frizzed curls and dark brown eyes, while the white GIs had soft yellow hair and piercing blue eyes. They were so tall—taller than any men we had ever seen. Their big boots, eyes, noses, and lips were larger than all of us combined, and they spoke a strange language that teased my ears, as though their tongues had been tied to coins inside their mouths and couldn't get free.

We shoeless and filthy kids stuck out our sweaty, dirty hands and shoved at each other with our elbows, fighting to get close to the uniformed strangers. Their rear tire had blown out, and they were stuck until they fixed it.

"You're on our road," we cried. "Pay up!"

Finally, they understood our demand to pay up gestures for stopping at our road, and the GIs stomped to the side of the truck in their shiny black boots and handed out square tins labeled with bold English letters and pictures of bright pink meat. The children weren't sure what the odd presents were, but the fact that the gifts were from America was good enough. They clutched their new treasures and sprinted home to gloat to their brothers and sisters who hadn't been smart enough to come out.

I wasn't so easily pleased. I shook my head when one of the blond GIs offered me a can. I had already spied my prize, and I wouldn't change my mind. Inside the truck, sitting on a crate, was a flat, hand-length package wrapped in dark brown paper. Shiny foil stuck out from both ends. I pointed to it, knowing the GIs were holding out.

One blond GI, whose boots looked as big as our rice pot, eyed me for a moment before giving in. He smiled and handed me the Hershey bar. I bowed to him, polite now that I had gotten what I wanted, and ripped away the slick paper and silver foil.

Inside, a perfect block of polished brown candy caught the reflections of the afternoon sun. I broke off one of the squares and placed it on my tongue, then closed my eyes. Creamy sweetness, better than anything I'd ever tasted, filled my mouth. Even the candy I'd bought at my aunt's store with a stolen egg hadn't been this delicious. I broke off another square and popped it into my mouth. My taste buds nearly exploded.

This candy had come from *Meegook*—America?

I vowed right then and there that when I was old enough, I would run away to *Meegook* and eat a piece of this delicious candy every day of my life. I didn't know how I would get there, but I would find a way.

Then I remembered my family. I didn't want to be a snake in my next life. Sharing a piece of this treasure with them was my duty, so I yelled at my mama, who hadn't missed a beat in her planting while I'd been gone, "Be right back, Mama."

I balanced the candy on my open palm, knowing that if I clutched it tightly, it would surely melt. I burst through the broken wooden gate of our house and called out, "Look what your big sister got for you from the Americans!"

My siblings, huddled around the open fire pit, barely looked up when I entered. Any other time, they would have danced around me, clamoring to see what I'd brought, but this time they ignored me. I tiptoed up behind them and peeked over their shoulders. My brother Junghee had a dead rat skewered on a stick and was holding it over the flame.

My siblings' eyes grew wide as the flames licked at the rat's body. An acrid stench filled the house.

"Are you going to eat that, brother?" Sunhee asked.

"Don't you tell Mama," Junghee said with a hiss.

"Try this instead," I said excitedly, holding out a square of that sweet chocolate. "It tastes like heaven."

Without taking his eyes from his roasting prey, Junghee put the candy into his mouth. Then he said, "This won't fill me, *Nuna*."

Annoyed by his response, I dropped a square into my baby brother Yonghee's mouth. His lips worked to catch my finger, thinking it was my mama's nipple. I gave Sunhee and Meehee a full square each, but they were too mesmerized by the rat to be impressed.

My heart hurt with disappointment. Who knew when I'd get heavenly candy like this again? I gave up trying to talk Junghee out of eating the rat and ran back to my mama. I could already hear her calling out, "Jeanhee ya!"

When I returned to the field, I was out of breath. "Close your eyes and open your mouth," I panted. "I have something yummy for you!"

She did as I said, and I dropped the last square of the Hershey bar onto her tongue.

"Is it good, Mama?" I asked.

My mama didn't even look up. She went right back to planting without even grunting an acknowledgment.

"Mama," I said. "This candy came from America. When I grow up, I'm going there to get lots of it."

"You crazy girl. First you want an *education,* and now you want candy. How are you going to get to America? Do you even know where it is?"

Unable to answer, I hung my head.

"*Michutsyu*—crazy!" she scoffed. "Get back to planting. We don't have much sunlight left. I have told you already, we must start on the soy beans tomorrow."

She really thought I was crazy. I remembered a few months earlier, I had told her about my dream of *boogo* the night before, and it arrived the next day just as I told her. I quit telling her about other dreams after she told me I was crazy.

But, I knew I wasn't crazy...

Chapter 7

Good Bye - Hananim

I WAS TEN YEARS OLD when my drunken father gambled away all of our rice paddies and farmland plot by plot, forcing my family to move into a town near the Makuly Brewery. There, he found work making cheap wine with flour for farmers. My mother had saved enough money to rent a small house with its own well about a mile from Bukil Elementary. Living in Sin Dong meant an end to farm work, and no more leeches chasing my skinny legs every spring.

That was the last time I saw God's face on the mountain. Not only was I leaving my rice paddy prison, but I was also leaving the circle of His protection. The day my father hitched the mule to the wagon loaded with all of our belongings except for the animals my mother had sold to pay a deposit on our rent, I stared, one last time, long and hard at my God's face.

I said, "Good bye, God, *Hananim,*" as if he could hear me.

During the three years we lived in Sin-dong, my dad seemed truly repentant drinking and gambling. He worked hard at his first ever real job and came home every evening to join my family before dinner. On Fridays, he turned his money over to my mother, keeping only enough to buy cigarettes.

After I graduated from elementary school, I took a National Entry Exam for middle school and waited for the test scores for days to get a notice in the mail. I was qualified to attend Namsung Middle School, the most expensive private girls' school in the city.

I was so proud to be accepted to Namsung Middle School. The school uniform was designed to symbolize not only Namsung School but test scores. From the moment my body perfectly fitted into a Namsung uniform, I was a new Jeanhee. I was on my way to steal Dam Keeper's life.

7th Grade - I was 12

My family was still poor. We didn't own land to grow food. We used a small lot that came with the house for vegetables, but the harvest was too small to feed all of us through the winter. My parents used what little money we had to buy groceries, and paying my middle school tuition was hard on the family budget. Guests were never allowed over for dinner.

My mama was so ashamed of our meager portions and cheap food that she always made sure the gate was shut when we ate. Meat was still beyond our budget, but, occasionally, Mama managed to save enough to buy a can of Crisco from the black market. Crisco, that white creamy lard, was as close to meat as we could afford. She would ration the white grease as long as she could, giving each of us a spoonful to mix in with our rice, soy sauce, and sprinkles of toasted sesame seed. It was so tasty. We couldn't wait for next meal time to get another spoonful of white creamy lard.

Though I had friends I hung out with after school and on Sundays, I never felt close enough to any of them to share my secrets. They were all two or three years older than I, and they knew stuff about boys that made me blush. The only girl at school from my town was a teacher's pet named Jungsil. Her family owned a small candy store and a few rental rooms near Wonkwang University. Jungsil and I talked on the walk to school, but once we arrived, we would part ways and she would never even acknowledge she knew me. Her snobbery didn't bother me. Actually, that is not true. It bothered me tremendously throughout school, even to the end.

Instead of trying to make friends with rich girls, I decided to focus on my studies and tried to be a model student, to show my mother and father how much I appreciated their financial sacrifice. I wished every day that Woojung was at Namsung with me, but she'd scored much higher than I and attended Iri Girls' school, the best public school in the city. She rode the bus, and I walked.

We never saw each other again. I had often wondered if she ever gotten over her illness.

Unlike Woojung, I wasn't born school smart. I had to earn every grade by studying twice as much as the other students.

I liked most of my classes although I struggled with math and science. But the class I hated with an all-consuming passion was music. The first day of school, Ms. Lee, marched into the room dressed all in white everything from head to toe—in a suit jacket, a miniskirt, sheer stockings, four-inch-high heels, see through gloves. She patrolled the classroom, peering down at each student searching for the smallest infraction. When she got to my desk, she told me to put out my hands, and I did. She smacked both of my hands with her thin white wooden stick and wiped it with her white handkerchief.

"Why didn't you wash your hands? Look, how filthy you are…." she yelled.

Covered with scars from frostbite and farm work, my dark tanned hands looked as if they belonged to an old man. I hid them under my desk and didn't answer her. No matter how much I washed, my hands still looked weathered and dark, and I hated Mrs. Lee for pointing this out to the entire class.

From that day on, I did my best to ignore music class. I hated Maria Calais's soaring voice and Beethoven's crying sonatas. Every piece Ms. Lee played created more resentment within me than joy. I fell asleep while the other kids nodded appreciatively to *Fur Elise* and woke when she slapped my hands with her cruel little white stick.

"Jeanhee, wake up!" "How dare you don't appreciate Fur Elise?"

Ms. Lee's lessons were a small price to pay for being in Namsung compared to working in the fields being chased by black demons.

My father's reformation didn't last. At the end of our third year in Sin Dong, he quit his job and fell back into his old self, drinking, gambling, and womanizing. His repentance came to an end. My mom was left to face being homeless with five kids.

My mama gathered all five of us together one afternoon, "Children, your father lost job, and I have no idea where he is. We need money to live. Your aunt from the brewery has a small hotel in the city. I begged for a job and she agreed to hire me as her manager. I don't know what all I must to do as manager, but I told her worry no more. I can learn very quickly to take care of her business like her own. She said that all of us can live in the spare rooms in the back of the hotel garden and guess what? We will have plenty of leftover food to eat, sometimes we may even get to eat meat." The most important thing all of us heard was "Plenty of leftover food to eat!"

My mama's eyes filled with tears. She reminded us that if she failed, we would be homeless. Mama needed to hear our confirmation as a family decision.

I was thirteen, Sunhee was twelve, Junghee was ten, Meehee was eight and my baby brother Yonghee was almost 6 years old.

We all nodded our heads.

"Yes, Mama," Yonghee, the youngest said. "I get to eat lots of food? Mommy?"

I nudged his rib and whispered at his ear, "Yes!"

While Yonghee was rubbing his small belly, I squeezed my baby brother ever so tightly.

Sinheung Hotel was in Iri City near the train station, in a seedy neighborhood filled with bars and prostitution, not at all a safe place for children. Nevertheless, it was a home to us. Mama's do-or-die decision to move into the city to manage the hotel turned out to be our saving grace. She learned the fourteen-room hotel business quickly, adapting well to overseeing four employees, two maids, a room service boy, and a cook. She welcomed customers in a good, old-fashioned way, bowing as guests checked in and out, always saying to them, "Please, come back and spend another night with us. I will have hot barley tea ready in your room just for you."

Her employees were very loyal and worked hard for her because mama treated them always with kindness. Soon business blossomed and my aunt was pleased with my mother. For the first time in my life, I could finally abandon my never-ending search for food. Since the hotel kitchen made quality meals for paying guests, the leftovers usually ended up on our table, dishes we never could have afforded on our own: grilled chogi, myulchibokoom, kimchi soup with pork meat and tofu, odenguybokoom, and sometimes even toasted seaweed. We didn't care at all that they were leftovers. For us, it was feasts we had never had. For the first time in our lives, we ate all we-can-eat food and were able to bring fancy lunch meals to school.

We no longer had to make outhouse visits on cold, wintery nights. Our bathroom was like the one I had used in Woojung's home. And as Mama made more money, our lifestyle became even more lavish. We each got our own toothbrush and had plenty of soap to wash our faces. She even bought shampoo for our hair. Soon, the never-ceasing plague of lice became only a bad memory.

The move to Iri City was my second relocation in three years, but I didn't miss life in Sin-dong any more than I missed the farm in Sinyong-dong. The city was a blessing for my *education*. The Sinheung Hotel was just a ten-minute walk from school, one block from a movie theatre, and three blocks from an open grocery market.

My grades remained mediocre. No matter how hard I tried to be in the elite student group, I was only an average student. The only class I excelled in was English. We weren't learning much more than simple grammar and basic words, but I threw myself into my English studies with passion. Soon, I ruled English class. If anyone had questions, they knew to ask me. I could pass a written English test better than the smartest student in our class. I was so proud that I'd finally found a subject where no one could outdo me.

No one understood why I was so passionate about the subject. I didn't share my dream about *running away* to *Meegook* with anyone, not even my new best friend, Oksoon. When my English teacher talked about his experiences in America as a young scholar, I propped my head on my hands and leaned in, listening to tales of this beautiful nation, *Meegook*.

Mr. Kim told me about his experiences in America. According to him, it was the politest society in the world. Before people passed each other on the street, they said "Excuse me," and apologized if their clothes brushed those of another. Everyone had a car and a room with beds, and they showered each morning with hot water. Every house had a kitchen and a dining room, and the bathrooms had toilets like chairs.

Schools in *Meegook*, Mr. Kim said, are easy. "There is no entry exam for middle and high school students, and there is no school on Saturdays."

I impressed Mr. Kim with how fast I learned and soon became his pet. He taught me *R, F, Z, PH, and TH* sounds that Koreans cannot pronounce.

I did it exactly as he taught me, mimicking his accent and inflection. I asked him how to write my name in English. The letters were alternately curved and stiff, different from the curved characters in Korean.

Jeanhee.

My American name looked beautiful. I wrote those clumsy letters all over my notebook cover. *Kang Jeanhee. Kang Jeanhee.*

"No," Mr. Kim said when he noticed my doodles. "Americans write the family name second. In America, you are Jeanhee Kang."

I didn't care how he changed my name—backwards, forwards, or upside down—as long as I got to use it in *Meegook*, the beautiful country called America.

As I progressed through school, my grade point average rose, mostly because of my high English marks. One day I found my name on the school's main bulletin board under the heading *Best Test Scores. Kang Jeanhee—Third place in Tenth grade.*

I couldn't believe it. Jungsil couldn't believe it either when she found out she wasn't even close to top ten.

Beaming with pride, I couldn't wait to go home and tell my mama.

"That's very nice, Jeanhee ya," she said. "Are you sure you didn't see it wrong?"

"Mama," I said, rolling my eyes. "I can read. That's what I'm best at."

I quickly surpassed the other girls I'd always considered to be smarter than I was and often stayed at school until nine o'clock at night.

I wanted go to college which meant I must prepare to score well on the national entry exam for college. We didn't' get to choose our college. Our test scores determined our colleges for us just as they had in seventh grade. In the 1970's, very few girls wanted an education beyond high school. A high school education was enough to get on the matchmaker's waiting list. But I had absolutely no interest in marriage, thanks to my father. My father's tempestuous relationship with my mother had dispelled any dreams I had of finding happiness with a man. I still remembered how my father beat us in drunken madness on icy snowy nights. Nevertheless, I did understand why only a few girls were interested in higher education. Girls were bred to be picked as the wife of somebody by a match maker.

No dating was allowed. Until the wedding night, she must remain pure as snow, ready to scream to announce her purity to her husband. Then she was expected to have several babies and hope to God that one of them would be a boy to carry on his family name.

"You might be able to go to *Meegook* if you're a reporter," Mr. Kim told me one day. "Your pronunciation is better than any student I've taught. You'll pick up the language fast once you get there. Times are changing. I see no reason why you can't make it as a female reporter."

For Koreans to score a visa to *Meegook* was like winning a lottery. If anyone did score a visa, the government routinely denied the applications from the rest of their family to make sure the departed family member had a reason to come back. Only a handful of Korean *Chebyuls*—super rich families—were able to travel freely along with diplomats and the top 1% elite students to represent Korean's proud nationalism.

Knowing how difficult it was for Koreans to study in America, I couldn't' help but ask how he did it. He told me that an American missionary had secured his student visa.

I advanced through the grades, envisioning myself as the winner of a scholarship to study abroad. Between studies, I read literature: Shakespeare, Ernest Hemingway, Mark Twain, Leo Tolstoy, Boris Pasternak, and O. Henry. Many were required reading for book reports to earn extra points to be considered a worthy intellectual among my peers.

Trying to fit in with girls with pretty light skin colored hands always reminded me of my past life as a farm girl. We had come from different places—they were from privilege, and me, from struggle. But my beautiful friend Woojung's lesson to "smile each day more than the day before" proved invaluable and again earned me the nickname *Smiley*. I learned to make fun of myself when my friends asked why my skin was so dark. Instead of wasting time telling them about my laborious childhood, I said, "I was adopted after birth. Because I was so dark, my real mama didn't want me."

One of my good friends, Jumsook, actually believed my story. She had the opportunity to meet my brothers and sisters, who were taller than I and had fair skin.

She said, "You truly were adopted. I thought you were only kidding. Does that mean you're the black sheep of the family?"

For some reason, I liked that description.

"Yes," I answered. "That's me. I am the black sheep, Jeanhee. Baa."

Attending an all-girls school was a coveted honor, and in order to stay enrolled, we had to follow strict rules. Our hair had to be parted from the right to the left and hang one inch below our ears. Everyone entered the same gate to reach their classroom, walking in a solemn line monitored by student guards, composed of the top performing students. Disciplinary teachers stood on either side of the line to inspect us. If a girl's hair appeared too long, the teacher would measure it with a ruler. If it was out of regulation, she would pull out her scissors and cut it in an embarrassing zigzag line as a statement to the rest of the school. colored hair pins, makeup, nail polish, and headbands were strictly forbidden. We were also required to wear white tennis shoes with four—not six— grommets, laced so the shoe strings overlapped rather than crisscrossed. If they could have standardized our height and complexions, I'm sure they would have done that, too.

The school's strict disciplinary policies extended beyond our appearance and dictated our social lives as well. We were forbidden to go to movies the school didn't pre-approve. We could socialize only in family-oriented restaurants, and only with girls. Pool rooms, adult coffee shops, and dance clubs were off limits. Getting caught with a boy, regardless of the circumstances, guaranteed automatic suspension by the school's disciplinary board. For those of us who dreamed of going to college, such a punishment was unthinkable.

Corporal punishment was practiced by all of our teachers, and each punishment was unique. Once a student ate lunch too soon, filling the room with the thick, pungent smell of kimchi, and the teacher whipped all eighty-three of us for the offense to his nose. Another time, a girl in the back of the room called our teacher *baldy,* and, again, he whipped the whole class. He didn't care who had said it, he simply refused to accept any disrespect. One girl, whose crime the teachers refused to reveal, was forced to kneel on ice in the center of campus and be whipped while the entire school looked on. The entire student body watched her cry in the snow that day.

Their fear tactics worked. I never wanted to experience such humiliation and vowed to always be a good student and to make my parents proud.

Every Korean's future was determined by education level, all the way from elementary school and the test scores. We were like machines, but in human forms. No exams were to be forgotten. Every point was counted for future reference.

But no matter how hard we tried, we were never able to satisfy all of our teachers. The P.E. teacher liked to pinch the skin on our rib bones when we didn't behave, leaving bruises that lasted for days. When he was extremely angry at us, we knew the hateful stair drills were forthcoming, sixty steps in all, we were ordered to march up and down without stopping for ten times. Afterwards, all of us would be limping for days. We weren't taught to do anything strenuous physically because they didn't want to create muscle-bound girls who looked like farm girls. Only poor girls who played basketball or volley ball to represent the school had muscles. Everybody knew they were from a poor family. Their only way to attend our school was to play sports and have their tuitions waived. Athletic figured girls were not in popular demand among a match maker's first round draft.

Our impeccably dressed tenth-grade English teacher, Mr. Bae, who always wore a bow tie and a bright pocket square in his tailored suit had a mean temper, and the slightest disrespectful act would set him off. He would beat us with his slipper at the slightest provocation.

One of Mr. Bae's tests was particularly hard for me, and although I could ace most English tests with my eyes closed, the test was exceptionally difficult, so rather than getting low test scores, I turned that particular test in blank. The day after the test, Mr. Bae angrily called out the names of the girls who had turned in blank exams and ordered them to line up, hitting them ferociously with his hard slipper.

When my turn came, he narrowed his eyes and said, "You go back to your seat!"

I shrieked and ran back to my seat before he changed his mind. My classmates watched me return to my seat with eighty-two pairs of searing eyes filled with jealousy. They were convinced I was Mr. Bae's pet.

I never knew why Mr. Bae had spared me that day.

Chapter 8

Forbidden Taboo

I HAD TWO SETS OF friends. The first was Oksoon, who never got into trouble. I'd met her in the ninth grade. She was shy, with brown, almond-shaped eyes and long, thick lashes. She reminded me of Woojung. And like Woojung, she never stepped one toe out of line. I don't think she could have gotten into trouble if she'd tried.

Our friendship had begun in a funny way. Whenever our eyes would meet, I could sense she wanted to be friends, but she waited for me to speak first.

So one day, I bumped into her shoulder on purpose.

"Oops," I said. "I'm sorry. I'm Jeanhee, who are you?"

She forgave me and introduced herself.

"Our friendship can begin in exactly one minute," I said, staring at the wall clock in the classroom until she burst out laughing.

"You're so funny, Jeanhee!" she said.

I smiled back, and we became best friends.

The other set of friends consisted of four older girls—Youngsook,

Jumsook, Moonsun, and Sungcha—who weren't serious about academics but were lots of fun to hang around. Older girls meant trouble. They knew things the rest of us didn't. I didn't dare invite them to my house. My mama would know right away that they were bad news. We often sneaked into movies to gawk at American stars and their on-screen adventures. As I became older, I grew increasingly fascinated by these films. The blonde women on the screen were so glamorous and risqué. I thought the movies portrayed America as it actually was and viewed them as a window into my future life.

At school I was an obedient student. I didn't get into trouble, and I didn't want my teachers to beat me. But American movies were my Achilles heel. I couldn't resist the temptation. Once, I borrowed a shorthaired wig from an older girl and sneaked into the theater by posing as an adult. Someone recognized me and told the school board I was being tainted by American filth. When Mr. Sun summoned me to his office shortly afterwards, I shook. Mr. Sun, a heavyset man with a mean, middle-aged face, never smiled.

"Kang Jeanhee, were you at the movies yesterday after school?"

"Yes, sir," I answered, looking down, unable to meet his eyes.

Luckily, Mr. Sun was my father's friend. They had graduated together from an elite college when Korea was a Colony of Japan. To honor his friendship with my father, he spared me. "Next time," he said, "you'll be suspended for ten days and have your name posted on the bulletin board."

I bowed and backed out of his office as quickly as I could.

My fear of Mr. Sun wore off in a few days. I was hooked. Whenever the movie distributor came to stay at our hotel, I would manage to get a free ticket. I knew spying eyes from the school board were everywhere and that some students even worked as double agents to curry favor with the board. I learned to wait until the movie had begun, when the theater was dark, to sneak into the back row, and then leave before the movie ended.

I saw most films by Charles Bronson, Clint Eastwood, and Sir Lawrence Olivier. I enjoyed *Dr. Zhivago* and most memorably, *Gone with the Wind.* I wanted to become Scarlett when I moved to America. From what I learned on the silver screen, it was a land of glittering white teeth, beautiful homes, sparkling clothes, fancy cars, and tall buildings. The movies only made my daydreams more vivid.

When we weren't at the movies, my bad girl friends found other ways to take me away from my studies. No one had a TV, and only a few of my friends had radios. Our afterschool or weekend activities didn't require money—hiking, visiting temples on the outskirts of town, and lounging around at each others houses. Though none of us had a boyfriend, we fantasized about them often. Boys our age hung out at a nearby mountain park, and we sometimes went there to sneak a peek. Though they were too far away for us to make out their faces, we would lie in the grass and watch them from a distance. An older boy, who just happened to be my neighbor, approached us and questioned me about my little sister, Sunhee.

"You're too old for my sister, and she's too pretty for you," I snarled at him. I went home that afternoon from the park to find my parents pacing beside the gate. My mother chewed her nails, and my father scratched the back of his neck, gestures that surfaced only when they were angry.

"You whore!" my father yelled when I stepped into the yard. "What were you thinking? How dare you throw manure in our face? You've shamed us!"

He pulled back his hand and slapped me across the cheek. He had never hit me while he was sober before, and I had no idea what had prompted his anger.

"I raised you better than this," my mama spat. "How will we hold our heads up on the street now?"

"I didn't do anything," I protested. Tears filled my eyes, and I pressed my hand to my cheek. "I don't even know what you're talking about."

My parents ignored my pleas.

In my father's eyes, I was already a whore. It infuriated me that my father, who had gambled away our family land, had questioned my integrity. I ran to the back of the house, buried my face in a pile of blankets, and sobbed my heart out.

I discovered that the boy who had asked about Sunhee had told my parents that he'd seen me kissing a boy at the park.

"Why do you believe that liar?" I shouted.

My blood boiled with hate. My father had never praised me for doing well in school or acknowledged how hard I worked to take care of our family. I'd been more of a father to them than he had.

I was in utter disbelief that my mama hadn't defended my innocence. I'd trudged along behind her, planting beans, working the rice paddy in my father's place, hauling buckets of water, and mopping dirt floors. I'd saved her life after she ate rat poison. Once, I picked pears all day for a fruit farmer just to keep a few so she could enjoy their sweetness. Her choice to believe someone else's words over mine was unacceptable. I would have died for Mama, and now she had betrayed me. I knew then that she would never be happy with me. To her, I was nothing more than a laborer. My soul had been ripped out and thrown onto the ground.

That evening, I cried until I fell asleep, and my parents didn't wake me for dinner. When I finally stirred, it was the middle of the night. The house had settled down after the afternoon's accusations. I picked up *War and Peace* from its place beside my bed and marched over to my neighbor's house. A cute boy, Heechang, lived there and had lent me the book. I planned to return it to him and give him something in exchange. I would make my parents' judgment official.

I would become a whore.

Just as I was about to knock on Heechang's door, a girl's voice echoed from inside. Girls were forbidden to be alone with a boy who wasn't a relative, and I didn't think he had any female relatives. Heechang was two years older than I with a handsome face with big almond eyes that could swallow me.

Heechang was approved by my mother, I could talk to him on the way to school since he was known to be straight A student and his father was one of my Dad's good friend. We walked to private classes side by side when regular school was out during summer and winter. One day he invited me to a donut shop before we walked back home an act which was forbidden by school. I was scared to death of getting caught, I looked around for spies who might report me to the school entire time, and I could hardly eat any bite of tasty donut. When he asked a second time, I told him my mama wouldn't let me. I had enjoyed talking to him, but the risk of getting caught by school board was not worth getting suspended for ten days or even worse.

Now I stood outside his house, wondering if he had a girlfriend.

My anger toward my parents had trumped my devotion to my *education*. I hid around the side of the house so the girl wouldn't see me when she left. I was glad he had a girlfriend. That meant he would know how to take my virginity.

After a tired-looking girl finally left Heechang's house, I knocked on his door. When he opened it, he was surprised to find me there in place of the other girl.

"I finished your book," I said, holding out *War and Peace*. "Thank you for lending it to me."

"Isn't it twelve-hundred pages?" he asked, looking me straight in the eyes. "You read it in three days?"

"I love Tolstoy," I lied. I hadn't even cracked at it yet. "It was better than *Anna Karenina*."

The expression on his face told me he didn't believe me.

"What's wrong? Why are you here so late at night?" he asked like an older brother. And indeed, since he was two years older, I called him *Oppa*, the word girls used for older boys. When I saw the worry in his eyes, I started to cry.

"Come here," he said. "Tell me what happened."

He wanted to hug me, but I could tell he was afraid to touch me. He had always considered me to be his little sister, acting with the utmost respect out of deference to my mama. He'd never made a move on me, and I would have refused to walk with him if he had. He put his hand on my shoulder, which shook as I cried. I clutched his arm. I didn't intend to go home.

"I want to sleep with you. I want you to touch me everywhere."

"What are you saying?" he said.

"Wasn't that your girlfriend who just left? Why did you let her into your room, and not me? What's wrong with me?"

"You can't stay here, Jeanhee." Obviously in shock, Heechang gaped at me. "You don't know what you're asking."

"Okay," I said, "Then I'll sleep outside your room. You can trip over me in the morning when you leave. I'm not going home."

"I should take you to your mama right now so she can lock you up. I'll be in so much trouble if you stay."

"I won't tell her. I promise!"

He stepped back from the door, and I walked into his house. He pulled a blanket out of a closet and arranged it on the floor for me, then waited until I tucked myself in to turn out the light.

Soon, the dark room became chilly. He lay next to me wrapped in a separate blanket—protection from me, I suppose. But I kept inching toward him, hoping he would have a change of heart and give me what I wanted.

The darkness made me brave, and I asked him again, "Please touch me. I don't want to be a virgin anymore. No one will know, *Oppa.*"

He wrapped me in his arms and touched his lips to mine. His heart beat against my chest. When he slipped off my panties, I stiffened.

"Are you sure? I can stop," he said.

I told him, "Don't stop, I want this."

I would be the whore my father had told me I was. I wanted to make him sorry.

Snug against Heechang's body, the cold night seemed an eternity away. After a brief flash of pain between my legs, my body relaxed. No one had ever touched me in that place before. The closest anyone had ever come was the monster man who'd groped me on the bus when I was a child. Yet this was different. I had no fear. Being so close to Heechang felt like I was loved. We were one. I felt I belonged to him. My lonely heart was filled with his touches, and I felt loved. I knew my action in madness was forbidden, an act that I could never undo.

I broke a centuries old Korean taboo to retaliate against my parents. I was too young and stupid to realize it meant my life had totally been reshaped forever.

Chapter 9

Subhuman

FROM THAT NIGHT ON, HEECHANG was my universe. He ended his relationship with his other girlfriend. She came back several times, and I knew from her tears that he'd taken her virginity, too. I told him not to talk to her or even open the door. I wanted to be near him every moment and was merciless in my possession of him. I had finally found someone who loved me back. And to my shame, I liked what we did in the dark.

For a time, I felt loved. As our relationship deepened, it became harder to conceal, and I wanted to be with him all the time. I struggled to act normal in front of my parents, and my friends grew suspicious of the sly smile that was constantly on my face. I wasn't spending as much time with them anymore, and my refusal to provide an explanation only served to make them more curious. My life became plagued by nights of elation and days of regret.

Guilt weighed heavily upon me. One day in science class, the teacher started the lecture by saying to all eighty-three of us, "I know which ones of you are not virgins just by looking at you. Shame on you!"

I wanted to die right there. I was certain he was speaking to me, and I sweated for the remainder of the lecture. But while our teachers were quick to condemn us, none of them ever bothered to educate us about our bodies. When I saw a small, bloody stain on my underwear at school one day, I panicked. The first time blood had spilled from between my legs was the night I'd lost my virginity. I'd thrown those panties away, fearing my mama would discover what I'd done. But this time I was at school, and Heechang was nowhere around. None of the other girls had mentioned anything like that happening to them. We never spoke about our bodies to each other. I spent all day worrying about how to tell my mama about the blood, sure it was because I'd had sex. When she saw that rusty, damning spot, she'd throw me into the street. I'd be ashamed and defiled, my future in America lost for good.

When I pulled my panties off that night, I mixed them in with the other dirty clothes, hoping she wouldn't notice. I stayed up all night, planning to confess what I'd done with Heechang, to repent and face the consequences. In the morning, I was surprised when my mama was kind and gentle.

She softly pushed the hair from my eyes and said, "This is an important day for you. You're a woman now. You'll bleed about the same time every month. It's something we all must bear." She handed me a clean, white cloth to fold into my underwear.

Then a few months later, my period didn't come. I grew concerned that I was sick, but continued to use the cloth my mama gave me, not wanting her to worry. Only after reading a book about pregnancy did I understand what was happening.

A baby was growing inside of me.

Oh, my gosh… What have I done? I hoped so badly that it wasn't true, wishing it was a nightmare I could wake up from and everything would be alright.

I was scared to death as I went to school for another month, hiding my secret. The shame was unbearable. One day I broke down in front of the only person who knew I was seeing Heechang—Oksoon. She tried to comfort me, but when I let her feel my tummy, now hard as a rock and beginning to bulge, she cried for my anguish.

"What should I do?" I asked.

Oksoon had older sisters who were well-versed in the way of the world. She dried her eyes and squared her shoulders. "I'll ask my sister tonight," she said. "She'll know."

The next day Oksoon pawned the gold ring her mother had given her for her 17th birthday. We skipped school, and she took me to the abortion clinic. I had never been to a hospital before. As the strong smell of alcohol of some sort hit my face, the cold sterile tables and surgical equipment frightened me. As I lay naked on the table, covered only by a thick cotton sheet, I cried. Then the doctor and a nurse came in. After inspecting my swollen belly, he asked me to spread my legs.

He said, "Open your legs wider."

I didn't want to, but I had to, and he touched my private parts. A tingle shot from the bottom of my feet to the top of my head.

"Why did you wait so long?" the doctor scolded. "You should have come in sooner."

The nurse took me to a back room and sedated me, so I'd stop shaking. Then they started the procedure. Seconds later, a searing pain shot into my groin and down my legs, as if someone were twisting my guts into figure eights. I cried the entire time, not only from the pain, but also from the embarrassment of lying exposed before two strangers. When the procedure was finally over, Oksoon wouldn't look at me.

"What's wrong?" I asked, angry she hadn't asked me the same question.

"I told. I called your mama. I heard you crying and thought you were going to die."

"Oksoon!" I was weak, but angry. "My mama is the last person I want to see right now. You broke your promise."

I didn't know what to do. I thought you were dying... you were hurting so badly. She's not mad."

My mama would kill me. My parents had been livid over the mere possibility that I'd kissed a boy, and now...

Oksoon left to go to school. "Take care," she said, patting my arm.

I couldn't even respond. If only I'd known her gentle pat would be the last time we touched, I'm sure I would have found something to say.

I lay in the hospital bed, wondering how I could ever be normal after this. I'd have to explain my absence to the school board and act as if nothing had happened. When my mama finally walked into the room, her face was a quiet mask.

"We can deal with this," she said. "Let's go home."

She helped me into my clothes and held my arm during the long walk. Every step sent needles of pain through my abdomen. Tears dripped down my face as we walked down the street in silence.

By the time the pain from my abortion finally lessened, I'd already missed three days of school. The school board confronted my mama and demanded the reason for my absence. Except for serious illness or a death in the family, they did not tolerate a student missing class. The principal informed us that they would have to review my case. I waited days for word from the school. Every time the phone rang, I jumped. When I picked up the phone on the tenth day and Oksoon's sweet voice met my ears, my heart fluttered with joy.

"Jeanhee..." she said, crying. "I can't... see you anymore. The school board and my parents have forbidden me from ever seeing you again. I'd get into so much trouble if they even knew I was calling you. I'm so sorry. I will miss you, my sweet friend. I was shocked to see your name on the bulletin board. It says, Expelled: Kang Jeanhee. *You're the gossip of the entire school.*"

A ton of brick landed on my chest, my body losing all its strength, and I fell to the floor helpless as a leech in the sun. Oksoon said, "I think Jungsil ratted on you. She must have seen you at Heechang's house. You know she lives not far from his house."

I cried out to my invisible God's face, "Help me!"

I prostrated myself, knelt before my mama, vowing never to see Heechang again. "He is nothing to me, Mama. I learned my lesson. I will never see him again as long as I live. Please help me to go back to school. Please talk to the school board, Mama. I want to go back to school. I will study day and night. I am sorry for what I have done."

"No, they won't take you back. It is over," she could hardly look at me, turning her face in tears. I had few choices as a taboo breaker. I could either drink rat poison to follow the taboo breakers who went before me to honor my culture, or face repercussions to live as an outcast for rest of my life. Or I could take the high road and disappear forever.

After a few weeks, Heechang gave a note to my little brother, Yonghee, demanding that I meet with him. I balled up the paper in my fist and threw it onto the floor. How dare he contact me? Didn't he know what had happened? Didn't he understand that I'd never graduate from high school and that no decent man would ever want to marry me? I was no longer the Jeanhee he had known. His existence was eliminated from my life then and forever.

In an act of utter despair, I shaved my own head to save my father's trouble to shave me to broadcast I was no longer pure as snow.

As each strand of black hair fell to the ground, lock after lock, my past mistakes fell from my conscience. The gesture was oddly freeing, and the weight of my sins lightened. I considered going away, deep into the forest, to live as a monk. But they, too, would likely cast me away because of my impurity.

I was wishing God's face was near me. I wanted to ask Him if He could see my sad face. I must runaway soon.

I was still remembering the Hershey bar, how it had melted on my tongue...I may have fallen, but I would not stay down forever. If anything, I only became more determined. I decided to stop dwelling in the past, and let it all go. Despite the hot throbbing in my swollen breasts, I forced myself to focus on the future.

The people who gave up on me have something else coming.

I will show them one day.

I deserve a second chance.

After I shaved my head as an admission of my guilt, my own mother didn't recognize me. The silky black hair that had belonged to her eldest daughter was gone, and my skull was now covered in dark fuzz. My feathery dome became another reminder for her that she had a bold, independent daughter—and *that* was another devastating blow to her as a parent. She had failed to raise me properly. She was so embarrassed that she immediately bought me a wig cut in a schoolgirl hairstyle— shiny, straight, and angled one inch below my ears. But the wig couldn't hide my dishonor. I was still the hot topic of neighborhood gossip. The wig was a small, inadequate consolation to her, but I felt obligated to wear it.

My brothers and sisters knew I had lost my virginity to Heechang and, naturally, assumed that was the reason for my expulsion. I had no reason to mention anything about the abortion to my brothers and sisters.

Watching my siblings leave for school each morning in their starched uniforms was torture. I longed to join them, to wake up and find my transgressions forgotten, my mistakes wiped out, to start fresh and smile again like Woojung had taught me. I so desperately wanted to graduate with my friends. From the window of my hotel prison, I watched my siblings walk toward school until they faded into the morning crowd. I found my battered old book bag and shoved my uniforms, school shoes, and even my English textbooks into it. Lastly, I slipped my school identification badge into the front pocket, but my fingers had trouble releasing it. After a few tortuous moments, I pulled out my empty hand and sealed the bag shut, hiding my lost dream from the rest of the world.

The days stretched out, and I longed to find some sort of distraction, but we didn't have TV or radio, and our rooms at the back of the hotel were too quiet. I tried to read the novels that used to entertain me, but the words were meaningless and found no footing in my mind. How could I care about the lives of imaginary characters when my own life was ruined?

I helped my mother check in guests or answer phones when she was short staffed, but she only allowed me to do so if I wore that hateful wig. I prayed to the invisible God's face, Buddha, my ancestors—even to the baby Jesus I had once seen at church, who was supposed to be born to save me from misery—and any other deity I could bring to mind.

In my heart, I wasn't ashamed of losing my virginity—I could always scream on my wedding night and pretend to be pure if any man would even want to marry me. My heart was broken for losing a chance get an education for life. I wasn't even going to be like my mother, who at least was respectable. I could become a prostitute, a servant, or if I was lucky enough, I could be some man's mistress, second or third wife to produce a son for a rich man. I became a subhuman at age sixteen.

My mama cried every time she saw me. When she cried, I cried back to her, hating that I had broken her heart. She cried for my shame, and I cried for her pain. More than anything, watching my mama cry was the hardest thing I have ever faced in my life. I was her hope. As her first born, I was to finish school, find a good paying job to take care of her. I desperately wanted to tell her, I could still do that, "Don't give up on me, Mama, I am not finished"

"Jeanhee ya," she wailed at me one day, "Has your grandmother come back to punish me again?"

"Mama, It's me. I made a terrible mistake. I did it to myself!" No way, I could ever tell her why I did it, not then, not ever.

She knew my run away days were closing in, and said, "Jeanhee ya, her voice breaking, "to be a big fish, fish must swim to ocean, as long as it stays in a small pond, fish will always be a small fish." It didn't make sense what it meant, but her word of wisdom somehow made me want to be a big fish instead of a small fish. I wanted to swim to the big ocean. I didn't know how big the ocean was nor how to swim, but I could learn. I had nothing to lose. and if I must die one day, I wanted to die as a big fish.

My father, for once in his life, held his tongue. Despite the pall of shame, I had brought upon the family, he didn't want my suicide on his conscience. Whenever we were in the same room, he simply turned his face away.

It was clear where I stood in life against Korean's iron clad culture. Yet I refused to die as a high school dropout. I refused to give up my childhood dream.

What if I really did run away?

What if I left South Korea?

No one here would miss me.

They would be glad to have one less bad girl to pollute their perfect world. I could leave and go to a place where no one would question my past.

What if I went to *Meegook*—America?

No one in *Meegook* would know of my shame. If I could find a way to get there, I would finish high school in the English language. I would put the words together like a puzzle to make sentences, and sentences into paragraphs, paragraphs into a new life.

Chapter 10

Ruŋaway

I WAS AWAKENED BY A strange dream that morning. A white envelope, boogo, was delivered to my house by a mail man. I asked my mama if someone died because I saw a boogo in my dream.

She looked at me like I was crazy, and said, 'No, no one died."

That was my second symbolic dream. I still remember my very first symbolic dream I had when I was eight years old. I remember telling my mama about it while working in the corn field. Next day, *boogo* arrived.

The day after my second symbolic dream, I was working in the front office to help my mama and, sure enough, a *boogo*, a funeral invitation in a white envelope arrived. I couldn't wait to open it. I forgot all about being sad for someone's death, consumed by my run away plan. Mama would be gone for at least two to three hours the next day to attend the funeral. I grew nervous and excited as the date drew near, and when the hour finally came, I followed her outside into the street, waiting until she disappeared into the bustling crowd.

When I was certain she wouldn't turn around, I hurried back into the hotel to steal money for train fare, food, and a suitcase. I sped to the open air market and bought the cheapest suitcase I could find. As I was looking for the cheapest bag, an old man in his sixties came to help me. I wasn't really looking at his face in fear he might know my mother, but once my eyes met with his, he stared at my face and said to me, "People will listen when you speak."

Yeah, sure they will, I was thinking to myself. They already have, and I didn't' even have to speak a word. I pretended that I didn't hear him and quickly asked him the price of bag. He said, "Yi-chun won," which was equivalent to $2.00. I paid for the bag and hurried back home to pack, and I was ready to become a big fish. I told my mama's workers I had stolen Yi-Man-Won from the register *to take with me.*

"Tell her not to worry about me," I said, "One day, I will be rich, and I will pay her back the money I stole."

My eyes welled up, and I cried in front of Mom's employees.

One of them asked helplessly, "Do you have to go?"

I didn't answer. They must have seen the determination in my eyes and known in their hearts that I had to leave.

"Take care of yourself, Jeanhee ya," one of the house keepers whispered in my ear. "Don't trust anyone, and don't let anyone trick you into doing something you don't want to do."

She tucked one thousand won, the equivalent of one dollar in American currency, into my pocket and gave me an even rarer gesture of affection—a hug. My mama had never hugged me, but it felt good as if I wasn't the only one who had broken taboo and was about to run away from home I had always wondered about her when she never went home for holidays. "You buy food with this money when you get hungry. I know how much you can eat."

After I said goodbye, I picked up the bag filled with a set of dictionaries, Korean to English and English to Korean, 3 note books, 3 pencils, and 3 erasers and my small wooden treasure box. I took one last look at my home, knowing I could never come back, especially where I was headed to... I could never be a part of my family again. I wouldn't be invited to any of my brother's and sister's weddings or graduations, and, who knows, I may never see them again.

The train station was only a five-minute walk from the hotel. Once I reached it, I walked up to the ticket window and purchased a one-way ticket. The whole time, I feared my mama would appear behind me, grab my neck, and drag me back home.

The half-hour waits for a train lasted a lifetime. Eventually, however, I boarded a train to Seoul, our nation's capital, four and a half hours away. Clutching my small suitcase, I meandered through the other passengers until I found a seat away from the crowd. Across the aisle a curious man stared at me. I avoided his gaze and looked at the ground between my feet.

"Are you running away?" he finally asked.

"Yes, I am," I answered, lifting my chin proudly. "And it's no business of yours." If I was still a school girl, I wouldn't have dared to speak to elders in such a tone.

My bold answer and the confident tone in my voice showed us both that I meant business. I had faced the worst life thus far, so a stranger's judgment on a train meant nothing to a fallen girl.

Flustered, he asked, "Where are you going? Where is your mother?"

"I've already said that it is none of your business, mister." I turned my face toward the window and refused to look at him again.

No one else dare to bother me all the way to Seoul.

When I got off the train, I planned to surprise my first cousin Youngcha, the daughter of my dad's stepbrother, who lived with an American in Itawon, part of Seoul, the largest American Army base in South Korea. I had met her only two or three times over the years, but I remembered her as being tall and slender, with long black hair. She smoked and cursed and did whatever she wanted, the exact opposite of how a Korean woman was expected to act. She had started out as a prostitute but had been pretty and clever enough for one of her customers to take her as his own.

Now she was the mistress of an American GI.

I wanted to learn her secrets and lose myself in the biggest city in South Korea, where no one knew about my past. No one would whisper as I walked down the street or refuse to look me in the eye, and my heart wouldn't break every time someone in school uniform passed me on the street.

And as a bonus, I could finally get rid of that ridiculous wig.

I wandered through the busy streets of Seoul with strangers bustling by, bumping into me as they pulled along their children, their arms full of groceries. I found myself surrounded by tall buildings, street kiosks full of pushy vendors, and aggressive busy crowds—all of it exhilarating. The best part was that no one cared about me in the least—and that was exactly what I wanted.

When I finally found Youngcha's house, I stopped and stared. Surely she didn't live in this beautiful two-story house all alone. It was brick, built American style, with a black-shingled roof. A thick concrete wall topped by fierce-looking barbed wire circled the property.

My heart racing, I pounded on the metal gate that led into the yard. I hoped she was home so I wouldn't have to sit on the curb and wait. When she opened the door, she raised her brows, squinted her eyes, and stepped toward me, searching my face.

"Hello, sister. It's Jeanhee, your cousin," I blurted, hoping she wouldn't shut the door in my face. "I've run away, and I need to stay with you for a little while. I want to learn how to meet an American GI. I want to go to America."

Youngcha was taller than I remembered—at least 5'9"—and was still very pretty, although she looked a little sunken around the eyes. She never smiled. She just observed. I could tell that somehow, despite her fancy clothes and home, her life had been a harsh one. Perhaps she recognized the same signs in my face.

Because like me, she had been a runaway teenager.

"Jeanhee ya," she said with a sigh. "What did you do?"

She stepped back to let me in, half reluctantly, but she was not so far removed from her Korean roots that she would refuse to take in a family member. I stepped into the house, my eyes wide as I took in a wall of bookshelves, a mahogany umbrella stand, and a black lacquer table.

"Do you live here alone?" I asked. "What do you do with all these rooms?"

She laughed. "These aren't mine. I rent the upper floor from a Korean couple. Come with me. I don't think they'll mind if you stay for a while. They probably won't even notice you're here."

Anyone who could afford to rent such a place in Seoul had to be rich, so I knew Youngcha's American GI must make a lot of money. As I later found out, he was a doctor, a truly exceptional catch even among GIs.

I found it easy to get used to a life with indoor plumbing, an actual bed, and a refrigerator full of food and delicious drinks. I drank Coca Cola every day. I was given my own tiny room off the kitchen and allowed to take a hot shower whenever I wanted.

The apartment was big enough for my entire family, although Youngcha had it to herself most of the time.

I fit into Youngcha's life easily and tried to be as little trouble as possible so she wouldn't send me home. I was careful to go to bed early so I wouldn't intrude on her time with her handsome GI. He was blond haired, with blue eyes, and he was very kind to me. I wanted desperately to say something to him in English, but because of his good looks, I couldn't bring to mind even the simplest words.

Youngcha was a good hostess, perhaps in part because she didn't want to face my mother's anger if she didn't take good care of me. She always made sure I had enough food and introduced me to modern technology, such as her record player, which I wasn't allowed to touch without supervision. After she got over her fear that I would tell my family she was living as a kept woman, she became prideful and hoped I would let everyone know how much wealth she had obtained.

Youngcha didn't work, and her days were free. If she wasn't shopping, her friends came over, and they gambled, smoked, and ate the afternoon away. Weekends were her time with her GI. They went out, while I stayed home alone. Youngcha really did look like a model—she had a sensuous, rhythmic walk that made men stare as she strolled down the street, and she had a closet full of beautiful, expensive clothes that fit her figure perfectly.

She had more shoes and jewelry than I imagined one woman could wear in a lifetime and kept her nails long and pretty, as only fallen women did. Her soft, pale hands told a different story than my own dark, calloused ones, and she held her cigarettes in the glamorous way American movie stars did. On date nights, she was truly stunning—her lashes coated with black mascara, her red lips pouty with lipstick—and I could see why her GI doctor paid so much to keep her. She belonged in that beautiful home, in a beautiful life.

Every day, she asked me, "Jeanhee ya, when are you going home? Your mother misses you. She calls me every day crying. You can't stay here and drink my Coca Cola forever."

"Soon," I answered. "I'll go home soon. I just need a few more days. You understand how hard it is there, don't you?"

"Yes, I know," she frowned. "I know it's hard. In a few years, you can find a GI. Right now, you're too young. Go be with your mother."

I lied and told her that I intended to return home. She believed me and even gave me some extra spending money for agreeing to go back to Iri City. What she didn't realize was that I was only using her as a stopover on my way to the Air Force base in Osan, about two hours away. According to her, that's where all the educated GIs lived.

Youngcha soon tired of receiving daily calls from my mother, and I knew I would have to leave before she put me on the train herself. I made the most of my time, asking her endless questions about GI bases, English grammar, and anything else that would prepare me before I got to Osan and then to America. After a few weeks, I felt I had gathered enough information about how to meet an American GI. Youngcha was relieved when I told her that I was ready to go back home to my mama.

"You're always welcome here, but this is better. You need to be with your mama. She misses you." She dug into her bag, her perfect nails clinking against tubes of lipstick, and pulled out some money. "Take this for your bus fare. And some extra—for food in case you get hungry. Do you need me to take you to the bus station?"

"No," I said quickly." I can find it."

"Are you sure?" she said, reluctance in her voice.

"Yes, sister. Thank you for letting me stay with you." I bowed to her and headed out to find a taxi.

Riding in the cab through Itawon traffic was a nightmare. I searched for a seatbelt to relieve some of my angst but couldn't find one, so I clutched the edge of the seat with my right hand and held onto my purse with my left. The taxi driver zipped through traffic, dodging cars, bikes, and pedestrians. I'm pretty sure he drove onto the sidewalk once or twice, before finally dropping me off at the bus station.

I wanted to kiss the ground when I got out.

I was on the road to a place I had never been and knew that once I got there, I would never be the same. I had dreamed of many things in my short life, but I had never imagined I would someday be one of thousands of hopeless, fallen Korean women—a grain of sand on the seashore. I had failed to keep my virginity for my wedding night. I had carelessly thrown away my future husband's prized gift. Little did I know that I was done with Korean men altogether. Heechang was the first and last Korean man I would ever date. They had given up on me, so I gave up on them.

Something was missing in my life, but at the time I had no idea what it was. I was too busy focusing on survival and on realizing my dream of finishing my education in *Meegook,* the beautiful nation. To do that, I needed to meet an American GI.

The bus bounced along the bumpy dirt road, past the busy markets of Seoul toward the small city of Osan. During the two-hour ride, I pulled off my wig and ran my fingers through my fierce spikes, now nearly an inch long.

I can do this, after all, I had been briefly trained by Yoncha, how to be a whore whether she knew it or not. I was plotting my next steps carefully, especially how I would protect myself from pimps. I couldn't wait to get to Osan, my gate way to *Meegook,* to get out of this hateful country forever. I pictured my American high school dream studying among American teenagers in English. The bookshelves there would be filled with thick English textbooks and note books for me to study.

I was already visualizing my future.... Garbed in a silky black robe, I would receive my diploma printed with my name in English: *Jeanhee Kang.* I planned the letter I would write my mother, bragging about how well I was doing and how my past didn't matter in America.

I would send her packages filled with Hershey bars and Coca Colas, gifts for my siblings that tasted as sweet as my new life.

I stepped off the bus in Osan on a sunny afternoon in April of 1974. The air was still, cool, and full of promise. I walked into a restroom and chunked the wig into a trashcan. The soft thud it made as it hit bottom brought a smile to my face. What a perfect way to start this new chapter of my life.

Osan was much smaller than Seoul, but the streets were still packed. Tall women in white go-go boots and short skirts strutted down the sidewalks, and American GIs watched their twitching hips from street side cafes. Older women called from their shops, yelling out, "Sister, I have a perfect blouse for you," and men in tie-dyed shirts and ripped jeans gave each other high-fives. Their eyes were tired and bloodshot, as if they had partied all night. People gave me second looks because they didn't know what to make of my short, spiky, boyish hair.

I hadn't been standing there more than five minutes when the pimps descended on me like vultures on a fresh kill.

"Do you need a place to stay?"

"Little girl!"

"I got a high-paying job for you, girl, come with me."

I told them I was waiting for my sister. My plan wasn't an innocent one. Innocence was no longer a luxury for me. Admittedly, my plan depended on the help of a pimp, but I wasn't going to go with just anyone. All of them had mean, tight mouths, and I was afraid of what they might do to me before I reached the brothel.

I had my eye on a stylish man with slicked-back hair who wore a tailored suede vest, when from behind me came a smooth, low voice.

"You need help with that bag? It looks heavy."

I turned to look at him. He smiled, showing one gold tooth. He wore a buttoned-up shirt and jeans, and unlike the other pimps, he looked like an average Korean guy. He was about five-foot-four and skinny, and he seemed kind. I measured him, trying to figure out if I could stop him if he tried to rape me.

I handed him my bag.

"I could use some lunch, too," I said, trying to act innocent. I wanted him to think I was a fresh young flower with no knowledge of the world. He'd be eager to take me to a brothel if he thought I was a virgin, a commodity worth far more than what an experienced whore had to offer. Besides, I didn't want to spend the money Youngcha had given me if I could get a free meal from him.

"What do you want to eat, little girl?" he asked. "My treat. I can always use pretty company at a meal. I'm Jinsoo."

"Toasted seaweed," I said. "And a big bowl of rice, please."

I didn't buy his comment about me being pretty. I knew I wasn't. I followed him into a nearby restaurant, where we sat across the table from each other. Jinsoo ordered two identical lunches: soybean-kimchi soup with stir-fried squid. After washing it down with barley tea, I sat back and wiped my mouth with my arm.

Jinsoo smiled his greasy smile. "Were you starving, little girl? I know grown men who can't eat that much, or that fast."

"I haven't eaten in days," I said, not wanting to explain that I had been hungry since the day I was born. "I would have fainted soon. Thank you for the meal, mister."

"If you can't afford food, then where will you stay?" His brow furrowed, "If you need a place to stay, I can take you to Mama sang. She'll buy you pretty dresses, feed you three square meals a day, and give you spending money. You'll be like a daughter to her. Any friend of mine is a friend of hers."

"Really?" I answered. I gave him a smile as fake as his own. "She must be a very nice lady to take in strangers. "Rubbing my fingers through my spiky short hair, asked. "Do you think she will like me?"

"Of course she will," he said. "She loves girls from the country, especially girls with new hair styles. Where are you from?"

"Junjoo city," I said. I didn't want to tell him I was actually from Iri.

He paid the bill, stood, and picked up my suitcase. "She's busy this afternoon, so I will find you a hotel room to stay until tomorrow." I thought he was acting strange because it was still early afternoon.

He was trying to pull a trick to get me to have sex with him—my cousin had warned me about that. I did need a place to stay if Mama sang was actually busy, and right then he was my only option.

I followed him down the road, passing through a busy open marketplace, live and dead fishes, fresh farm vegetables everywhere, a butcher shop with a pig head hung by the window, dog meat shops displaying live and dead dogs. After turning down several twisting streets, we reached a run-down hotel at the end of alley. The attendant, an old lady, called him by his name, and, instantly I thought to myself, he must bring all of his aspiring whores here before taking them to Mama sang. The room he rented was small, with peeling flowered wallpaper and bedding folded up in the corner.

He pulled out a blanket and made a pallet on the floor. "Come on over here," he said. "Be a good girl and repay me for that meal before I bring Mama sang to see you."

"No!" I shook my head. I stood in the corner far away from him, ready to run if I needed to. "I'm fine over here, thank you."

His face hardened. He marched over to me, gripped my arm in annoyance, and dragged me over to the bed. I pulled back, but I was no match for his strength. He grabbed my shoulders and threw me down onto the blanket, then fell on top of me.

"No!" I yelled again. He pressed his chest against mine. I spoke to him in a voice barely louder than a whisper. "I know you're taking me to a brothel, and that's fine. But you won't be able to sell me as a virgin if you have me first—and you'll get more money if I'm pure." I continued, "I will tell Mama sang you touched me."

"You're crazy. How do you know any of that?" He stopped, his face just inches above mine. He had specks of red pepper on both sides of his gold tooth.

I inhaled his nasty kimchi breath and prepared to push him away and run, but to my surprise, he rolled over.

"You win," he said. "I won't touch you. But you'd better not run away. I have eyes all over this city. I'll find you, and you'll be sorry. I'll be back at ten o'clock tomorrow morning to take you to Mama sang."

He left, probably heading back to the streets to find another girl, and I locked the door behind him. Exhausted and full, I slept until the doorknob rattled. A new day had dawned, and I was surprised to find the sun's soft rays streaming through the window. Where had the night gone? For a second, I thought I was still in my small room at Youngcha's house. I listened for her voice and a pang of guilt slid through me. She would be so worried about me. I had lied to her, and she deserved better after all the kindness she had shown me.

When I opened the door, I was greeted by Jingo's gold-toothed smile.

"Hello, my little virgin girl. Are you ready?

Chapter 11

The Lucky Club

THE NEXT MORNING, MY SUSPICIONS concerning Jinsoo's plan to rape me before he took me to Mama sang were confirmed. This time, he bypassed the narrow bustling market tour for his next victim and led me directly to a shabby two-story building that read in bright red, Welcome to the Lucky Club. To my surprise, it was located only two blocks from the bus station... I was so glad I didn't come straight to Osan. All the little bits and pieces of beans Yongcha had spilled in my naïve ears kept me safe. Getting raped by a pimp as an initiation before I start my hooker training course wasn't exactly on my do list in Osan.

Jinsoo took me inside the building and lingered in the hall of the brothel while Mama sang spoke with me. She was in her mid-fifties, her face weathered and weary, and her eyes sharp. I was sure she had once been a prostitute herself and had worked her way up. In her I saw ambition and a keen intelligence way beyond that of the average whore.

"Hello, Jeanhee," she said gently. "I'm Mama sang. Do you know what you will do in the brothel?"

"Yes." I nodded. "But I've only had one boyfriend, and I never went all the way with him. I wanted to be a good girl. I'm embarrassed to let a man touch me that way."

"You'll get used to it," she said, while she stared at my short hair. "It's not that bad. And life here is good. I'll buy you a bed, clothes, shoes, makeup, and feed you three meals a day. Once you've paid me back with interest, you're free to go. She ran her finger through my inch and half short hair, and said, "I will buy you a wig as welcome package, how about that?" Somehow her touch gave me a sense of security.

"I want to meet a GI and go to America," I said. I needed to share my dream with someone, and I didn't find it odd that one of my only confidantes so far in life was an aging whore. "I want to finish high school there."

"If you want that so much," she said, her eyes sad for reasons I didn't understand, "I'm sure you'll get it. We have enough GIs in this town to take the whole city to America. If you find one who'll make you his wife, you won't be the first or the last."

She paid Jinsoo for his trouble. The lie about my virginity had increased my value tenfold. Then she led me back to the brothel, a two-story building made of concrete and brick, with dark screen windows. Mama sang led me through two red vinyl doors into the Lucky Club.

The first floor was a nightclub, where whores danced and solicited customers. Lit only by dim sunlight filtering through the windows, the place looked shoddy, with the mirrored walls smeared with grime and dust. The air reeked of stale smoke and sex, and spilled liquor made the floor sticky. My shoes stuck to the dirty tiles.

I followed Mama sang up a creaky flight of stairs to the living quarters on the second floor. Some of the whores stayed there, while others had homes nearby. Each bedroom had a separate entrance and a common bathroom with running water, washboards, soap, and shampoo. Several whores lounged in a bedroom, gossiping and smoking. When we walked in, they immediately stopped to check me out. Their partially exposed bodies were draped in cheap, gaudy clothes that advertised that they were for sale. Some were old enough to be my mother—their soft, florid curves barely constrained by their dresses—while others were still filled with the allure of youth. None of them had Youngcha's class, and they all looked, at first glance, like straight trash.

"Hey, green bean," one of them greeted me. "Heard you're a virgin."

"Were *you* ever a virgin?" another one asked the first whore. "I can't remember."

"Hush," Mama sang said, and the other whores laughed. "One of you needs to take her shopping. Here's some cash. Bring back the change, or I'll take it out of what you make tonight."

A whore named Youngmi heaved herself off the bed and gestured for another girl to join her. "Come on, Yuna. Let's get the little bean ready for tonight."

The other whores smiled kindly, all except for the youngest, Choi. She had sloping, cat-like eyes and sharp cheek bones. She had clearly been the babe of the club until I got there, and she eyed me with fierce jealousy.

As we walked to the market to purchase clothes and makeup for my first night, I learned that Youngmi had been married and had two children, but now she was Jinsoo's girlfriend. When she found out I had turned down his sexual advances, she laughed and laughed. We became close friends. She treated me like a sister.

Later, I would learn that Youngmi wasn't a very good whore. She didn't like GIs, and because she was not very pretty, they didn't like her. She rarely had customers, and without income, would be stuck paying off her debt to Mama sang forever. Though I couldn't understand why, she was in love with that grease ball Jinsoo and wanted to be with him every chance she got.

Yuna was pretty and quieter than Youngmi, and did not yet look like a whore. Her face was bright with the hopeful bloom of youth. Her short hair was dyed light brown, and she wore much more makeup than Youngmi.

"This life isn't so bad. We'll watch out for you until you get on your feet," Yuna promised. "Don't sleep with anyone until we look at them first. Some of those GIs are not for first-timers. And if your first time is awful, it'll be harder to get used to it."

We spent the afternoon buying cheap outfits and makeup. The white high-heeled shoes they picked out for me pinched my feet. I found walking in them nearly impossible. I'd felt safer walking in the rice paddies with snakes winding around my feet, but I was determined to learn how to wear them. If I could carry water buckets up an icy slope in winter, I could certainly learn to teeter around in heels. The girls also let me pick out a pair of white go-go boots. I felt chic and sophisticated with white leather wrapped around my ankles.

Makeup was not my strong suit. As a school girl back home, make up was forbidden. At first, I slapped it on like a geisha from hell, not understanding how the thick white powder, fake eye lashes, god awful color shades on my eyelids and blushes made me prettier. An older whore was teaching me how to look like a cheap whore. To finish her skilled, make up lesson, she chased my lips with red lipstick. I back away, refusing outright to put on that red lipstick. I was willing to be made over to her satisfaction, but when it came to red lipstick, I drew the line. I said, "No lipstick for me." I just couldn't bring myself to do the lipstick thing. Somehow putting that nasty red lipstick on my lips was like giving up my last rite to be a school girl again. An older whore shook her head, and said, "You don't gotta wear lipstick to sell sex around here. As a matter of fact, you don't gotta wear anything in this hell hole, green bean."

I'd never before had so many outfits nor had anyone spent so much money on me. I could see why girls like me, who had lived in poverty their whole lives, would be attracted to this lifestyle. Lying on my back a few times every now and then seemed like a fair trade.

Despite my reservations, the cheap hooker makeup did empower me. When I looked into the mirror, I didn't see the old Jeanhee, the one left brokenhearted by her mother's sorrow and her father's disdain. Instead, I saw the new Jeanhee, a girl in search of a second chance at any cost. I was determined to end up in America on my own two feet. This pit stop was to serve one purpose. To earn a one-way ticket to America so I could graduate from high school.

The first thing I did when I returned to the brothel from my shopping trip was to plea again with Mama sang about my dream, the very reason that I ran away from home to be sold to her brothel.

"I turned seventeen less than two months ago," I said, "and I've never slept with a man. I promise I'll be worth your investment if you let me pick who I want to sleep with until I get used to it."

I wasn't exactly lying. I *was* a virgin of sorts. A GI virgin, anyway.

Mama sang already knew about my *runaway* dream, which I had told her the day she bought me She hadn't scoffed at it, so I thought she might be open to this deal. Plus, I knew there was no way in hell I would be staying in this whore town long. If I could meet a GI fast enough, maybe I wouldn't even have to sleep with anyone at all. Maybe my GI would buy my freedom from her by paying off my debt.

Mama sang had a reluctant look on her face, but I kept talking so she couldn't interrupt me. "I'm scared to be alone in a room with those big men, Mama sang. I'm afraid it will hurt. I want to pick someone gentle."

The truth was, I wasn't scared. But this was my body, and I wasn't going to let a man touch me unless *I* wanted to be touched. Of course, I knew, she could refuse my request since she owned me now.

The evening was quickly approaching and all the girls were bustling about, getting ready for GIs, putting on their makeup, slipping into sheer dresses, gluing on false eyelashes, and securing their glamorous wigs with bobby pins. They talked casually amongst themselves about how much they were going to make, some teasing the others about their prospects. Mama sang gave me a wig to cover my short hair.

Rubbing my new hair, which took me months to grow, I said "I like my hair as it is."

"Youngmi, you'll be lucky to make enough to gamble tomorrow," Yuna said jokingly. "You don't even try to get the GIs to notice you. You need to forget Jinsoo, you know, he is bad for your business?"

Choi glared my way, her eyes narrowing to slits. "I'm sure *she'll* make more than that little country chicken over there," she said, referring to me. "Who would want such a skinny thing? Not even for free, probably."

I ignored her and followed the others downstairs. Mama sang still hadn't answered my plea, and in that moment, Choi's curse sounded more like a blessing. I hoped no one would want me. Not yet, until I was ready.

In the soft light of the Lucky Club, even the older prostitutes looked young and pretty. They had smoothed their wrinkles, hiding away years of hardship beneath elegant scarves and hairpins, like a scene cut from an American movie. I had been drilled with a price sheet, so I knew what kind of acts the prostitutes carried out and how much money they made for each of them—five dollars for blowjobs, ten for a short session, and twenty for a long session, or an overnight sleepover. If a GI wanted anything kinky, he paid more money. When Yuna first explained that to me, it repulsed me.

"Yuck!" I said. "That is disgusting. If somebody wants something kinky, he'd better marry me. What does *kinky* even mean, Yuna?"

"Shee! Jeanhee ya, shut up." Yuna looked around to see if anyone else had heard me. "You'd better not let Mama sang hear you say that."

I murmured, "Okay, sister." I understood.

She smacked me lightly on the shoulder. "You have to pretend to enjoy it, or you'll never pay off your debt. You'll be here forever, like Youngmi."

Oh, no! I wouldn't be there forever. I was getting out of there as soon as I met the first GI who would fall in love with me.

She pitied my daring determinations, and said, "Sure, you are." I don't think she believed a word I said to her.

Later, she told me stories about how far some of the girls went in the bedroom to make more money. "I'd never do those things, and neither will you." I quickly agreed with her. Whatever she didn't say, it must be really harrowing to endure...

It didn't' bother me, I was ready before I got there. What I was about to do was for my childhood dream besides more than anything, I wanted to prove Korean's iron clad culture dead wrong about me in *Meegook.*

Mama sang instructed Yuna and Youngmi to escort me downstairs, to the clubroom, at seven o'clock. The other whores distributed themselves at several tables near the dance floor. I wore a baby blue miniskirt, a sparkly pink halter top, a pair of black fish-net hose, and my new pair of white go-go boots—clothes unlike any I'd ever worn before.

The Lucky Club was hopping. Whores danced, rubbing their bodies against GIs. Their goals were to get them to buy a drink or an hour's worth of pleasure. I was appalled. I tried to go unnoticed, staying in my seat so as not to draw attention to myself.

Night had transformed the filthy clubroom into a shadowy den of pleasure, the grime now concealed by soft lighting and the flash of a disco ball spinning overhead. The DJ played five fast songs in a row, and then one slow song over and over. After hearing the songs so many times, I learned a few lines of lyrics, funky music, *California dreaming, Stairway to heaven*, I will survive, and *lay your head something, something.* During slow songs, the GIs and whores would grind their bodies close together, as if they were really in love.

Laughter and raucous voices spilled through the constantly opening doors and onto the streets. From upstairs, I could make out softer, more private noises. Yuna taught me how to entice a GI with my eyes, holding his gaze seductively until he approached me. Everything I was taught not to do as a school girl was happening right in front of my two eyes. I had never seen women shake their hips move sensually, their sole goals were to attract GI for sex. I didn't' know much about hell, but if there was one, this could fit the description. And I was in it with them.

I was drilled by the older whores to accept the drinks the GIs sent my way to help out Mama Sang. I pretended to drink every one of them to run up their bar bills. If I wasn't going to make any money for Mama sang from prostitution, at least I could boost her liquor sales. I never once drank any alcohol, though. I hated the flavor, and even the smell of it turned my stomach. It brought back too many memories of my drunken father. Eventually, the bartender caught on and sent me water or Coke, but still charged the GIs for liquor.

I managed to escape that first night with my make-believe virginity still intact.

As the days and nights went by, I got used to my new life in hell and started getting braver in the club, dancing baby steps to the disco songs, flirting with GIs, and laughing at jokes I didn't understand. I learned how to cross the floor in my go-go boots without stumbling, how to catch a man's eyes and then look away, knowing that in a few minutes he would send over a drink and perhaps join me for conversation. I only spoke a few words of English, but that didn't matter. Most of them just wanted someone to listen, to laugh at certain points, or make a sympathetic face and stroke their arm.

For any conversation beyond that, I had to pull Yuna over to translate for me. I could say *yes* and *no, hi,* and *how are you,* or tell a man he was handsome. Soon, I learn to ask for food and drink, and, of course, recite Mama sang's price list. Since most of the club girls couldn't speak English, many relied on body language more than anything else. Sometimes, the nights flew by, and other times they dragged. Holding on to my *virginity* was always a fight.

During the daytime, the other girls whiled away the hours smoking, drinking and gambling, but I never joined them. I was there to carry out my plan, I knew if I joined them, I might get hooked as they did, and I might be stuck with them for life. No way was I going to ruin my dream. I made every excuse to avoid them during the day. I often hid in my room studying English words, memorizing definitions with the dictionaries I brought with me. I wanted to be prepared for high school in *Meegook*.

The longer I delayed picking a man, the higher my price became. The GIs were intrigued by me with my two-inch short hair. They thought I must be something special for Mama sang to allow me to hold out for so long.

The higher my price rose, the angrier Choi became. She was the youngest, the most wanted one until I came. She'd walk by and blow yellow smoke in my face after a deep cigarette drag, another time with dope smoke with her bad ass two-inch blood red claws. She couldn't stand the way men flocked around me instead of approaching her. Everybody was afraid of her. Yuna said she was born to be a bad ass hooker at birth and I totally believed it. Choi happened to have a steady significant other, a GI who always managed to find her. However, to my detriment, no one ever made it clear to me exactly who her GI was.

All the other whores treated me like their long lost sister, and that also infuriated her. None of them liked her, and whenever I walked by, she would cluck like a chicken, hissing, "Hey, country chicken, why don't you go home? Go back to your rice paddy. No one wants to sleep with a skinny thing like you with short hair like a pitiful boy." I cringed and said nothing in fear her long claws.

One night I wish I could forget, I did the unthinkable. I accidentally caught the eye of her GI, unbeknownst to me, and he immediately approached. "Hi, little virgin girl. May I buy you a drink?"

Before he could even order it, Choi crossed the room and slapped my face. She grabbed my hair, yanked me from my seat, and dragged me toward the front door, swearing the entire time. I struggled, but she had a fistful of my short hair.

"Little bitch!" she yelled. Her blood red long, curly nails were about to come off her ten fingers, to claw my face in pieces, "I told you to stay away from my GI! You no good *yissipalyon, galboya!* No one wants you here!" I had rarely heard those words spoken and had certainly never been called a *fucking whore* before.

"I am going to kill you!" she screamed. "I've been waiting to beat the crap out of you from the day you first walked in, you little country chicken. Let me show you how a *real* bitch fights!"

She hurled every curse word she'd ever heard at me, punching me in the mouth, ears, and forehead. I fell to the floor and curled into a ball as she kicked me. Youngmi and Yuna pulled her back, but when I staggered to my feet, she lunged at me in a final, mad-as-hell effort to shove me out the door, screaming, "Go home! Get the hell out of here! You are not welcome here!"

I tumbled through the plate glass door, landed on my side, and curled into a fetal position, lying in a soup of blood and shattered glass.

The club fell silent.

Youngmi hurried outside, pulled me up, and lifted my left hand gently. A jagged shard of glass was imbedded deep in my arm, and blood poured from the laceration. My vision swam, and I nearly collapsed. Youngmi put her arm around my shoulders and murmured in my ear. "Jeanhee ya, Jeanhee ya, you're fine. You'll be just fine. We're taking you to the hospital, sweet bean."

Yuna ran into the street to hail a taxi.

When we stepped through the doors of the town's only hospital, the pungent odor of rubbing alcohol filled my nose and made me cough. I cried, not because of the pain, but because of the blood that poured from my body. Youngmi held my uninjured hand, while Yuna hovered nearby. Before long a doctor and a nurse rushed in with a syringe. After numbing my arm, they picked out the glass, piece by piece and dropped the bloody shards onto a metal tray. I watched in disgusted fascination as the doctor's needle and thread wove in and out of the cut, stitching it closed with black sutures. When they finished, they wrapped my forearm in stark white gauze. Mama sang, who had shown up while they were working, watched me with concern.

Youngmi paid them, and Mama sang turned to me, her voice frantic, "The police will be looking for you. Please, please, don't tell them your real age, or we will all be in big trouble. I will lose the club, and Youngmi and Yuna and all your friends will be out on the street. You must lie. Promise me, Jeanhee ya, promise now."

I nodded silently, and we turned together to leave.

A squat policeman confronted me as I walked out the door. "You must come to the police station," he barked. "Right now. And we don't need your friends. Just you."

The police station was less than a hundred feet from the brothel. Prostitution was legal in South Korea, but underage prostitution was not, and the police liked to crack down on it whenever they could.

The station held six desks and six uniformed police officers. The captain sat me in a chair across from his desk and hammered me with questions. He was heavy-set, middle aged, and strutted around as if he owned the town.

"How old are you?" he demanded.

"Eighteen," I told him, trying not to let my voice shake. I had never been in trouble with the police before. What if they put me in jail? Or worse, what if they sent me home?

"You! Stupid girl!" He slammed his fist against the desk, and his face turned red. "You are a lying *galbo*. You tell me your correct age, or I will throw you in jail—and you won't last a day with the murderers and rapists in there."

"I… I'm seventeen," I said, singing like a bird. My resolve had lasted less than sixty seconds. The interrogation was probably the easiest he'd ever had. "I'll go home. Please don't send me to jail."

"What year were you born?"

"1957, sir."

"What day?"

"February twenty-second, sir."

"How long have you been working in that whorehouse?" he asked, slamming his fist against the desk again, this time so hard the agonizing vibration soared up my newly stitched arm.

I wiped the tears from my face. "I... I got here two weeks ago, and a pimp sold me to Mama sang. But she never forced me to sleep with any GI, or even let them touch me. I'm just living there. Please, sir, please. Let me go home."

"You can come back tomorrow morning after I arrest Mama sang." With a satisfied look on his face, the captain sat back and folded his hands over his gut. "You'll have to be here to press charges. Don't go back to the club."

"I'll take her to my house and watch her," Youngmi called from the door. She had been standing outside, watching us through the window. She'd followed me to the station, but the police hadn't allowed her to come inside. "I'll bring her back tomorrow and help her get a bus ticket home."

"Why should I let her go with you?" the officer asked Youngmi.

Youngmi glared at him. "Because I'm her friend."

"You're another galbo at the Lucky Club?"

"Yes, sir," she answered.

"I don't know why I should trust you, but I can't take her home with me. I have children. Take her and bring her back tomorrow, or I'll arrest you both."

I was shaking by the time we reached the sidewalk outside.

"Youngmi, what should I do?" I asked in despair. "I can't go home."

"We're going to see Mama sang," Youngmi answered, putting her arm around me. "We'll work it out."

"What if the police are watching us now?" I pulled back. "She'll be so mad at me. I don't want to see her."

"We can fix this, but you have to follow my lead." Youngmi's face grew stern, and for a moment she looked like my mama. "Okay?"

"Okay, sister."

Once we reached Mama sang's house, I stayed behind Youngmi with my eyes downcast.

"Mama Sang, the police want you to report to them in the morning. Jeanhee will not press charges if you wipe out her debt and mine," Youngmi said. "Let us go free. And give her *Sasipmanwon* for the damage." She pointed at the stitches on my arm and the bruises on my face.

I gasped. She had asked for more than six months' pay for an average Korean back then—the equivalent of four hundred American dollars. I was sure Mama Sang would never hand over that much cash, but she immediately started counting bills. The gentle manner in which she'd always treated me had disappeared. If she could have beaten me right then, I'm sure she would have.

"You country girl from Jolla Do," she snapped. "I should've known your kind. This is my savings for the whole year. I was good to you. And this is how you pay me back? You whore. You'd better watch out, or I will tell every mama sang in town about you. Get out! Both of you!"

Youngmi and I backed away.

"Don't let her come anywhere near my club again, or I'll lose my brothel," Mama sang said with a hiss at Youngmi. Then she slammed the door.

Youngmi and I walked to her home without saying much. She caressed my short hair and said to me, "You're going to be okay."

That night I slept like a baby, lying between Youngmi's children, the first full night of sleep I'd had since arriving at the Lucky Club.

The following morning, I went back to the police station and refused to press charges against Mama sang. The Captain was so angry and tried to intimidate me, but I held my ground. Little did he know that Youngmi had coached me and that we had rehearsed the conversation in great detail.

"Don't be scared when he yells at you," she'd said. "That's how they talk. Remember, he's not going to beat you up. You didn't do anything illegal, so he can't send you to jail."

I would never go back on my word to Mama sang, not after she had paid me off. When the officer realized I wasn't going to press charges, he asked if she had paid me to refuse.

"She did, didn't she?" he asked.

I shook my head. "No, sir. She didn't force me to sell my body, either."

He seemed disappointed that he couldn't arrest Mama sang, and he made me promise to go home. I tried my hardest to look meek and repentant, and then I lied and told him I would call my mama as soon as I left the police station.

"Be sure you do," he snarled. "Because if I ever see you again, I'll arrest you and put you in jail."

"Yes, sir!" I backpedaled out of the police station and ran as fast as I could until I could no longer see it.

For months, I worried that he would dart around a corner and take me into custody, but when I finally did run into him again, I found our exchange oddly pleasant.

"You're still here?" he asked, amused.

"Yes," I said. "I met a nice family, and they're taking care of me. I'm a good girl now."

"Oh?" I could tell by his face that he didn't believe me, but he nodded and said, "I'm going to pretend I didn't see you today. And don't let me see you again, or it's off to jail with you."

Chapter 12

Twenty Dollars for Sex

I STAYED AT YOUNGMI'S HILLSIDE home that was only slightly better than the house where I'd grown up. Youngmi, her parents, and her two children all shared two rooms and a small outdoor kitchen. The children reminded me of my brothers and sisters, whom I missed deeply. I felt like a part of family I no longer had. They all knew their mother was a prostitute during the nights, but during the days, she was their loving mother.

Youngmi was sweet to me, too, and treated me as if I were her prized possession. She was proud of how she had rescued me from Mama sang and had gotten our debts wiped clean. Her grease ball boyfriend, Jinsoo, drifted in and out. He smiled at me and occasionally would reenact the night of his unsuccessful conquest and try to lure me into the bedroom.

"Little girl, you still owe me for that lunch," he would say. "And there is a special kind of payment I want, not cash."

"Go away, grease ball!" I would shout, laughing, and he would laugh, too. I'm not sure he would've slept with me even if I'd let him. We had become friends and had developed an odd mutual respect for each other.

I called my Mama for the first time. She was crying, I wanted to cry like a baby but I couldn't. I didn't want to worry her.

"Are you alive, Jeanhee? Are all your limbs attached to your body? Any of them hurting you?" she asked

"No, Mama, I am not hurt, I still have all my limbs."

"Guess what? Mama! I have found a really good job that pays me a lot of money. They feed me three times a day, give me a place to sleep, and buy me fancy clothes to wear."

"Algo….," she cried again. "Where are you?"

"I am in Osan. I have some money saved just for you. Will you come to get it?" I asked my mama.

I met my mama at the bus stop the next day. We both knew the questions and answers about my job were not going to take place. I gave her most of the money I got from Mama sang, and I told her to come back every month to get more. I saw my Mama weep as she got on the bus to go back home, a home where I was no longer welcome. I wanted to cry but I couldn't. I left all my sad tears at home before I ran away.

I never once lost sight of my goal while I was in Osan I needed to get to America and finish high school. I needed to find me a GI as soon as possible to marry me before I got too old to go back to high school.

I had enough money left to get a little room with a kitchen near Whore Alley, two blocks from the GI base. Bars adorned every corner of the alley. Drugs, drunks, gambling, fights, and craziness I had never have imagined went on every day and night. I was on my own—with no supervision—no pimps forcing me to sell myself. I was fortunate in that regard since most prostitutes found themselves working for years to pay their debts to Mama sang.

Yuna, who was able to pay off Mama sang's debt a few weeks before Choi attacked me, was from the same region as I, Jolla Do, so we had a special affinity for one another. I followed her from bar to bar as she worked, and she became my personal bodyguard. Any GI who wanted to approach me had to go through her first.

"Not him," she would say. "He's no good for you." Then she would shake her finger at the man flirtatiously. "Talk to me, handsome soldier. You stay away from her."

I always listened to her. I had trouble keeping the GIs away, though. They followed me as if I were a magnet, offering to buy me drinks and meals. In my heart, I still hoped to land a GI without prostituting myself.

When Yuna finally approved a GI for me, I knew I was about to have sex with a man I'd probably never see again. I was about to sell myself, body and soul, for twenty dollars. I reminded myself, *this is for my second chance at the American dream. I can do this.*

I was scared and unsure of what I was supposed to do, so I let him kiss me on the lips. He fondled my breasts as he undressed me, and soon my underwear dropped to my feet. He picked me up, laid me on the bed, and said something I didn't understand. I made twenty dollars. The next day, he came to find me. Yuna asked him if he was married, and he said that he was. He started crying when I refused to see him again. I didn't understand his tears. I needed to find an unmarried GI and had no time to waste on tears.

With another GI few days later, I got undressed, only to find blood flooding between my legs. Embarrassed. I started crying while squeezing both my legs trying to stop the bleeding. In that moment, I felt naked as I never had before. I was thinking he was going to get the hell away from me instantly. Instead, he brought Kleenex, crying with me while wiping blood off my legs. He comforted me by hugging me sweetly and by gesturing with both of his palms together next to his face and his eyes closed…he told me that we won't have sex, we. would just sleep together

"Sleep… Ok?" he said.

I said to him, "Ok, GI, we sleep…"

He held me like a baby girl in his arms all night long. For the first time since I ran away from home, I slept peacefully all night.

I tried to give him his money back the next morning, but he pushed it back to me and said, "Thank you!" I was astonished. I was the one who should have been thanking him. I saw him from time to time after that night in different bars>. He would always wave hello and send me drinks, but he never asked me for sex again but always stared at me sadly as if he was wishing for something I could never give to him…

In the summer of 1974, the day arrived that I had been waiting ever since I had come to Osan. It was the day that would change the path of my life, and Yuna was the one who started it all. She couldn't wait to introduce me to John.

"Jeanhee ya," she said. "Guess what?" My eyes went wild and crazy waiting for her surprise.

"I think I found one for you. He is a young cowboy only nineteen years old, two years older than you."

Chapter 13

GI John

JOHN HAD JUST ARRIVED TO Osan US Air Force Base in South Korea. He wore cowboy boots, blue jeans, button-up shirts, and a ten-gallon hat. The only thing he was missing was a horse and gun holster on his waist. He was the funniest GI I had ever met. Though I already smiled a lot, thanks to Woojung's teachings, he was the first man who had ever made me laugh out loud. Conversations were impossible tasks because of the language barrier, but he used every technique available to tell me what he was thinking: body language, drawings, and even charades. Once, he stood against a wall and pretended to be a clock, moving his arms at angles and making tick-tock sounds, sending me into peals of laughter. When we were together, the world faded into the background.

He wasn't a big man like most of the blond-haired, 5'8", blue-eyed GIs I'd been chasing. He had a head full of dark hair and hazel eyes. He'd been in the Air Force for only six months. He was from Mexico, Missouri, a place I had never heard of, but it sounded fascinating because it was in America.

"Yuna, you can't keep Jeanhee forever," he said. "I want her. I'll take good care of her."

"You might not be able to afford Jeanhee," Yuna said cleverly. "After all, she is a virgin—men ask me for her every night, and I send them away. They're not good enough for my Jeanhee."

"How much?" John finally asked.

"Two hundred dollars a month, plus her expenses," Yuna said. "No less!"

"Done," John said, and he shook her hand. "I would've paid more than that."

Then he scooped me up and twirled me around, laughing.

Yuna laughed, too. "You two are big innocent babies," she said. "You deserve each other. Neither of you should be out on the streets."

John joined me in the little room I had rented. He always called me *honey,* and I thought it was because he thought I was sweet like honey, but later I found out that's what American boys call their ladies.

John and I felt so connected from the moment we met even though I didn't' understand what he was saying. Just the way he looked at me wasn't enough. He would buy me roses and tell me he loved me every chance he got. My past shame was not mentioned. Besides, I couldn't' speak enough words to explain my past mistakes nor why I was in Osan. For both of us, it was apparent that our relationship wasn't based on sex even though it started with asexual arrangement. We both were teenagers. He was lonesome being away from home and I was too.

We soon fell in love.

I knew that John would marry me one day soon. My days of hanging around bars searching for a GI to take me to *Meegook* were over. I had found my *GI. John.*

I pieced together phrases in English, and he learned a few words in Korean. With my dictionaries, I learned a word a day and practiced difficult tongue-tied- English pronunciation. My key words in order of I am hungry, I like to eat, and I love you. We loved going to the movies on base, I didn't understand a word, but it was one of the perk for GI girls. I would always ask for popcorn, a Coca Cola, and, of course, a Hershey bar. I would unfold the silver foil slowly and drop those perfect rectangles into my mouth, one by one, remembering the day I had first tasted the heavenly sweetness when I was eight years old.

After the movie, John would take me to the Non-commissioned Officer's Club— better known as the NCO club—and feed me hamburgers and French fries with pools of ketchup.

"Slow down, honey," he would say as I gobbled my food. "Nobody's going to take it away from you."

When I was growing up, I never had enough food or affection, but now I was getting plenty of both.

Two English phrases I had to learn were *Excuse me!* and *Thank you!*

If I passed too close to an American, I had to say, "Excuse me!" and I had to say it back if they said it to me. "Excoosemeeee!"

I couldn't help but think to myself how strange Americans were, saying the same words again and again all day long. I never heard my parents treat each other so politely. But if I did anything nice for John, he would always say, "Thank you!"

Within a short time, John had given me more hugs and kisses than I had gotten during my previous seventeen years combined. Actually, I had never gotten a hug from my mama growing up, not even once. She may have when I was born but I couldn't remember that far back. I was in love with American culture and all of its hugs and kisses. I was taught to speak with body language, but I adapted to learn gestures of emotions in speaking language.

I didn't need John to go down on bended knee or to hear the swell of violins to know that he loved me. His smile was enough, and I smiled back. I missed his physical affection while he was at work and couldn't wait for him to come home to me.

We had been living together for about six months when I noticed he was grinning more than usual one evening. Through a mixture of hand movements and broken English, I asked him, "Why you laughing?"

He replied,' Uhmmm! Jeanhee, I," he pointed to himself," I want to marry you." …. pointing at me. "I want to take you," …motioning airplane in the sky... "home with me to *Meegook*, America."

I didn't understand much of what he said, but I heard going to *Meegook,* and I knew the word, America! I smiled so big that I thought my face might split and threw myself into his arms.

"*Chungmal?*" I cried in Korean. "Yes, me be your wife? John, I

...so happy!"

He may not have understood my words, but he understood that I was ecstatic. The news was almost too much for me—a GI was going to marry me and take me to America. That meant, I was going to high school in *America!* I danced around our tiny room in a circle until I got dizzy.

The following week, John hired a marriage broker to start the paperwork. We quickly realized our wedding plans would be more difficult to carry out than I had initially imagined. Because I was only seventeen, I needed my parents' permission to marry. The day the marriage broker told me this news, John came home and found my face clouded with fear. My father would be less than glad for his shamed daughter to come home. On top of that, he would never allow me to marry an American.

John didn't seem as worried as I was, but, of course, he had never met my father. He wanted to meet my mother and my siblings and offered to accompany me on the trip home, but I had already brought shame to my father. Bringing an American GI would broadcast my profession to all the neighbors. No decent Korean girl would marry an American GI.

I packed my little satchel for a one-night stay and called home to tell my siblings I would be arriving on Friday by train. I made sure they understood I wasn't coming home to rejoin the family, but to get my father's permission to leave South Korea.

The train ride home was different from the one that had taken me to Seoul. Instead of being excited for the next step in my journey, I was filled with shame. I wished I had a mask of a pretty girl's face—maybe Oksoon's or Woojung's—so I could hide behind it. Despite my conservative clothes and makeup-free face, I was sure everyone knew where I'd been and what I'd been doing. While I was living in Osan, my shame had receded. Most of my friends were prostitutes, and around them I felt shameless. Living with John was no big deal. Returning to my hometown and its strong Korean traditions made me recognize that I had become a different kind of Korean, one my family would never be able to accept.

By the time the train chugged into the station, I shook from head to toe. I was sure my brothers and sisters had learned my secrets and wouldn't show up to greet me. I had protected and loved them for so long, and I couldn't bear the thought of their disapproval.

I clutched my bag and held my head high as I marched across the platform.

"Hi, sister!" Meehee shrieked, running toward me, her eyes wet with tears, her crazy hair as big and uncontrollable as ever. I couldn't believe how much taller Junghee and Yonghee had gotten, and how quickly Sunhee had matured. The chatter of familiar voices filled my ears, and as I hugged each of them, I saw in my siblings' eyes how upset they had been during my seven-month absence.

Sunhee ran her fingers through my hair. "I'm glad you decided to let your hair grow out again, sister," she said. "When you left, I thought I had three brothers instead of two."

"Sister or not," I said while my siblings fought over who would carry my bags, "I can still take Junghee if need be. So you had better behave while I'm home."

"Sister! This is heavy!" Junghee complained. "Did you fill it with bricks?" He wanted to know what goodies his sister had brought for him.

I smiled at him. "It's filled with presents for you and the others."

As I wove through the crowded streets toward the hotel, I felt as though I had never left. Only when I looked down at my simple dress that in no way resembled a school uniform was I reminded that this was no longer my home.

As we neared my old house, my brothers and sisters grew tense and passed secretive looks between each other. Junghee tightened her lips, and Meehee crossed her arms over her chest. Our pace slowed. Finally, I halted.

"What's going on?" I demanded, looking them over. "Why are you all so nervous? Did Dad tell you I couldn't come home? He doesn't want to see me, does he?"

"No, sister." Junghee looked away. "He knows you're coming, but he doesn't care. Mama's gone. We didn't tell you because we didn't know how to reach you in Osan. Mama wouldn't give us your address or phone number. She ran away."

"What?" My question came out as more of a gasp than a word. "She ran away? She wouldn't leave you. Never. What happened?"

"Dad brought home a second wife," Meehee broke in, bursting into tears. "Mama won't come home. She comes to work, and then she leaves."

"Meehee, stop crying," I pleaded. "It'll be okay."

I ground my teeth the rest of the way home. Every step sent a jolt of anger through my body. I couldn't believe my father had done this. My mama had worked her life away for our family. For a moment, I forgot the purpose of my trip. All I could think about was giving my father a piece of my mind and running his new whore out of town. I stormed through the hotel door, dispensing with niceties and confronted the workers who stood behind the reception counter.

"Where is she?" I asked.

"She who?" they said in unison, playing dumb.

"It is good to see you, Jeanhee ya," one woman said. "Your mama will be happy."

"Who?" I said, ignoring her pleasantries. "That young bitch my dad brought home. Is she here? In our mama's room?"

I could see in their eyes they knew exactly who I was talking about. They looked down and kept their mouths shut.

"I'll look in every room in this hotel," I said. "I'll find her and throw her into the street."

"She just wants money. Then she'll leave," another one of them said. "She's so young. She doesn't have anywhere to go."

"Oh, no!" I yelled. "No whore of my dad's is going to take the money I send to my mama."

I shoved past them into the kitchen, dropped my bag onto the tile floor, and grabbed the biggest butcher knife I could find. The wooden handle was worn smooth from years of sweaty hands, but the blade was sharp. A thin string of gristle still clung to its glistening edge. I stormed toward the bedroom, and my brothers and sisters ran out of my way, their eyes wide with the image of crazy sister. My father had been irate when I had dishonored the family, yet, he dares to bring a whore to replace my mother, no way was I going to let her be my sibling's step mother not then, not while I was breathing.

As soon as I entered my mama's room, I halted. My father's new wife, a tall skinny woman who was much too young for him, cowered in the corner. She wore the makeup of a whore.

"Get out of my house," I hissed, holding the butcher knife high. "Or I'll slice you in half and throw you in the river!"

I swung at her, close enough that she felt the wind of my blade. Then I noticed her quivering lips. In her face, I saw myself and my friends, Youngcha and Youngmi. Somewhere she had a family who had thrown her away. She had been unlucky to land my father, rather than an American GI.

Then I put away my thoughts and did what I needed to do to protect my family.

"If you don't leave right now, bitch, I will kill you!" I yelled. "This is where my mama lives!"

"Sister!" Junghee cried, running into the room behind me. "Don't hurt her! You'll go to jail. Sister, stop!"

I knew he wouldn't try to grab me while I was swinging the knife, so I pulled my hand back and said to the woman, "My brothers and sisters live here also. You want my dad, take him with you. We don't want him, and we don't need you. Get out!"

One of my mother's workers grabbed me around the waist, and a second one twisted my wrist until I dropped the knife. Sobbing, the girl slung her clothes into a ragged suitcase.

"You're crazy!" she shouted, holding a framed picture to her chest, mascara running down her cheeks. "You're a crazy girl!"

"That's right!" I yelled back. "I'm crazy, and if I find out you've come back, I'll get that knife and finish what I started!"

Within a few minutes, she ran out of the house and onto the street. My mama's workers let go of me, and I turned to face my brothers and sisters, my heart still pounding in my chest.

"Where's Mama?" I asked. "I want to bring her home."

My brother told me she was staying in a nearby motel. I ran to find the Chanhyundong Motel. A little old lady in the front office told me my mama's room number. I entered her room without knocking. My poor mama lay on the floor with a wet towel on her forehead, crying. When she saw me, her face crumpled.

"Jeanhee ya, my daughter."

We wrapped our arms around each other, something we rarely did, tears streaming down our cheeks.

"Mama, I'm going to America," I told her. "I'm marrying a GI, and I'm going to live in a nice house and have nice things and never be hungry.

Every month, I'll send you money so you'll have plenty of food and be able to afford somewhere to live if Dad should bring home another slut."

"I won't go home to your father, Jeanhee ya," my mama said. "He's had that woman in our house. I won't go there." She shook her head vehemently. "I've put up with enough from that man."

"You must go back," I said, taking my mama's hands in my own and looking her in the eye. "Junghee, Sunhee, Meehee, and Yonghee need you. If you don't raise them, she'll take your place. Do you want a woman like that to raise your children? What will happen to the girls with a mother like that?"

I helped her pack her things, and we returned home together.

Meehee and Sunhee had already removed all traces of my father's second wife from the house. Somehow, they had even gotten rid of the smell of her cheap perfume.

I turned to my mama again.

"This is your home, mama. Don't ever let anybody run you out of here again. You tell him to leave and take whatever whore he brings home with him. One day, I'll buy you your own home with a garden full of flowers. You'll wear the prettiest clothes, and I'll shower you with lots of jewelry to show off to the neighbors." My mama smiled.

"Mama, you can still come to get money from me once a month as you have. I am not leaving Korea yet. Guess what? Mama, I am planning to go back to high school in *Meegook*." She didn't' believe me but I wanted her to know that I hadn't failed in life yet. I got choked up and had to stop talking. I desperately wanted to tell my mama how much I loved her but I couldn't. She herself was never taught to say "I love you" by her own mother.

My father didn't come home that evening. I hoped he'd show up the next morning. I sat with my mama and brothers and sisters, and we talked long into the night, gorging ourselves on Hershey bars, M&Ms, Snickers, and cookies I'd brought from my new life. They gobbled the exotic treats by the fistful. I had also brought some black market items, including Vaseline, instant coffee, Spam, toothpaste, soap, shampoo, and Marlboro light cigarette for my Dad. My family had never seen any of those items from America before.

My skin had grown thick. I'd been forced to grow up while I was away. I would never voluntarily tell them how I had met John, and they would never ask. I think they knew the answer would be one they didn't want to hear. Mother was the only one who knew, because she came to collect money from me every month. I wanted them to stay as they were with their ideals intact and their minds naive.

I described John as best I could, drawing a picture of a nineteen-year-old redneck dressed in cowboy boots, cowboy shirts, and Wrangler blue jeans whenever he wasn't in uniform. I told them I had an electric stove and had learned to cook Ramen noodle soup. And of course, I told them I was moving to America to finish high school.

"Will you come get me one day, sister?" Yonghee, the youngest, asked, his eyes shining. None of the others cared. Immigrating to another country was an unthinkable dream to them, and they didn't care to venture beyond their walls. They were perfectly content in Iri.

"Yes," I said. "I'll come get you, Yonghee. One day we'll live in America together."

After my siblings went to bed, my mama put her hand on my arm and looked at me intently. "Jeanhee ya, tell me. Are you happy?"

"Yes, Mama," She cried with me for the past two years of broken hearts and shattered dreams for both of us. Our destinies were going to set us apart thousands miles away from each other. She was losing her daughter for life.

"Mama, I'm going to high school in America and I'm going to be rich one day. I have to study all the time to pass the test in English. Once I register for school, I will send you a picture of me sitting in an American high school. Okay, Mama?"

I don't think she believed me about going to high school, although her pitiful eyes brightened up when I said I was going to be rich one day.

"I don't want your life to be as unhappy as mine. I don't want you to struggle like I have."

"Don't' worry, Mama, I won't."

"Guess what?"

"One day, I am going to be rich and I will take care of you, I promise, Mama"

The following morning, my father gaped at me as he stumbled in through the door.

"You're still around?" he asked with a sneer. "You have no right coming back here for anything. "You've cast shame on our *chosang*— our family tree. If you marry an American, I will mark you out from our family tree. Don't you ever forget, you will no longer be my daughter."

"I know that." I said, pressing the paper into his hand. "Sign this, and I'll be gone forever." My last protest to the mean culture into which I was born was directed to my father. "Don't worry about me coming back here, because I will never come back!"

I didn't tell him how I really felt—that I'd never wanted to be his daughter in the first place—for fear he'd storm out without signing the form.

Once my father sealed the paper with the Kang family stamp, I clutched it to my heart as if it were made of gold.

Nothing stood in my way now.

That afternoon, my mama and my siblings walked me to the train station. Unsure of when, or if, I would ever see them again, I boarded the train with a heavy heart.

"Don't forget us!" my mama cried as the train left. "Jeanhee ya, don't forget me!" she was chasing the train car I was on waving, her hand, sensing I was leaving Korea.

I looked out the window as their tiny outlines faded into the cityscape, and I spent the rest of the train ride thinking about how my childhood had ended. I was relieved when the brakes squealed, signaling our stop in Osan.

Here, I was no longer Jeanhee ya, shamed daughter, but Jeanhee, soon-to-be bride, future American high school student. I hid my permission slip in a small box under my bed.

Finally, in September of 1974, John and I took a morning train to the American Embassy in Seoul, holding hands all the way. People stared at us as we climbed the embassy steps, most likely assuming I was a prostitute.

Our marriage ceremony was brief. I couldn't understand most of the words, except when the judge asked, "Will you be John's wife?"

"Yes," I said, lifting myself up on the balls of my feet and nodding, so happy I could have jumped and touched the moon.

Then it was John's turn to take his vows.

"Yes, I do," he said, the sparkle in his eye turning into a giant smile by the time it reached his lips.

With those words, I changed from Kang Jeanhee to Mrs. John Thompson.

The official stamped our paperwork after we kissed, officially proclaiming us man and wife. I was so excited to be married to a GI who didn't question my purity nor past shame. He loved me as I was.

More than anything and beyond love, soon, I was going to *Meegook* to go back to high school.

I must prove to the Korean people that I wasn't just a loser. I must get back in high school soon.

Chapter 14

Second Chance

JOHN AND I WERE BARELY able to communicate in English. We did our best through use of my dictionaries, gestures and body language.

I was getting used to newly married life. I had no idea what a wife's duties were, but I was so happy and my sex-selling days were over.

Three months passed, and John slipped a slender gold band onto my finger. Five tiny sparkles glistened beneath our lamp light. Wearing a ring, to signify marriage, was an American custom.

"For me?" I asked. I was shocked to see the ring. I didn't' think I was fit to wear a wedding ring. The very idea of wearing a ring as a symbol of marriage, a celebration of my wedding night as a pure virgin bride had left me when I broke taboo, which seemed like a life time ago. I knew that I didn't deserve to wear such a cherished symbol.

"I love you." John sweetly continued.

Umm...I murmured... "I love you, too." I was hesitant but I let it stay on my finger.

John was kind and never raised his voice to me or treated me as if I were less than he unlike my father's treatment of my mama. I began to like showing off my ring to my friends. I became their idol. I was living their dream. Though most of them would never make it out of Osan, I gave them a glimpse of hope.

As weeks passed, I was getting more anxious to go to America, I couldn't just ask him right after we got married. I knew John wanted me to stay with him while he finished his tour in Osan. I taught myself how to say, "I want to go to high school in *Meegook, please.*" I begged him to send me on ahead to *Meegook*. I was so afraid that I may not be accepted to high school for being too old. I was already eighteen years old.

"John, please… I want to finish high school. Please, John? Please? Please?"

"Jeanhee, we don't have enough money to buy you a plane ticket yet."

I hounded him every chance I got.

"Okay, okay," he said, finally, "I've been saving money to buy your airplane ticket. You can live with my parents until I can come get you to the next base."

I received the passport, but they had spelled my name wrong.

"Chin Hui Kang?" I said with a frown. "My name is Jeanhee Kang."

"We're not asking them to change the spelling," John said. "It would probably take them another six months." I decided they could call me whatever they wished, as long as I could land myself in *Meegook*.

Two nights before I was schedule to leave for America, I called home from a pay phone.

"Mama," I said, cradling the phone. "You can't come here to get money anymore. I am leaving Korea."

"Guess what? Mama, I am going back to high school as soon as I get to *Meegook*."

"One day, I am going to be rich. I plan to buy you a pretty home, pay off Dad's gambling debt, and give you plenty of spending money. You never have to work again. It is going to take a while, but I promise I will take care of you, Mama. Please tell Sunhee, Junghee, Meehee, and Yonghee I left Korea."

She started wailing louder and louder ..." *My baby girl, all grown up... Algo...Chal gala, nettal...*"

"Make me proud, Jeanhee ya, okay?"

"Yes, Mama!"

"Don't forget about your mama!"

"I won't, Mama!"

The time came to get rid of evidence! *What happened in Osan must stay in Osan.* Where I was going, I was never going to be needing to wear hooker outfits. My favorite white Go Go boots, six inch FMP, sequin halter, wig, matching miniskirts, fake eye lashes, make ups, all of the slutty outfits were thrown into a dumpster.

I immediately went to the market with Yuma to buy new clothes to make me look like myself again, a school girl my age.

As we were shopping together, Yuna, said, "I'm going to find my GI one day, just like you did." I quickly lost my happy face. I felt Yuna's sadness come upon me and I wished that she had found her GI and that we were shopping for both of us.

"Yuna, you are so beautiful, I know there is a GI just for you waiting to find you soon.'

Yuna's eyes brightened up with hope.

"Jeanhee ya, chalga," as she waived good- bye in tears

"Okay." I nodded in tears. I wish I could find another GI John to marry her so she could go with me. I hated to leave Yuna behind.

As soon as I came back from the market, I started packing. There were a few items I that I remembered to pack before anything else. I made sure both dictionaries, Korean to English, and English to Korean, 3 pencils, 3 notebooks, 3 erasers and my treasure box were in my bag. I packed and unpacked everything, then repacked while John watched. He was both sad and happy. Happy, only because he saw how excited I was to be going back to high school.

On October 16, 1975, exactly ten years after I first dared to tell my mama I was going to America, I proudly stood at a boarding gate about to prove I wasn't crazy after all. All around me, families hugged and cried and waved goodbye. I didn't search for my family amongst them. I knew none of my family had come to see me go. I had no time to be a cry baby.

John slipped two twenty-dollar bills and a hand written note in English in case I got lost into my hand. He told me I would change planes in Alaska, and then fly on the same plane all the way to St. Louis.

He had a downcast expression on his face, but he knew I was happy.

"I love you," I said, wrapping my arms around his neck and kissing him over and over. My cheeks were wet with his tears.

"If you get lost, find a soldier or someone in uniform. Make sure he's in uniform, not civilian clothes. Remember what I said about strangers."

"Okay." I nodded.

I'll see you in six months. I love you."

"Thank you," I murmured. I was sad to leave, but knew that being left behind was even harder for him.

We hugged one last time.

Stepping onto the plane, I believed I was climbing aboard my own dream. I became so giddy, I missed a step and stumbled. The stewardess led me to a window seat and showed me how to buckle in. I'd never been on a plane before, but I wasn't afraid. I would soon be flying over the Pacific Ocean on my way to America. I studied the picture of John's parents and memorized their faces, hairstyles, and smiles.

Like an eagle, the plane flew into the sky, soaring over stark white clouds and a brown-green patchwork landscape. Darkness came, and I slept.

When I awoke, I peered out the window to see an ocean of ice. The plane had stopped in Alaska. This was America, but not my destination. I had to get off the plane, but because I was afraid I would miss my connection or that someone else might take my seat, I didn't leave the gate to get food.

Finally, I arrived at my dream destination in *Meegook—America. The land of opportunity, land of free, land where I will find my second chance.*

I stepped into the terminal in St. Louis, Missouri, and glanced around the corridor until I saw an exit sign. John had promised that his parents would recognize me when I got off the plane. Even though I had memorized their pictures, I took another look at them just to be sure. I glanced at the pictures, and then at the crowd. Glanced at the pictures, and then at the crowd. Until all at once, I spotted a group of people waving excitedly. The family of four rushed toward me, holding up my picture.

"Jeanhee?" They had a photo of me and were taking turns to compare the photo to the real me standing before them to make sure I matched.

"Yeah, it matched!"

"That is her"

They were all much bigger than I, and I decided they must be very wealthy to be so fat. I bowed to John's mother and his father.

"Hi," I said. "I am Jeanhee."

They attempted to bow in return, then grabbed me and gave me a giant hug—a big hug, from big people. I couldn't understand why John was so skinny and thought maybe they hadn't given him his fair share of food.

John's mother hugged me first, then his father, his sister Karen, and Drew, his younger brother. Each took his turn. They stared at me and tried to engage me in conversation, but I hadn't yet learned enough English to go beyond the basics.

John's father grabbed my tattered satchel from the luggage carousel, and his mother led me to a station wagon. I wanted to jump around and yell, "I'm here, America! I finally made it!"

But I didn't want my new family to think I was crazy, so I kept quiet.

Exhausted from the twenty-three hours long flight, I fell asleep as soon as I got into their car. During the ride to my new home, I awoke a couple of times. The air had grown chilly, and night had fallen. The yellow splash of streetlights cast shadows into the car. Within moments each time, I slipped back to sleep, only jerking awake again when the crunch of gravel told me we'd turned off the main road. We were in their driveway.

"Come, Jeanhee," my mother-in-law said. "Welcome to Mexico, Missouri."

I got out and found myself standing in front of a long, narrow, white box-like 'thing.' A trailer, with metal sides. I had never seen one before and thought it might be a train car they could move whenever they needed to, although I didn't see any train tracks.

Inside, the trailer was dim and messy. John's room was tiny, with a few decorations and a narrow bed sporting gray sheets. I peered curiously into the other rooms. They weren't much different. This wasn't how America was supposed to look. I had expected every home to rival Woojung's, with high ceilings and grand windows. The trailer wasn't any bigger than my apartment back in Osan.

The next morning, I saw that all of the other homes in the neighborhood were trailers, some sitting directly on the ground, and others on wheels. Either way, they all looked the same.

I didn't waste any time. I had my book bag I had brought with me from Korea on my shoulder, and I was ready to ask. With a mixture of sign language and broken English, I let John's mother know I wanted to start high school right away.

"Don't you want to rest a little first, Jeanhee?" she asked. "You just got here a few hours ago."

"No," I said, shaking my head, "I am not tired."

"I want to go high school today. I must."

If John's mother only knew what I had done in order to earn this chance... I had been dreaming about this opportunity of my life day and night for past two years. I refused to lose another minute waiting.

After a meager breakfast, John's father left for work at a brick company, while John's brother, Drew, and his sisters Karen and Sherry bustled around the house, preparing themselves for school. I checked the supplies I'd brought with me, a set of dictionaries, Korean to English and English to Korean, 3 notebooks, 3pencils, and 3 erasers. When we were ready, John's mother drove us to town in the station wagon.

The school was a large red brick one story building, the only high school in the city, and had what seemed to be an infinite number of classrooms. I wondered how I'd ever find my way around inside. Students milled about on the fresh green grass, chatting and wasting time before starting the school day. The girls wore makeup and nail polish. The boys had on shirts and jeans, not a uniform in sight. When I saw a boy and girl kissing in a hall way, I was searching for teachers to cast them away. We would have been suspended just for holding hands back in South Korea. I could tell right away that no one here would ever have to kneel in the snow as punishment. I was too busy staring at the other students to notice they were staring back.

John's mother accompanied me to the office to help me register for classes. The administrative workers smiled at me, nodding a lot, trying to be encouraging. They registered me for English, history, home economics, math, speech, and study hall, and then asked for a transcript from South Korea. I hadn't expected to be asked for a transcript. I was in America to get a fresh start. In fear they wouldn't accept me, I lied and told them it would arrive soon. No way was I going to spill the beans about getting expelled for life from high school in Korea. Holding onto my dictionaries, I said to myself that I wouldn't screw up again and reminded myself how I had earned this precious second chance.

A blonde girl escorted me between classes that first day, and I memorized the route so I wouldn't get lost. I couldn't believe how often we changed classes, once each hour. In South Korea, we sat in the same desk for three or four hours at a stretch and the teachers came to us. Here, we went to them. And the classes were much smaller. Instead of eighty students, each class had no more than twenty. Students daydreamed and passed notes during class. Students in America seemed to have no fear of their teachers.

I was lost in all of my classes. The teachers talked too fast, and I never knew what they were saying. I decided to focus on English and home economics, two subjects where I was sure I could make some progress. Every day, something took me by surprise. Kids made out in the hallways, the cafeteria, or anywhere they could. The library was bursting with thousands of books … more than one person could read in a lifetime. The large, sunny cafeteria looked like a fancy restaurant. I took my Korean-English dictionary with me everywhere, determined to learn as fast as I could.

Despite my best efforts, my English wasn't good enough to help me make friends. My inability to communicate made me feel invisible, but it was better than the social shunning I'd experienced in South Korea. My favorite teacher was the special English teacher the school brought in just for me.

At least she understood some of the things I said.

My teachers never pronounced my name correctly, not even once, but that didn't bother me. I was in *Meegook,* attending an American high school, studying English every day. So many other Korean girls would love to be in my shoes. During the 70s, only the best of the best Korean students, who could basically recite Genesis to Revelation forward and backward with eyes closed could earn such a chance to attend an American school.

I had made it back to high school my way. It didn't matter to me how I did it. I had earned my second chance, and I swore to myself no one was going to take it away from me. Not now, and not ever. I wished the school board, my teachers, and my friends from Namsung could see me now. I could just see their shocked faces. I had just won the lottery, one in million chance. I would have posted it on Facebook but Mark Zuckerberg's parents weren't even dating yet.

If the teachers would just slow down, I could understand each page better. A one-page letter to John took me four hours to write. Thank God, I could read faster than I could write. I asked John's mother to send it to him, along with the cowboy shirt I had made for him in my home economics class. In his letters back, John always wrote about how proud he was of me.

I was the first Asian student in the school's history, and my name, picture, and an article about me appeared on the front page of the school newspaper. I couldn't wait to cut it out and send it to my mama.

Within one month, an envelope with six international stamps arrived from my Dad from Korea. I never thought I'd get a letter from my Dad, so it was a big surprise. I was shocked, happy, nervous, and scared. I still remembered his last comments like yesterday as he stamped his seal on the marriage waiver to marry John, "You are not my daughter anymore!"

Holding his letter in my hand nervously, I told everyone that I was going to my room. I sat on my bed and carefully removed the sticky seal to slide out the letter he wrote. Every sentence was written in a formal letter format Chinese style Koreans used, top to bottom, rows reading from left to right.

Dear my daughter Jeanhee,

This is your father. I saw your picture in American High School. I had it framed and hung it on my bedroom wall. I am so proud to have a daughter like you. I always knew you were the smartest of all my children.

I want you to know, I didn't mean what I said when you came back home to get my permission to marry GI. I was angry, just angry about losing you to an American man. You are my daughter, no matter what.

My dear daughter, Jeanhee, I am truly sorry for being an unfit father for you while you were growing up. I am drinking less now. I quit gambling for good after you paid off my last gambling debt before you left South Korea. I just want you to remember you are my daughter no matter how far you are from home.

From Your proud father,
Kang Palhyung

I wept…
and wept some more….
All of the emotions I had tucked away, held deep in my heart for so

many years, hatefulness against him since I was a child, beatings he gave my Mama and us in his drunkenness all came upon me as I wept.

Old tears mingled with new tears, and all together poured down my face as I read the letter over and over, holding it tightly to my chest.

My Father *did* love me.

I forgave my father. His letter washed away all the wrongs he had ever done to me and my mama.

Kimchi and rice became a thing of the past, as Mexico, Missouri, had no oriental grocery stores. Ordering food at school was a challenging. The only words I recognized were *hamburger* and *French fries*. Those were the only items that were familiar, and I could say it without trouble. One day in the cafeteria, a boy approached me from behind and poked me in the shoulder.

He lowered his face to mine and asked, very slowly, "Why do you eat the same meal every day?" He drew out each word so I could understand what he was saying.

I don't know why it bothered him so much that I always ate the same thing, but after that I learn to try fried chicken and mashed potatoes.

Whatever fears I'd had about John's family's reservations about me quickly disappeared. I always behaved respectfully as I was taught in Korea, respected my elders, helped with chores, washed dishes, and helped them cook. On their pay days, they took me bowling and to McDonald's.

I studied non-stop. My English teacher was so impressed with my progress that he gave me an A for effort. I was so proud of that grade. It made me believe I could do better in my other subjects.

Time flew by, six months later, John finished his tour in South Korea and returned home. When we picked him up from the St. Louis airport, he was beaming with no sign of tiredness... He wrapped his arms around me and kissed me firmly on the mouth, then hugged his mom and his sisters. I was so happy to see him. He held my hand all the way home four hours away.

"Jeanhee, your English is so good," John said. "I'm so proud of you."

Not long after he got back, he broke the news that we were moving to Luke Air Force Base in Glendale, Arizona. That was fine by me. I'd held out on giving the school my Korean high school transcript as long as I could, and the administration was growing weary of my excuses. Besides, life in Missouri wasn't what I'd envisioned. My dream of a pretty home and delicate, beautiful clothes was nowhere in sight. John's family wasn't wealthy by any means. I had noticed they ate a lot of cheaply made food like sloppy joe and macaroni and cheese or bread and hamburger meat mixed with flour and milk. We never dined out either.

The move didn't benefit me as much as I had hoped. My new high school in Glendale, Arizona was even more difficult. There was a large number of Latino students, and the administration couldn't afford to find an additional English teacher for me. John worked two jobs, during the day on base and at nights and weekends working for local construction company to make ends meet. We were living paycheck to paycheck, barely paying our bills on time. Except for an occasional trip to McDonalds, we cooked food at home to stay within our budget.

Our one-bedroom studio apartment in a low rent housing neighborhood ten miles from Luke Air Force Base was glorious compared to my school life without a special language teacher to help me with English. After a few months of struggling, I was compelled to quit high school.

I was a high school drop out. What I did to earn a chance to go back to high school back in Korea began to haunt my conscience. I did all that in Osan for this?

I was already nineteen years old, married to a poor GI with no high school diploma.

Chapter 15

Broken Dream

AS POOR AS WE WERE, John pressured me to have a baby. I think his parents suspected that my motives for marrying him hadn't been pure, and he wanted to affirm my commitment by starting a family.

When my period stopped for two months, it made John very happy. He couldn't wait to get the doctor to confirm that I was indeed pregnant. He hugged and kissed me and laughed, and then called his mother. Calling my mother about my pregnancy had never even crossed my mind, besides I hadn't' yet to be able to send her any money yet. My dream to finish high school was drifting farther and farther away.

I was still unable to communicate with John freely. I wished to God that I could just once tell John in plain English about my past mistakes, why I had sold my body for $20.00 back in Osan, how badly I wanted to be a school girl again, and I was no way ready to be a mother. None of it could be explained to him. Instead, all I could do was to lock myself in the bathroom and cry for hours.

"This is a happy time for us, Jeanhee," he said through the door. "Every married couple wants to have a baby. I've never met a woman who wasn't excited about becoming a mother. What's wrong with you?"

In my frustration at being unable to communicate, I cried even harder.

I wished I could scream, throw fits, or even curse but my limited English language denied my tongue.

I picked a set of dictionaries, now tattered with use, and I looked up the word for *abortion* under A in the one that translated Korean to English. I shoved it to John, my finger trembling as I pointed.

"I want this, John. I don't want a baby." I didn't care how much the procedure hurt, or what it might cost. If I had a baby, I would never live out my dream. I'd promised myself as a young girl that I would never have children. Having a baby meant I would be trapped in a sad life like my mother.

John jerked the book from my hands and placed it on the table. "Hell, no. Abortion is illegal here, Jeanhee," he said angrily. "That is *my* baby. If you ask a doctor about abortion, they'll throw you in jail. We don't do those things in this country."

I was deathly afraid of being deported to South Korea and having to work in a brothel again.

My first son, Joshua, was born at the end of sixteen hours of labor. I cried a lot during childbirth, not only from the pain, but also from the realization that I could never return to school. Then *he* came. A tiny, helpless baby, and he was all mine. After the nurse wrapped him tightly in a blanket, she let me hold him—a little bundle of life, a life that depended *completely* on *me*.

I had no idea how to be a mother.

We couldn't afford disposable diapers, so washing dirty diapers and constantly feeding the baby became my daily routine. I was completely worn out. Taking care of a tiny baby's need at all hours, I forgot to eat. Trapped, overwhelmed, and exhausted, I became anemic. The doctor instructed me to eat liver every day for the next six months.

Two months after Joshua's first birthday, I had another son, whom we named Jason. I now had two babies and a poor husband, and I was a high school dropout.

I had become my mother.

John was assigned to Lackland Air Force Base in San Antonio, Texas, two years later. John's new status as a *Drill Sergeant* meant that he received a higher paycheck, but not by much. Determined to be a skilled drill sergeant, he brought his lessons home to me. He practiced commands and sang marching songs in our bedroom, and I rolled on the ground with laughter when he made his voice deep and harsh.

Soon, however, his behavior ceased to amuse me. He started barking orders and trying to run me as if I were one of his basic trainees. Despondent, I wondered where his boyish sweetness had gone. Where was the man who used to tick-tock like a clock and tell me jokes late into the night?

As I saw our marriage disintegrating, looking more and more like that of my parents every day, I wanted to be free. I didn't want to be married. I was wasting my life away... still without high school diploma. What I did in Osan was coming back to haunt my soul.

I told John that I want to end our marriage. John didn't take me seriously at first.

"John, I want a divorce," I told him over and over. "I don't want to be your wife anymore." Lacking English still, I couldn't clearly explain what all I wanted in my life before it was too late, before I got too old, and I wanted to give it another try to get an education. I wanted to taste freedom and to find out who I was. I knew he wouldn't hear any of it even if I could tell him.

"We'll work things out, Jeanhee." he said. He was in denial and thought I'd get over it.

"I am leaving you!" I screamed at him. 'When you come home from work, today, I will be gone."

He quickly jumped up from the couch, and said, "No way am I going to give you a divorce. Do you hear me? We're *not* getting a divorce,"

He shouted like a drill sergeant.

I left John. I packed my clothes, taking what I could in my little bitty beat up car. I left my wedding ring on the counter, a note next to it letting him know where the boys were. I swung by on the way out and left my boys with my best friend and neighbor three doors down, Moonsook. I hugged my boys tightly, crying my heart out as an unfit selfish mama. Holding their tiny hands to my heart, I promised them that I would come back to get them as soon as I could I kissed their sweet cheeks, took a one last look at my poor boys, and got in the car, only to jump out again. I went back to hug them one last time and told them that I would bring them a lot of toys when I came back.

They were only two and three years old. I begged my sweet girlfriend, Moonsook, to take good care of my babies for me. Moonsook cried with me and said, "Don't worry, I will take good care of those babies just like my other two. They will have fun together.

Through Moonsook, I had met a Korean girl my age named Miye, who had a beautiful oval face and a perfect smile. She was newly divorced with no kids. She had told me that her husband had left her for a blonde haired American girl... We hit it off right away, and she let me move in with her.

Miye and I worked as waitresses at a popular Chinese restaurant called The Golden Wok in San Antonio. My very first real respectable job. The Wok's authentic noodles and vegetable dishes were so good that a line formed out the door at dinnertime, and on good nights I made as much as two hundred dollars in tips. I got along fine with the chef, who was from Hong Kong and spoke no English but had a wonderful toothless grin. But I did not get along with the chauvinistic manager, Luciano.

I had Luciano pegged from the moment I started working there. I had learned to spot his "type" while interacting with some of the bolder GIs in Osan. It would always start small, with a little gesture here, a phrase there. As time went on, he began acting creepier and creepier, not even trying to hide his gaze. But for the most part, he kept it just this side of offensive. That would change one day after my lunch shift.

Luciano must have felt it was time to make his move. One day after lunch hour was over, everyone was finishing up to close for a few hours until dinner hours, and he took off his shirt in an attempt to impress me with his physique. I couldn't help laughing at his bravado, "Yeah, yeah, you are showing off."

"Too dumb to get a high school diploma?" he asked with a sneer. "You will always be a waitress. Why do you need high school diploma? Huh?"

His words propelled me to start night school to study for my GED. I didn't care how I got my high school diploma, and now that I was twenty-two, a GED was my only option. I was glad to be back in the classroom. Twice a week, eleven other high school dropouts and I would meet in a local church to study for our high school equivalency exam.

He didn't take rejection nearly as well as that grease ball pimp had back in Osan. He was using his power to punish me, making me clean the toilets and scrub the cracks in the tile with a toothbrush.

I got sick and tired of cleaning toilets, one day, I made a pact with Miye and one other girl to get back at Luciano for the harassment. So one Friday morning, the busiest lunch day of the week, we clocked in, and then clocked out two minutes later, walked up to his face all together, shouting, "We quit, Luciano! Enjoy the lunch crowd!"

As we knew she would, the Golden Wok's owner, Lily, called me to ask why we'd quit without notice. I couldn't wait to tell her what had been going on with Luciano. She demoted him that day and gave us our jobs back.

The next day, we found Luciano in the kitchen making egg-rolls. To make his humiliation complete, I asked him if I could show him how to roll the dough faster.

In a few weeks, I realized I may had eaten too many egg rolls. I was gaining weight and was no longer able to fit into any of my clothes. I had gotten fat. I needed to do something about my double-stacked tummy. Losing weight didn't require a high school education. I went to Walmart, bought a book entitled *How to Lose Weight Fast.*

Be a runner, the author said.

"Why not? I said to myself. I won my first race beating all those tall leggy girls once."

"How hard can it be?" I didn't look as pretty as Lyndsay Wagner from *Bionic Woman* on TV, but I could run like her.

I bought myself a pair of cheap running shoes, running shorts, and a T-shirt with a large neon check mark on the front. I bought a cassette player with headphones like the ones I had seen in a fashion magazine.

I started with one mile per day and extended my distance as running got easier. Soon, I ran from three to five miles a day religiously. My daily runs exhilarated me, and as the sweat dripped from my body, my worries and fat melted away.

I was hooked on endorphins. My daily run has remained a part of my fitness regimen to this date.

Chapter 16

An Offer I Couldn't Refuse

I WAS AT AN OFFICER'S club on Lackland Air Force base with Miye on our night off when Robert first approached me. He was dressed in a one-piece, hunter-green flight suit and was exceptionally tall, slim, and good-looking. I soon learned that as a young man, he had run away from home, contrary to the wishes of his wealthy parents.

He had volunteered for the Air Force at age eighteen and served in the Vietnam War. After ten years overseas, he decided he wanted to become an officer, so he finished his bachelor's degree through the University of Maryland's overseas program for active GIs. When I first met him, he was just one-month shy of finishing the United States Air Force Officer Training School. He wanted to be a pilot, but because of his age, he no longer met the requirements and had to settle for becoming a radar controller for an AWACS spy plane.

Robert was the exact opposite of John. He was well-bred and came from a wealthy, successful family from Syracuse, New York. His father worked as a chemical engineer for the Bristol-Myers Company, and his younger brother, Jeff, studied at Harvard Business School. His youngest brother, Adam, had earned a full basketball scholarship at USC, and his mother was a professor at Syracuse University. I was drawn to this well-educated man with piercing blue eyes. Robert conveyed a caring warmth I had never felt before. He was almost ten years older, so caring like a father I had never really had.

Robert was as surprised as I was by his infatuation with me. He had never before met a woman he wanted to come home to every night. During all the years he had spent in Vietnam, the Philippines, and Thailand, he had never before met a lady who tempted him to give up his carefree bachelor lifestyle. He later explained that he fell in love with me the first time I smiled at him. Woojung's lesson had gotten me into trouble.

Robert and I went on a date the following day. Over the next few weeks, he asked me out to fine restaurants and showered me with compliments, always telling me that I was beautiful. He was a perfect gentleman. Much time had passed since John had shown me any tenderness, and I hadn't even realized how much I missed it.

A few days before Robert was to leave for Tyndall Air Force Base to begin the final stint of his training, he took my hands in his and squeezed them gently. Then he reached into his jacket and pulled out a round-trip ticket to Panama City.

"Jeanhee, I love you. Will you fly to meet me?" he asked. "You don't even have to sleep with me. I'll take care of you while you get your GED, and I will even send you to college if that's what you want. I'll help you get your children back. And after Panama City, I'm deploying to South Korea. I put in a request to go there in hopes that you'd come with me. I know you miss your family."

He didn't let me get a word in edgewise. I could see how desperately he wanted to convince me, he had made plans for my life. "And in case you change your mind, I bought you a round trip ticket so you can return to San Antonio anytime you want."

For once, I was speechless. I was overwhelmed by a man I hardly knew saying everything I wanted to hear.

I accepted the tickets. I couldn't believe I had just been offered a round trip air ticket with no strings attached from a man I hardly know. I had been enjoying my new single life, and now another man wanted to put me back in a cage. Robert was not part of the plan. But at the same time, I was deeply tempted.

"I'll keep the tickets for now," I said. "But that doesn't mean I'm coming there. May I have some time to think about it?"

"Of course, sweetheart," he said. "I'm a patient man. I can wait."

I certainly didn't want another husband, but that's what I ended up with, almost before I knew it.

On graduation night of officer's training school, Robert's parents flew in from Syracuse, New York, and he insisted I meet them. At the celebration dinner, his parents scrutinized me carefully. The pressure made me uneasy. Robert's mother was blonde and beautiful, her makeup flawless, and she had her hair pulled back into a perfect sleek ponytail. Her dark coral lipstick accentuated her egg-shaped face, fair skin, and gleaming white teeth. And on her delicate finger sat the biggest rock I had ever seen. It sparkled like the disco ball in the Lucky Club. Despite their social class. His mother and father were nice and welcoming, with the same air of serenity Woojung's mother had conveyed so effortlessly. But I sensed their apprehension. What did their handsome, accomplished son see in this little scrap of a woman? They didn't understand. To be fair, neither did I.

On Robert's last night in San Antonio, he and I stayed together at the Hilton Hotel on the River walk. I reluctantly gave him my promise that I would join him in Panama City, but also warned him that I still needed some time.

Sweetness was longing for a man I hardly knew yet. I felt right to spend the night with him, and we fell into bed naturally and effortlessly, our bodies working in tandem. Afterwards, he held me so tightly against his hairy chest that I thought I might smother.

I pondered Robert's offer all night long, wondering if I could learn to love him one day.

We had only dated for four weeks. I had not had a chance to spread my wings wide freely as single woman yet. Marrying again was the last thing on my mind. As days went by, I was missing my babies desperately. John rarely let me see them thinking I would come back by baiting me with my babies.

I asked Miye for an advice. She was close to my age, but she often acted like an older sister.

"You have nothing to lose," she said. "Keep your ticket, and if he turns out to be a horrible man, come back. You can always live with me again."

A few days later, I called Robert. "I've thought about your offer, and I've decided to take it. I'm coming to Panama City."

"I'll make you so happy, Jeanhee. I promise I will be so good to you. You won't be disappointed."

Miye and I both cried as my plane pulled away from the gate—we had grown so close. I wasn't ready for another relationship, and yet the burdens of life have a way of clouding one's judgment. I needed financial security, my babies, and to get my GED to go to college.

Robert had promised me all three.

When I stepped off the plane in Panama City, Robert rushed toward me with tears streaking down his face. After a long hug, he put his hands over my eyes and led me to the parking lot. When he took his hands away, we stood in front of a brand new red Firebird. He pressed a set of keys into my hand.

"This is your car," he said. "You can take it anywhere you want to go."

Grateful and confused, I kissed him long and hard in the front seat of that beautiful car. His generous gift made me grateful, but conflicted. What would I ever achieve for myself if I kept taking handouts from men?

We had dinner at a restaurant perched on the edge of the seashore, with the gentle crash of the waves underscoring the seriousness of our conversation. While the sun set, Robert poured out his heart and attempted to convince me that I had made the right decision in joining him. Eager eyes watched me as he poured our champagne and made promises I hoped he would keep.

"I'll help you register for school tomorrow, and then I'll find the best lawyer in town. We'll get Josh and Jason back. I want us to be a family, and they're young enough to accept me as their father. We can make this work, Jeanhee. I promise."

He was true to his word, and I soon started school on the base, taking a business and typing class. Robert rented a beautiful condo on the beach and hired a maid. The place was fully furnished and had more than enough room for us, with two red L-shaped couches in the living room and sleek black appliances. The furniture had a beach theme, and the green and beige curtains were made from a pretty palm-tree print, with beige carpet throughout the condo. It was very cozy.

We went out to dinner every night after his training class, and every weekend he asked what *I* wanted to do—and that's what we did. He never tired of being tender toward me and made it his mission to make me happy every single day.

In his eyes, I was precious.

I, on the other hand, didn't feel as if I deserved so much attention. I believed that if he knew the truth about my past, he would no longer be able to look at me. I wondered from time to time if I should reveal my secrets, but I decided to stay silent. If I were to move forward in life, Osan would have to stay far behind me.

In September, as Robert was preparing to deploy to South Korea, he proposed with a beautiful diamond ring. Everything in me wanted me to say no, because I believed that marrying him would only sidetrack me again. But how could I refuse the sweetest, most loving man I had ever met?

Looking him in the eye, I listed my shortcomings in hopes he may change his mind "I don't know how to cook, and I hate housework," I said, "I'm independent, I follow my heart, and I fight back whenever I feel the need. I would be a terrible wife, Robert."

"Shh." He pressed his fingers to my lips. "We already have a maid, and we'll get a cook. Once we get your children back, you can join me in South Korea and see your parents. Jeanhee, I love you. Be *my* Jeanhee, will you? We'll be a family, and I'll be the best daddy ever to your boys."

"Robert, you are the sweetest man I've ever met." My eyes welled up with tears, but I still held on to my resolve. "I don't deserve your kindness. I'm not sure I'm ready to marry again. I'm not sure if I'm really in love with you."

"Okay, sweetheart." My words would have been a crushing blow to any other man, but Robert just laughed them off. "Then you'll learn to love me. I'm willing to wait."

I said *yes*. How could I have ever said *no*?

Robert had promised all the right things, and he followed through. Soon, I was in San Antonio to get my babies back in my arms. I stayed with Miye while I anxiously waited to get my babies. Robert gave me more than enough money to hire an attorney. I ended up paying to represent both John and me since John claimed that he couldn't afford to pay. John wasn't thrilled about letting me have my boys. He came up with a solution best benefiting him, knowing that the ball was on his court. He said, "I will agree under one condition."

"Not a problem, you don't have to pay child support, ever!" I said.

All I wanted was to get my babies back to take them with me to Korea. The judge was not so convinced by my willingness to give up child support. She asked me if I was in anyway being threatened by John on this peculiar custody arrangement. I lied to the judge, telling her that I didn't need money because my new husband was very rich.

The judge asked one final time, "Are you sure, Ms. Kang?"

I said, "Yes." I was just so truly thankful, John let me have my babies back. Besides I owed John for bringing me to *Meegook*.

Within two days, my babies and I were to South Korea to join Robert. I found a job to die for at the *Education Center* on Osan Air Force Base, working as the field assistant for the Los Angeles Metropolitan College Overseas Program for GIs. I was in charge of registration for college program using GI bills and Accounts Receivables.

My position at the *Education Center* was a dream job, one of the most sought-after positions on Osan Air Force Base and the highest paying position for a Korean. Because I was a U.S. citizen, they paid me more than five times what the average Korean in the office made, some of whom had worked there for over twenty years.

If only they had known the truth. Just six short years earlier, I had stood outside the base's main gate, selling myself for twenty dollars to any GI who would have me.

My life was luxurious.

I had a loving husband, beautiful home, live in maid to take care of my boys, cook and serve me, and had the most prestigious job any Korean woman could have.

Chapter 17

GED

FINALLY, IN THREE MONTHS OF studying for GED test, I received my long awaited high school diploma. I passed the GED test in English. I was the first Korean to ever obtain a high school diploma after being expelled from a Korean school on Korean soil.

I cried tears of joy for my redemption. I felt like I had just received a degree from Harvard. I was jumping around so excited, barely able to stand, wishing to yell and scream at the Korean culture that had been so quick to give up on me and shut the door on my *education dream*, "Look, Koreans! Look at my high school diploma!" I knew no Koreans were there to hear about a taboo breaker's tainted excitement.

I immediately went out to purchase the most beautiful mahogany frame I could find for my GED certificate and hung it right behind my desk on the wall in my office, for everyone to see. Nobody could miss it unless they were blind. Though it was only a GED, to me it symbolized the redemption of my dark past, the fruits of my life to that point...What I had done in Osan just a few years before was transformed into worth doing by a single piece of paper.

With my freshly minted GED certificate on my office wall, I was able to enroll college classes at night, tuition free because I worked for the college program. I could have never imagined, a taboo breaker, a former prostitute, me, taking college courses in English with Americans. I didn't see that coming. It was an impossible dream on Korean soil during the 1970s.

There is no reason whatsoever that I should have ever gotten restless being married to Robert. I was living Dam Keeper's life, yet I wasn't happy. Taking college courses at night reminded me that I was missing out on my chance to be a school girl. I was already 24 years old, and I felt I was racing against time. Before I got any older, I wanted to reclaim my stolen high school years.

First, I wanted to be free. I wanted to experience college life like a real school girl without being married. I wasn't giving much thought to how I could afford to go to college with my two young sons. My heart was longing for my missed school girl years and I would deal with the finances when I got to *Meegook*. I wanted to walk freely on a campus with my peers, smell books in a library, and study to pass exams.

I had to choose. school or break this man's heart? There were no right words to say to a man who loved me so deeply.

I begged for his mercy as I told him what I wanted the most in my life. I told him that I felt like I was trapped by marriage, I wanted to smell the air without bondage and be a school girl again before I get too old. He knew I wasn't ready when I married him. He was hoping I would settle in and love him back.

"Please forgive me, I want to live out my dream." I begged Robert, "I will never be happy unless I finish college. Please let me go. I just can't be a wife for you," I said to Robert. "I wasn't ready to be married then, and I still am not ready. I am sorry.

I broke Robert's heart. "I love you, Jeanhee," he cried and stroked my hair in anguish. "I'd never keep you from anything, I will let you go because I love you so much. One thing I would like to be remembered as the "Bridge' I built for you in your life." Robert said tearfully.

Marriage as a permanent state of being—living happily with a man, content and warm in his love—had not been on the top of my list of dreams growing up. In fact, I still remembered vividly watching my parents fight and swearing to myself then that I would never be married. It seemed that being stuck with the same person for life, doing the same thing over and over was not my forte. It was like repeating my mother's life all over again. I wanted the freedom to go to college without being tied to marriage. I wanted an adventure instead of having a stable home, being loved, and happily settling for what I had.

A little over a year after we moved to Osan, I divorced Robert in a Korean court. The day that the divorce was granted, I was set free. If I were a bird, I would have flown for days, forward and backward and around the world, both wings stretched as far they could reach, stopping anywhere I wanted to live and experience real life—with no boundaries.

I was consumed by day dreaming of walking across a beautiful campus filled with rows of impeccable, perfectly lined trees, envisioning myself studying with my peers at the library full of books The day I received my *college degree*—would be the day I might consider being trapped again...

I shared my dreams with Sooncha, my new friend while we were having lunch at our favorite Kimhi House on the corner of whore alley, At nineteen, Sooncha was five years younger than I—a baby in my eyes. She called me *sister* since I was older than her. Sooncha was unfailingly sweet, with her big heart mirrored in her shimmering dark eyes. She had caught the attention of Thomas, her GI, when she was a go-go dancer at the Officer's Club, before he married her. *Tom,* as she called him in her thick Pusan accent, worked in Robert's squadron.

"It's time for me to go back, Sooncha," I said. "Robert and I are divorced." "I want to go to college in *Meegook,* but I don't really want to go back to Texas or Arizona, and definitely not to Missouri."

"I know what you can do," Sooncha said excitedly. "You can come to Oklahoma and live with me and Tom. I will be lonesome since Tom will be flying AWACS plane all the time. I am sure Tom will say yes."

I was sure he would, too. He absolutely doted on Sooncha.

When Sooncha told me the next day that Tom had agreed, we were both so happy. We chatted the afternoon away making plans for our new lives, sitting over bowls of kimchi soup at Kimhi House I mostly talked about college, and she talked about having a car to drive and spending Tom's money while he was away. Neither of us could even pronounce *Oklahoma* correctly, but we knew it was somewhere in America and that was enough for us.

"Home of AWACS spy plane, Tinker Air Base in Oklahoma," Sooncha said, excited and jumbling the letters. Then she laughed.

"Who cares how you say it? I am going to America."

She was thrilled. I was glad she had fallen in love with her GI before her face took on the ragged, worn look of a whore.

Sooncha and Tom left me their new address and phone number the following week when they flew to America. Within two weeks, I sold everything to raise money to take with me. With the money I had saved, I would hopefully have enough to get by until I could get a part time job. At the end of November 1982, my boys and I were on an airplane back to *Meegook*.

I closed my eyes and imagined myself soaring above the clouds on my own wings, swooping and diving over the dark ocean below. My boys were excited about flying again. A bumpy landing startled me out of my dream as we touched down in chilly, windy Oklahoma City. Tom and Sooncha were waiting to pick us up. Sooncha bounced up and down on her toes and yelled, "Sister!" over and over in excitement as we neared the exit. We hugged, and she scooped both of my boys up into her arms.

Tom drove us to their new home in Midwest City, in a quiet, middle-class neighborhood.

Josh, Jason, and I were soon settled in Sooncha's small guest bedroom, all three of us sharing one bed. I woke up with a foot in my face more often than not. We were crowded, but comfortable, and Tom was absent much of the time. He was careful not to mention Robert, for the sake of their friendship, and also because Sooncha had requested it. Tom seemed genuinely interested in helping us.

Perhaps he believed he was doing Robert a favor by pointing me in the right direction.

Chapter 18

Jesus and Angels

THE FOLLOWING MONDAY, TOM AND Soncha drove me to Rose State Junior College to register for classes for the spring semester starting in January 1983. By then, I spoke English well enough to register myself.

I squeezed Josh's hand as we walked out of the administration building. We had met with a financial officer who had approved a Pell Grant to cover my tuition and books. I couldn't stop thinking about how great America was. Because I was poor with two boys to raise, the government was going to *pay* for my education.

"Mama is going to college," I told my boys happily as Tom drove us home. "One day, you'll go, too."

We registered the boys at an elementary school near our new apartment close to campus so I could walk to school. The school bus would pick them up and drop them off each day, so it worked out perfectly.

Then Tom said, "Jeanhee, you can get Government assistance while you are in school." What is that? I was intrigued.

"It is called a Welfare program. They will help pay for rent and give you food for your family since you don't have a husband."

"Welfare? Free food and help paying for rent?" I was encouraged because I had been worrying about working and trying to study 10 hours a day to pass tests in English."

I was still in disbelief, I had to ask Tom, "When do I have to pay it back?"

Tom said, "You don't have to pay it back. It is for single moms who don't have enough money to go to college."

I didn't know what to think about getting something for free.

The next day, Sooncha drove me to the welfare office in Oklahoma City. My boys sat on either side of me in the wide front seat, gripping my hands. The building was tall, and its glass windows reflected the city around it. People bustled in and out, some in suits and some obviously very poor.

I had trouble believing that in *Meegook,* the Beautiful Country, the government would give out money to help poor moms eat and pay their rent.

We sat in hard metal chairs as we waited to be called for our interview. Many of the applicants were African-American, while others were white and Native American. A diverse group, yet all of them stared blankly at the stained white walls because they had lost hope and resigned themselves to mere survival.

I was so ashamed and embarrassed to be amongst them. Knowing that I was about become an official beggar asking for handout. I looked around to make sure no other Koreans were there who might recognize me.

"What is this place, Mama?" Josh, who was five years old, noticing something strange about my nervousness, whispered into my ears.

It hit me right then. I was there waiting for a handout among women of all other ages.

"This is a government building." The last thing I wanted to tell my boys was that they were a beggar's sons. Quickly, I gathered my thoughts to make some sense of it all.

I said, "We are going to talk with some people who will give me a test to see if I can pass a test in English to go to college. College tests are really hard to pass."

"Are all these people going to school, too, Mama?" Josh continued with his finger pointing at an old lady with gray hair." Her, too? Mama?"

"Yes, son, she forgot to go to school when she was young and stupid. One day, she got mad at her mama and daddy, and she quit school and ran away from home." Sensing uneasiness in my facial expression, he pointed at another lady.

"Yes, Josh, all of them are going to school, trying to make up for their mistakes." It had been selfish of me to divorce a man who loved me to death, I had it all. The reality of living as a single mom hadn't sunken in yet. I was still lost in the madness of chasing a school girl dream.

When the woman at the desk finally called my name, I left Sooncha and the boys in the waiting room and met with my caseworker, Melissa. She was a cheerful curly blonde in her early thirties, blue eyes not yet jaded, and surprisingly friendly.

"Hi! How do you pronounce your name? Chin Kang?" She said, "Ms. Kang, please fill out all of these forms in front of me and ask me if you have any questions. It took her less than 10 minutes to determine I was a dead broke single mom. Food stamps and monthly rents were approved. She told me what I couldn't buy with food stamps such as cigarettes, drugs, and alcohol.

I said, "Thank you so much."

Just as I got up to leave her office, she said, "Oh, by the way, you must report to me once a month. Do you have a car?"

"No, I don't." My face frowned.

"How are you planning to get to school?"

"I plan to walk to school, it is not that far...' I began to sob again, wiping my tears with my bare hand, quickly preventing from my boys from seeing me cry.

I think she felt sorry for me. She said, "You are going to college to get a degree, and you are going to get a good job when you graduate. I promise you this hard time will pass., I know it will. I have an idea, Ms. Kang. I will come to you every month instead so you don't to have ask someone to give you a ride, how about that?" She sounded like an angel instead of a welfare case worker.

"Thank you!" I said to her.

She instantly replied back, "You are very welcome."

After the shameful stint at the welfare office, I tucked my boys in to bed after a quick dinner with Sooncha. My heart sank watching my boys fall asleep next to me. How selfish it had been of me to give up everything without making financial plans to take care of my boys. I had been reduced to a being beggar. Becoming a beggar in *Meegook* was the last thing on my y to–do- list.

My heart raced with shameful guilt as I remembered tagging along behind my mother while she worked in the field to grow food for us to eat. I don't ever remember her taking us to beg for handouts. We were dirt poor, but we had pride.

The money I had brought with me from Korea for a rainy day would not last very long, and doubts and self pity were ganging up on me. My heart grew heavy and filled with remorse. Studying the innocent faces of my boys as they slept, I realized that they were depending on a stupid dream chaser, a selfish mama. I was all they had. Watching my boys sleep with tears in my eyes, I rubbed their heads and turned my face into my pillow and wept. What had I done? Weeping became crying out in the dark, I wondered if I should just end my misery. At the thought of dying, I realized how my poor mother must have felt when I was only two years older than Josh, the night she drank rat poison.

My Korean pride had been crushed. The reality had sunk in, and all of the responsibility fell into heavy heart. I was a single mom with two young boys without financial security.

I was broken. My childhood dreams were diminishing. I cried profusely, gripping my mouth shut, trying not to cry out too loud at first until my cry became unstoppable. I used a pillow to muffle my cries, and I cried some more, wishing my pillow would smother me to death. Sorrow won the best of me that night. I was lost in the darkness. I lost my war. I lost the will to live.

A bright, shining light invaded my dreams.

A man in his thirties with long blond hair finely dressed in a beige and gold robe tied with a pale blue satin tassel in the waist was standing next to my bed. I had had strange dreams all my life but never one like this one. I knew instantly He was Jesus. Frightened and unable to move a single limb, I froze. The only part of my body I managed to move was my eyes to see Him.

Jesus grabbed my right arm with his right hand gently and asked ever kindly, *"Why aren't you going to church?"*

"Going to church? Me? Why would anyone like me go to church? You must not know of my dark past."

I was questioning Jesus as if He could read my mind while I was glued to my bed completely immobile including my mouth, but that didn't keep me from expressing my doubt of His presence and I couldn't help wondering if Jesus have made a fatal mistake thinking I was someone else with no dark past.

The surreal nature of His presence overwhelmed me. I wondered if I hadn't imagined the entire dream. I was unsure of what to make of any of it.

How did Jesus know where I lived?

DANG! Did I cry that loud? Did the Baby Jesus from the church when I was seven years old on Christmas Eve remembered me? I was sitting in the back, there's no way he could have seen me.

Had he been following me ever since? How in the heck did he know I was crying in despair anyway?

Why would Jesus even show up in my dream to ask someone like me such a question? Wait a minute. Did my God's face tell Jesus about me to feel sorry for me? The last time I saw my God's face was fifteen years ago. I clearly remembered the yellow pencil the pastor had given me instead of that sweet rice cake and the resentment I had harbored toward the church ever since.

Still shaken by the out-of-nowhere visit from Jesus, I gathered my wits and slid off the bed to turn on the lamp. I pushed the shade aside so the light wouldn't shine in my boys' faces and reached into my suitcase. Pulling out my worn out treasure box, I opened it and took out the pencil I hadn't touched since that night so long ago.

Why me? Why going to church? Those church goers with unjaded faces will know in a heartbeat what I did in my dark past as soon as I put my right foot in their church.

I was certain Jesus had mistaken me for someone else, as I climbed back into bed without waking my boys and forced all thoughts of Jesus out of my mind. Eventually, I fell back to sleep, promising myself, not to cry too loud next time, in fear that Jesus might come back to ask me, *"Why aren't you going to church?"* again.

The next night I had another dream, only this time it wasn't Jesus.

An old lady was dressed in a pure white linen Korean traditional dress—a *hanbok*. She had her hair perfectly combed and tied with *bynyu to the back*. Her pure white-white linen dress was impeccable, without a single thread of wrinkles. As I held my breath, my body froze again exactly like the night before. She sat on the floor in a shadowed corner and ducked her head as if she didn't want me to see her face.

"Your grandmother sent me to give you a message," she said, "It is not your time to die. We are not ready for you." She also said to tell you, "All your childhood dreams will come alive, and you must live to see it."

She disappeared quickly just like Jesus did. Startled wide awake and chilled to the core, I sat up in bed and looked around the room. Not once, but twice.

No one was there.

After those two strange nightmares, I gave up any thought of ending my life for good, and I knew not to ever fall asleep crying like a baby again.

I never did go to church in fear that those unjaded faces might find out what all I did in my life. I had literally broken all of the Ten Commandments by the age twenty-five. I could just see it already. As soon as those church people found out my dark shameful secrets, surely they would have kicked me to the curb.

True to her word, Melissa came to my apartment each month to visit with us and to get an update on my life, to check on the kids, and to review the condition of my apartment. She also needed my signature on the required paperwork. When she discovered I ran every morning before

I went to class, she learned my routes and would stop me along the way.

"Jeanhee, stop! Please!" she would shout. "Stop for a few seconds! I need your signature!"

With a smile, I would jog backward to her car, sign the paper, and get my aid for another month. She always made small talk while I signed.

"You're making me breathless, and you're the one running," she'd say with a laugh. "I wish I had the same motivation to run every day as you do, Jeanhee!"

She had apparently forgotten about checking my apartment or checking on my kids after school. I think she probably thought I was a good mother and a responsible person. Perhaps, she hadn't met too many welfare recipients who were also dedicated runners.

I wasn't as young as the other students, but I didn't let it bother me. I walked tall and proud as if the people in South Korea could see me walking into my American classroom thousands of miles away.

I was back in school. That was what mattered the most.

Walking to class that first day, I clutched my books and sharpened pencils to my chest and recalled that skinny little girl who was barely six-years-old, the skinny little girl with a dream who walked beside her mama on her first day of school in South Korea.

"This is *my* second chance," I said aloud. "I am not going to be expelled this time, and I am going to pass every class, and I will graduate."

I had originally wanted to enroll at the University of Oklahoma, home of the Sooners. I spoke with my counselor about the possibility of transferring to OU one day, and asked if my grades would transfer if I was able to save up the tuition fees. She recommended the ROTC program for the U.S. Air Force, and that seemed like a perfect solution. I would get my degree at the junior college and then switch to the university, where ROTC would pay my entire tuition, including textbooks and even some of my expenses. In return, I would serve *Meegook,* which had given me the second chance.

The idea seemed too good to be true. I visited the OU campus one day and fell in love with OU. I wanted to be a part of the Sooners. The visit motivated me to study even harder, and I began scribbling OU symbols on my notebooks as a reminder of why I was studying so diligently. I might as well have been chanting the phrase *'Go Sooners!'* over and over at football games along with tens of thousands of other fans.

Although I had big dreams of attending a major university, my boys kept me grounded, and during this time, I had to truly embrace the responsibility of motherhood. My sons and I did everything together. I didn't know much about how American mothers raised their children. I hadn't been taught the importance of physical and verbal affection growing up, but I did my best to mimic what I'd seen other families do for fun. We played soccer in the park and hide and seek inside the apartment. We swam in the complex pool and watched TV together at night. At Christmas, I bought a small pre-lit tree from the store and gave them the few small presents I could afford.

During the week, I dedicated myself not only to my own studies, but also to theirs. I tried to instill Korean-style discipline and the importance of education in my boys. I had extra homework drills they had to complete daily for at least an hour before they could play. On the first day of school, I sent a note to each teacher that read: *Dear sir or madam, you have permission to spank my child if he doesn't behave.* I read it to my boys before I tucked it into their backpacks so they knew they had better listen and do what they were told by their teachers at all times.

After they were in bed, I studied. I was sure some professors only gave me a passing grade because they saw how hard I was trying. They all knew I had difficulty understanding English, but they also saw how hard I worked. I felt immense pressure to pass every test and stayed up late into the night studying.

I often found myself overwhelmed with all of the responsibilities I faced as being both a single mother and a full-time student, unable to communicate fully with anyone except Sooncha. Turning in my thesis in English was utterly nerve-wracking.I just knew I was going to fail. Despondent, I wrote at the bottom of the last page: *Dear Professor, this is the best I can do. English is my second language. Jeanhee Kang.*

I often left my grades at the mercy of my professors.

As I struggled with the stress of school, raising my boys, and managing our meager income, I focused on our future rather than fretting over our present circumstances. I had not bought a single outfit for myself since I had moved back to America. I spent the money I had left over each month on my boys because they needed it more than I did, but I didn't have time to mope around or be depressed.

My daily jogging routine soon became an obsession, a way to release the stress that dogged me without having to spend any money. I loved *The Bionic Woman* television show. The star of the show ran so fast she was nearly a blur. I wanted to be like her—powerful, strong, and determined. No matter how I was stressed from studying to memorize vocabulary or study for a test, I could simply strap on my running shoes and let all of the stress fade into the background. It truly kept me balanced, and focused.

My college game-plan was to try as hard as I could and hope my professors believed in me as much as I believed in myself. I looked at every subject as *the subject* to pass. English was extremely hard for me to understand at times, so I would ask my professor which topic he would cover at the next class. I would read the whole chapter beforehand to familiarize myself with the foreign vocabulary. Then after each class, before my memory wandered off, I would go back and read each chapter again word by word first, sentence by sentence once I understood those together, then I would read the whole paragraph at last. If I misunderstood one word, it would throw me off and I had to start over. If I didn't know how to spell or pronounce a word, I assumed it would be on a test. So I would write it, then rewrite it ten more times, or until finally I could write it without the dictionary. If it took twenty times to write until I could memorize the definition, I did it. That was the only way I could learn the English language. I was on campus every chance I got, studying as much as I could take all in, my dream—and this time, I wasn't letting my education pass me by. The other students had no idea what it was like to be a single foreign mother on welfare. But around them, I was a carefree college girl.... In a way, I was still a girl in my heart living my school girl dream.

My best subject was creative writing. I befriended my creative writing teacher, Susan Mansour, who always took a group of students under her wing. With her caring help in English, I learn to communicate, express my thoughts in English. Soon, I was shocked to realize that I had actually been *thinking* in English, instead of Korean. What a strange, yet exciting realization.

Between raising my boys and studying, I didn't have much time to socialize. I was too immersed in my education, mesmerized by every new thing I learned. I was finally fulfilling my dream, and even though I was poor, I was *so* happy. The eight years since I'd been expelled from Namsung might as well have been a lifetime. Since the expulsion, I'd had enough adventures to fill one life, maybe two. And I knew that no matter what life threw at me, I could overcome it. I could run. I could get out of the apartment, take a deep breath of fresh air, and run until my mind was no longer racing, run until I forgot the challenges threatening to weigh me down.

I was free.

Chapter 19

Fell for a Devil

I TOOK A MUSIC APPRECIATION class as an elective in order to help my grade-point average. In that class, I met a tall, dark-haired Palestinian from Kuwait named Hamid. He was in and out of class. His attendance was terrible.

While our fingers tapped out simple notes on the piano, filling the air with jangling discord, he would raise his eyes to mine and look me over. He would smile at me with beautiful, perfect teeth and ask how I was doing, hold doors open for me, and surprise me with coffee. He was silly, always joking, and when he first asked me out, I didn't take him seriously. I lacked social skills when it came to meeting men. I had gone straight from my Korean school days, where we were forbidden to even look at boys, to life as a prostitute, to the position of wife. Besides, dating wasn't on my agenda.

"Hamid, how old are you?" I finally asked him one day. He still had that young, baby-faced look about him, whereas my reflection in the mirror revealed an unmistakable jaded look—tightness in the cheeks, and shadows beneath my eyes. I didn't see that we had a single thing in common.

"Old enough to buy you dinner," he said, smiling back. "Come on, Jeanhee, let's go on a date."

Eventually, I gave in. I couldn't resist his charm. He five years younger than I. While I had been getting knocked around by life, he had been catered to by his wealthy father in Kuwait. He was 6'2", breathtakingly handsome and physically fit. He had creamy brown skin, thick black hair, and gleaming white teeth. When we kissed for the first time, I forgot all my mama's lessons about having married my father for his looks.

At first Hamid was a joy, always smiling, doing, and caring especially for my boys... He took me to movies, out dancing, and paid for expensive dinners. Having Hamid by my side exhilarated me. I wanted his youthful carefree life. I wanted to be a young girl again, to make up for everything I had missed during my teen years. Hamid began to spend more time in my apartment than his own.

Completely blinded by his charm, I ignored our more divisive differences from day one. I knew he was from the Middle East but I wasn't aware of his radical beliefs. He showed no respect for Americans and their culture—two things I loved dearly.

A few months into our relationship, Hamid started to show his true color. His mood swings shifted day to day, hour to hour. One minute he would be jovial and smiling, and moments later a black cloud would descend upon his brow. He grew jealous of other men who were my friends. We spent less time whispering sweet nothings and more time quarreling over trivial offenses. As our relationship deepened, so did his moodiness. Small disagreements sent him into a rage. His face would turn red, he would clench his teeth, and then he would mumble a mishmash of English and Arabic. I wasn't exactly an angel either. I have always been a feisty, stubborn person at heart, and I refused to let him off the hook for anything he did wrong. I would never allow anyone to ever treat me as a subordinate again.

Once our arguments blew over, his temper would fade. Within a few hours, Hamid would resume his sweet, loving persona and lure me into a night of make-up sex that scorched the sheets. I had never made love like that before.

Hamid became increasingly abusive verbally. "Stupid Jeanhee, you're never going to get out of this crappy college. You should have stayed in South Korea and grown rice." and "You're lucky I took you in. You've already been used up and rejected by two other men. Look at yourself in the mirror. Look at those wrinkles beneath your eyes." I think he got a sadistic high from making me crumple in tears.

In his worst rages, he would rant about the American infidels, talking about the Bible and how Jesus was just another figure, not the Son of God. I was not a Christian at that point in my life, so I had no idea about who Jesus was but if what he preached from the Koran made him act the way he did, I didn't want any part of Islam.

He kept trying to break me, to brainwash me and turn me into a zombie who would always bend to his will. It was all about him. Despite the vow I had made after leaving Robert that I would remain a strong, independent woman, my strength waned under Hamid's ill treatment. The first time he hit me, leaving a red-hot hand mark across my face, I flew into a rage. I feared I might kill him, but then he begged me to forgive him, telling me he hadn't meant to hit me, that he just had a temper and would *never* do it again.

"Jeanhee, I love you. I'm so sorry," he sobbed. "Why did I do that? I would never hurt you. You just made me so mad. Don't leave me. Please. I'll never hurt you again."

When he hit me again, the same sincere, sweet as ever promise continued. I kept thinking and I kept believing he would change. He didn't' mean to hurt me. I lived under his control and allowed my kids to endure his tyranny. As soon as he and I raised our voices, the boys would scurry into their bedroom, shut the door, and cower behind it. Sometimes, I would find them under the bed or in a closet, and they were always crying. He never hit them, but they were terrified of him, nonetheless. They cringed whenever he walked by and refused to hug him when he attempted to do so, only making him angrier.

Too calm down, he would go into my bedroom, shut the door, and listen to Arabic songs for hours, followed by his favorite song, *"Hey, teacher, leave those kids alone! We don't need no education!* I thought if anyone dared to play such a song in South Korea, they would be stoned to death before the day was over.

I reminded my boys we would be alone just three of us one day, just the three of us. I promised them I would find a way out somehow and that we would get away from him. I made sure to spend special time with my boys, picking pecans from trees outside, cracking them open with a hammer, taking turns to crush them to bake their favorite chocolate pecan cake. Life wasn't perfect, but it wasn't unbearable. At least, not yet.

A few months before I graduated, I had a brief moment of hope. I received a letter from Norman, Oklahoma. Inside was an acceptance letter for a full ROTC scholarship to the University of Oklahoma written on OU letterhead. I cried out with joy.

"I was going to OU!"

The United States Air Force offered to pay my full tuition and cover my books and spending money. In return, I would serve as an officer in the United States Air Force for four years. The country of my dreams, *Meegook*, had already provided for me financially, and now they were going to put me through college at OU. Who wouldn't be proud to be an American? This *truly* was the greatest nation in the world, and I would serve twenty years if that was what they wanted of me. I was one step closer to leaving Hamid and reaching the next level of my education. I would finish junior college in a year and a half. I would have to study even harder, but I had no time to waste to get to OU.

As soon as Hamid found out my future plans which didn't include him, he instantly became irate. Not only he wasn't in my future plan, he hated the thought of my serving a country he despised. I could almost see fumes coming out of his ears.

On May 10, 1984, I prepared for my long awaited triumph, my special day of redemption— my junior college graduation, soon I will be in Norman, Oklahoma, studying as University of Oklahoma student and cheering for the Sooners wearing red. I hummed as I got out of the shower and dried my long hair, so excited to put on my silky black graduation gown. I was two hours away from receiving my associate's degree in elementary education from Rose State Junior College. The happiest day of my entire life had begun to unfold.

Satisfied at the way my robe swished as I turned from right to left, I smiled at my reflection in the mirror. I pulled my cap down over my hair, trying to decide where to put the tassel. It tickled my face, and I rearranged it at least ten different ways before I was happy with it. Everything in me wanted to let out a shriek of joy.

Suddenly, the front door opened and then shut. Hamid had entered the apartment. Brisk footsteps approached me from behind. When he saw how happy I was, he became enraged.

"You think that is good for you?" he snapped, apparently eager for a fight. "You don't look pretty. You look ridiculous. Look at yourself under your eyes. See those wrinkles? Do you know why they are there? Because you are old!"

Monster, Evil, Satan whatever... He was one of those or all three. This was the day I had lived for, had given up a loving husband and luxurious life for, and he came to spoil it all. I had heard the words he threw at me, before, so they didn't bother me as much as the reason he had come. He knew I had a temper too, and that, eventually, I would fight back.

"Those professors passed you just to be nice," he said. "They felt sorry for you. You'll never make it at a real college. They'll laugh you right out of the classroom at OU."

"Please get out of my way, Hamid," I said. "I can't miss this. I have been waiting for this day my whole life."

"I am not letting you go! Do you know why? Here is why! You are going to fight against us one day as an infidel soldier if you go to OU."

"Hamid, please," I was trying not to cry in fear of smudging my makeup. I knew that if he tried to stop me, I wouldn't be able fight him. This is what I had worked for. I had studied ten hours a day to pass test, finished in a year and half to graduate. This day meant more than anything to me. I was trying to get on his good side, but he wouldn't budge.

I knew I would regret it for the rest of my life, but I knew I must tell him that I would give up ROTC at OU in order to attend my graduation ceremony.

"I'll do anything. Just let me out. Please don't make me miss this day. I'm begging you."

My cries grew more frantic with his silence.

"Please let me enjoy my proud moment." I sobbed in fear of missing the celebration, the moment the dean would call my name aloud and I would walk onto the stage to receive my degree.

"I'll do anything," I repeated desperately. "Just please, please let me go to my graduation. I will do it, just let me go to my graduation!!!"

"Anything?" He halted and stayed silent for what felt like an eternity. Then finally, he asked again carefully, "Anything?

"Yes!" I yelled. "Anything you want."

The Devil's horns were sticking out of his head by then, and he said, "Okay, then. We are moving to another state soon. You agree to go with me?"

I screamed, "Yes!"

He finally got what he wanted out of me, and said," Go get your stupid degree."

I had less than twenty minutes left to get to school and catch up with my friends before my graduation ceremony.

I would have sold my soul to the devil for the chance of my life time, my college degree. I did sell my soul to a devil but I was too excited to think about what had just happened. I literally raced against clock the whole way to school, my black robe flapping behind me, holding my cap in my hand. I barely made it to the ceremony on time, sliding into my seat with my robe twisted and my face flushed. When my turn to walk finally came, I was filled with nothing but pride despite Hamid's earlier taunt. I walked as slowly as I could, savoring every second of that special moment, thrilled by the cadence of my name over the loudspeaker and my chance to shake hands with the dean.

I reveled in the polite applause from the audience, although I received much less than the other students because I didn't have a single family member or friend present. I had been so busy fighting with Hamid lately that I had forgotten to invite even Sooncha, who would have stood up and yelled for me. Even so, I was still smiling as I sat back down, fighting back tears of joy and holding the small scroll as gently as if it were a newborn child. It was a day I would treasure for the rest of my life.

As soon as I got home, I carefully hid my diploma instead of hanging it on the wall. I didn't want Hamid to tear it up in pieces.

I, Jeanhee Kang, was on record as a graduate of Rose State Junior College.

I was screaming to Koreans thousands of miles away. *Look at me! You gave up on me, refused to give me a second chance. Look at me! I graduate from college!*

No Koreans heard me.

If they heard me, they would still turn their heads, *No, Jeanhee Kang, you should have gone to Harvard University. By the way, what about what you did in Osan?*

I could never be good enough for the Korean people.

Rose State Jr. College Graduation May 10, 1984

I treasured this photo of me. And one day in the not too distant future, I would earn my bachelor's degree. I dreamed of putting on an Air Force uniform and serving the country that had given me a second chance. The celebration in my heart didn't last very long. I was now in debt to Hamid, and to him I was nothing more than a chess piece. While I had been celebrating, he had been plotting his move. His intent was to steer me away from the University of Oklahoma.

Hamid wasted no time to move us to Baton Rouge, Louisiana. Less than five days after my graduation, we moved. I loved him and believed I could change him. Completely blinded by what I thought was love, I gave up my scholarship at the University of Oklahoma. Sadly, Hamid had no intent to change.

Once we were settled in at apartment five minutes from LSU, Hamid dropped out of school, began to gamble, smoke dope, and drink. His father refused to send enough money when he found out Hamid dropped out of school. He wouldn't work, claiming that he wouldn't want to work for infidels. I pushed my education aside and looked for a job. Meanwhile, Hamid's violent episodes grew worse.

He had become my father. And I was living my mother's life.

Whenever Hamid yelled at me or came at me with his fist raised, I saw my father's face snarling at me. When I looked in the mirror, patting concealer around a black eye or a bruise on my collarbone, my mother's sad eyes stared back at me. I could find no escape—I saw no way out—and I felt helpless to protect my boys.

As the weeks passed, Hamid became even more obsessive, claiming he loved me more than anything, saying that he would change, begging for yet another chance. I kept believing him.

He wouldn't allow me to register at nearby LSU. He had me exactly where he wanted, trapped, lost, and brainwashed. I cried every time I heard the LSU Tigers roaring thunderously during football games.

To make ends meet, I waited tables at El Chico, a Mexican restaurant about ten minutes from our apartment. Hamid couldn't stand the thought that some of my tips came from men. He often showed up at the restaurant unannounced just to make sure I wouldn't smile at them. Each night he questioned me relentlessly about my conversations and accused me of flirting and of cheating on him with my male patrons.

The manager, Ali, who was from Iran, had genuine sympathy for me. He knew what was happening with Hamid but avoided talking about it. He didn't want to embarrass me. Whenever Hamid stormed in through the door and slumped onto the bench in the foyer, my heart would pound. I was sure I was about to get fired, but my manager always said, "It's okay, Jeanhee. He's not bothering anyone. As long as he's quiet, it's fine."

Eventually, Ali allowed me tend the bar to keep from having direct contact with customers. I couldn't mix a drink to save my life, but he gave me a Rolodex full of ingredients and taught me how to follow the instructions. He told me to take my time making the drinks, too, so I could avoid the male customers. Another waitress would deliver them to the tables.

Despite my troubles with Hamid, I showed up at my work, smiling, hiding my broken life. At least I got out of the house away from him. For a few hours a day, I was happy—protected from another black eye, if only for a short time.

Our fights soon became even more vicious. Hamid punched walls, broke door frames, and screamed violent threats at me. He got tired of me calling 911 and started hitting me more carefully, just as hard, but with fewer bruises and always where my clothes would cover the evidence.

After five months in Baton Rouge, I realized Hamid would never change. I longed to find a way to get away from him. The only person I could think who could drop everything to help me was Robert. I got his number from Thomas. Robert was stationed in Florida when I called him shamelessly. I knew he still loved me. He came to Baton Rouge the next day, in hopes of whisking me away—ready to take me back as his wife and make us a family again.

I met with Robert at a nearby Chinese restaurant. I could sense, that two years after our divorce, he was still broken-hearted. I had no choice but to tell Robert what I had been through with Hamid. As I expected, he was ready to take me back in a heartbeat, but he was still cautious.

"My sweet Jeanhee," he said, "you know I love you so much. You are the love of my life I can never let go of, but I don't want you to break my heart again."

Robert knew I was truly a terrible liar.

"You know I still love you. I'm ready to take you back as my wife right this minute and be a father to your boys and love you forever, but, first, you have to promise you'll never leave me again. And you have to look me in the eye when you say it."

A dumb ass, me. I couldn't do it. I could not lie to Robert's piercing blue eyes. I may have done a lots of shameful things in my life, but I was never a liar. I couldn't lie to save my life.

I was so close to being swept off my feet again—to stepping back into the life of a commander's wife in the Philippines where he was about to be deployed, living a posh and secure existence in a nice house with a maid and a cook. But I couldn't lie nor commit to *forever* and *I won't hurt you again.* As badly as I wanted to be swept away from the hell of my miserable life with Hamid, I simply couldn't bring myself to lie to a man who loved me so much.

I cried out to Robert, 'I am sorry, I just can't promise to never hurt you again. Robert cried with me. "I wish to God, I could tell you what you want to hear, but I just can't."

Oh, my sweet Jeanhee, are you sure? You need me now more than ever."

"I know, Robert"

As Robert got up to leave me, he asked for my final answer once more.

I shook my head, and we cried some more.

After a long, tearful hug, Robert and I went our separate ways. That was the last time I ever saw him.

Not long after our most vicious fight ever broke out and erupted into a screaming match, with Hamid's face turning blood-red and the veins on his forehead ready to burst. I thought he might scream himself into a fit, and I wished he would just fall down dead. He went absolutely crazy when he found out I had gone to church.

Like a life saver or something, a few weeks before, a preacher had knocked on my door while Hamid was away. He stood there holding a Bible at my door and asked me if I wanted to hear God's promise at his church.

"What is God's promise?" I asked.

He said, "If you believe in Jesus, you will be saved from my misery."

"Did you say that I will be saved from my misery?"

He said, "Yes, all you have to do is believe he is your God."

There is my answer I thought to myself. I didn't need to call Robert to make him cry over me, I needed a God in my life.

I said, "Sign me up, preacher! Where do I sign to come to your church?"

He chuckled graciously and said, "God don't need your signature. You just show up, He will be there waiting for you. Here is the address. We are less than a mile from here."

I was seeing a glimpse of hope already.

"Okay, I promise, I will be there this Sunday at 9:00."

That was it!

I needed a savior to save me from my misery, and I agreed to attend. The only time I had ever been to church was twenty years before when I was seven years old. I was lured go to church then, but this time, I wanted to go. Besides, the pastor didn't promise any rice cake. I wanted to go to church on my own free will. I was ready to hear what went wrong with my life.

The Jesus dream I had two years back during one of the darkest nights of my life had never crossed my mind nor did I remember the angel who came to tell me that it wasn't my time to die. Maybe, I subconsciously remembered. Maybe Jesus knocked on my door disguised as a preacher. I went back to church a few more Sundays when I could sneak away, comforted by the welcome I received and eager to escape Hamid if only for a couple of hours Those unjaded faces seemed not so judgmental. Besides I wasn't there to confess my sins. I was there to be saved from Hamid.

The pastor of the church told me that baptism would save me from my sins altogether. I asked him to baptize me so that I could become a brand new person. I followed the pastor's instructions to the letter and repeated every word he said. I expected him to cleanse me and make me a new person—a born again Christian, whatever that meant.

As I walked back home, however, I didn't feel any different than I had the day before, even though the pastor had told me I was saved and I was a brand new person. Despite this hefty burden, I remained hopeful because every time I went to church he proclaimed that I was saved, and I believed him. I thought that because I had broken so many commandments that it was going to take much longer to cleanse my sin.

I was without transportation, and one of the kind member of the church gave me her old car. I loved it. Having my own car came with shining independence. Hamid hated it. It was a death threat to him.

The devil went crazy, intent on destroying the car, snapping off the side mirror, bending the antenna, and smashing his fist into the windshield.

"American infidels!" he yelled. "Trying to buy you with their false prophets."

He became even more disgusted when he learned I had allowed the pastor to baptize me without asking *him* first. I initially didn't want to tell him about my baptism, but I eventually told him out of a desire to hurt him. I huddled in a ball in the corner and covered my head as he screamed at me and punched me with his fists. I didn't even try to fight back. I just cried for my existence in life. I remember thinking blankly that this time, he just might kill me.

Yet he didn't.

As quickly as he had turned on me, he wheeled around and ran out the door. Holding one shaking hand to my split lip, my eye socket throbbing, I ran to a neighbor's apartment to call 911. The whirring blue lights and sirens filled me with almost as much dread as Hamid did. Trembling and nauseous, I allowed them to drive me to the station to make a statement. Afterward, they picked up my boys from school and took us to a battered woman's shelter in Baton Rouge.

We stayed at the shelter for a week. I hadn't realized so many other women were in the same situation. We shared stories, went to in-house counseling, and helped each other tend to the children. All of us were scared and filled with different levels of sadness. But mostly we were just ashamed because our futures were so uncertain.

I was relieved to know that I was the only Korean there. The last thing I need was another Korean mocking at my failed life. We spent a lot of time in group sessions, sharing our feelings and experiences. The husbands and boyfriends of the other women sounded like Hamid. They would be sweet for a while, and then a time bomb would go off and they would explode with anger. Most of the women had escaped once but had been lured back, thinking that the next time would be different.

I couldn't stay at the shelter forever. I had to think about my next move. I had a friend, Lee who lived in New York City. She had been my neighbor back in Osan. We had become close friends, and when she left Osan before I did, we promised to keep in touch.

I called Lee out of desperation instead of calling Sooncha. I wanted to go to New York where Hamid could never find me.

"Jeanhee!" she said. "How are you, honey?"

"I'm so sorry I haven't kept in touch," I said, doing my best to hide the fear in my voice. "I need somewhere to stay. I've been with a bad man—a man who hits me—and I have to get away from him."

My voice broke, but she jumped into the gap. "You have to come here, Jeanhee! I don't have an extra bedroom, but the living room is big, and I won't mind your boys staying here with us. Do you have a ticket? Write down my address."

The battered women's shelter agreed to pay for three one-way bus tickets and $20.00 for meals for the three of us to travel to New York City. My counselor reiterated daily, "Men don't change. Abusers *do not change*. If he gets your number, do not answer the phone. If he finds out where you live, do not answer the door. And never, *ever* call him."

The counselors at the shelter wanted us to get as far away from Hamid as fast we could and never come back to Baton Rouge. They were very hopeful, believing I could be one of the few women to permanently break the cycle of abuse.

The small van the shelter owned dropped us off at the Baton Rouge Greyhound bus station, to catch a bus to New York. Josh and Jason each clutched a garbage bag full of clothes and pillows we had retrieved from our apartment with the help of a police escort. I had trembled the whole time, terrified of what Hamid might say or do, but he only mumbled incoherently because he was too afraid of the cops.

The boys wanted to say goodbye to him, but the police pulled them away. I didn't meet Hamid's eyes the whole time, and I didn't feel safe again until I was on the bus headed north. The trip reminded me of my bus ride to Osan as a young girl, but this time the stakes were even higher. I was responsible for two more lives. I was exhausted and held my boys tight to my sides as the steel grip of sleep took hold of me.

I didn't know it yet, but an entire spate of new problems loomed on our horizon. In a matter of hours, we would be surviving in the Bronx, New York.

All thoughts of the church I had attended in Baton Rouge and being saved went out of my head. No one had saved me. I'd had to save myself.

Chapter 20

To New York City

THAT BUS RIDE TO NEW YORK was summed up with two garbage bag full of clothes, three pillows, and my boys with a $20.00 bill. I was a twenty-seven-year-old, dead broke with two young sons, ages six and seven.

The Greyhound bus stopped in every little town and city along the way and took short detours off the highway for meal breaks at McDonald. Twenty dollars was just enough for my boys to eat two meals I skipped one meal to make sure my boys had enough to eat. The bus rolled through swamps, forests, and plains. I was finally seeing America, even if it wasn't under the best of circumstances.

Unanswered questions plagued me all along the way, causing my heart to palpitate from drowning in shame and self-pity. We were exhausted from the constant state of fear of unfamiliar destinations with strangers on and off the bus at every stop. Josh and Jason tried to be brave, but their wide, trembling eyes broadcast the truth. All they knew was that we were running away from Hamid. I felt sorry for my boys and kept asking myself what had I done to them and why I had fallen for such a violent man.

Regrets piled upon one after another. What could have been, should have been… there were no right answers… I could be at OU in Norman, waiting to be a lieutenant in the United States Air Force, in a crisp uniform and shiny boots, serving the country that gave me second chance.

Instead, my boys and I were on a Greyhound bus to New York City, homeless.

Lee met me at the Port Authority terminal, the main bus station in New York City, late that night. The time was well past ten, and we were dragging. Lee greeted me with a warm hug and instantly welcomed my boys, showering them with compliments. I never felt like we were a burden to her. Koreans always stick together and protect their own, and she was no exception.

Lee hailed a cab and after stuffing our meager belongings into the trunk, we headed to the Bronx. What an odd sensation to wake up the next morning to honking cars and the screeching grind of a garbage truck. The shiny high-rises I had seen in movies were nowhere in sight. Our view was of a trash-strewn, traffic-clogged street, with only decaying buildings with broken windows looming above us.

We lived at Anthony Avenue in the Bronx on the seventh floor—in the heart of the Puerto Rican district. Lee had warned me about this place called The Bronx, but never in my life would I have believed how dilapidated it was. Paint peeled off the walls of her apartment, the ceiling was cracked, and the linoleum was wrinkled and warped. Our door had five locks. Drug deals went on in the shadows of almost every corner in our neighborhood. I didn't allow Josh and Jason to play outside unless I could watch them. And I never let them go downstairs alone, even to check the mail.

Lee had left her GI husband to become Choi's mistress. Choi, a tall Korean with a crazy gleam in his eye, was a leader of a Korean mafia who was married to a former Miss South Korea. He was one ugly man, though. His face was a *ggombo*, marked with scars from a bad case of chicken pox. He never went anywhere without an army of men to protect him.

At first I didn't believe her about her lover's occupation, but one night when we were all together at Kim's Korean restaurant in Flushing, Choi thought it would be funny to give me a demonstration of his power. I had wondered why numerous frightened Koreans had bowed to him during our meal. When the owner of the restaurant came to the table to see how we liked our food, Lee's boyfriend grabbed the man's neck and said, "If you don't pay me back, I will kill you and add you to the menu tomorrow."

Then he laughed loudly and looked around to see who else had been intimidated by his show of power. Over dessert, he casually told me he had once taken off a disrespectful Korean gang member's knee cap with an ax to teach him to respect his elders.

"I still don't believe it, Choi," I told him.

He laughed and said, "Yes, you do."

Lee had a job waiting for me alongside her in the accounts receivable department at a small publishing firm on 32ND Street in Midtown Manhattan, right next to Korea Town. We rode the D train from the Bronx to the heart of New York City every day, then walked two blocks toward the Empire State Building. I was a fish out of water in NYC, unsure of how I would ever be able to reconcile my unfinished business—completing my *education* and raising my two boys—with the hectic lifestyle of this crazy city. I had never seen so many tall buildings, people, or so many taxi cabs in one place in my life.

Before long I was forced to leave my job due to relentless sexual advances made by my boss. Soon after that, Lee quit her job and moved in to a nice condo in Manhattan with Choi, leaving me to pay the apartment bills alone.

I found a new job in a few days. It was my dream position at Gold Spoon Investment Company on 29th Street and Broadway in the heart of Korea Town. I felt safe there even though I was no longer a part of that rigid culture. Korean men wanted nothing to do with me, which was more than okay with me. The last time I had been with a Korean man, I had ruined my life.

My job title was *Public Relations Specialist*. I served as the liaison for my Korean bosses who didn't' speak English fluently. I was their go-to person to interpret real estate business meetings with powerful business tycoon in New York City. The company paid me well, paying for expensive tailored suits, salons, and often escorting me to a private tailor to custom make a suit to fit me perfectly. I loved my dream job.

The apartment in Bronx was unsafe for my boys. My neighbor, Sonya, watched them for me until I got home. After a few months of tortuous deliberation, I decided to send them to live with my mom and attend a math institution in South Korea. They would be safe and better off with my mother for the time being. I would save money to bring them back when I could find safe place for us to live. Sending the boys to South Korea allowed me to move into a one-room occupancy in a Korean home in Flushing for $500.00 a month. All I needed was a place to sleep so their large extended family didn't bother me.

Life propelled me forward. I had found a sense of purpose and direction, even if I didn't love New York. Without the boys to occupy my evenings, I found a second job in Greenwich Village working at a Korean owned Boutique.

I had time to enjoy going out occasionally on weekends. Lee and I would meet when she was free from her mafia boyfriend at our favorite club called *Lime Light*. I wasn't looking for a man. I knew most of them wanted only a one-night stand. It was a familiar scene except it was in *Meegook* instead of Osan. I didn't' drink, but I enjoyed dancing to songs like Madonna's "Like a Virgin, "Blondie's "Call Me," and "Girls Just

Want to Have Fun" by Cyndi Lauper.

One night a good-looking, curly-haired blond man in his late thirties approached me. He'd spent half the night staring at me before working up the courage to come over and talk.

"Hi!" he yelled over the music. "I'm Paul, and this is Luke." He motioned toward his friend who had followed him to meet us.

We decided that they were interesting enough followed them to VIP room. They tried to impress us by claiming they were movie producers, but Lee and I could care less about their occupations. Neither of us wanted to be famous anytime soon. We sat in that room and drank. They were getting drunk, and I was the only sober one drinking Coca-Cola. We chatted until closing time.

"Let's go to my place," Luke said then, slamming his drink onto the table in excitement. "We can keep partying and watch the sun rise from my balcony."

"Why not?" I looked at Lee, and she smiled. "It's the weekend."

Four of us took a cab to Luke's high-rise overlooking Central Park. The place reminded me of a picture perfect apartment out of a movie— with incredibly beautiful décor, expensive lamps, creamy marble floors, and glass windows from floor to ceiling. Lee flirted heavily with Luke, and I could tell by Lee's body language that she would have taken Luke right there on the floor if she could. What Choi didn't know wouldn't hurt him.

Still, I felt pressured. I wasn't sure if I wanted to have sex with Paul, but he kept lying to me about how beautiful I was and how attracted he had always been to Asian women. If he would have said, "You look nice this evening" instead of "You look beautiful," I would have believed him. Anyway, I let him lead me to his bedroom thinking maybe I will try this guy out to see if he is better than Hamid. But instead of urging me to lie on the bed, he pulled a briefcase out of his closet, popped the clasp, and took out a baggie of white powder. The briefcase was full of neatly stacked bags I couldn't believe what I was seeing, and even country chicken like me knew what was in those bags because I had seen them on Miami Vice—cocaine.

But how had he gotten so much of it? He tapped some out onto the counter, divided it into straight little lines, and snorted them through a rolled hundred-dollar bill. When he had inhaled all of it, he brushed his index finger into the bag and rubbed some on his gums. I had never actually seen anyone do drugs before. My sixth sense was waving a bright red flag toward the door to get out of there immediately.

What if the cops showed up? What if I got caught with this guy? I would never be able to bring my boys back to live with me.

He recognized my panic. "It's okay, baby," he said. "Here, try some. You'll feel better in no time. It will put you to the top of the world."

"No," I yelled. "I don't do drugs."

"Are you kidding?" he asked in surprise. "You dare to turn down coke? Isn't this what you wanted?"

"No." I shook my head and edged toward the door. "I'll be right back. I have to talk to my girlfriend real quick. I will be right back"

I backed out of his room butt first, closed his bedroom door, and found Lee on the couch with Luke, half-naked, with his hands running all over her breast.

"Lee!" She didn't hear me at first, so I yelled again, "Lee! Get dressed!" I said. "You can do that later with Choi. We have to leave, right now."

"What's wrong?" She looked embarrassed, clamping her arm over her breasts as she shoved Luke off her and reached for her shirt. "Did he hurt you?"

"I'll explain later," I said. "Let's go."

Paul and Luke attempted to talk us out of leaving, but we were out of there in minutes and took a cab to her apartment on 32nd street.

"Those guys must have been drug dealers," I said, "not movie producers. Paul had a whole briefcase full of cocaine."

"Luke had a little bag, too."

"Did you snort it?" I asked.

She didn't answer my question.

That was the only time I ever left the Limelight Club with a man and after that, I stuck to a dancing only rule. Men in New York were very forward, coming after me and professing their love in a heartbeat. I grew sick of those empty, insincere encounters. But mainly, I missed my boys. An unrelenting void grew inside my heart.

Despite all that had happened, a dream job in the heart of New York

City, I began to wonder what Hamid was doing. I missed his silly, stupid jokes and the passion we had shared in bed before everything went wrong. I hadn't felt that kind of raw lust and the subsequent primal satisfaction with any man since. I had forgotten all about that sad, long bus ride with my boys and had *made* myself forget about the abuse. I selectively chose to remember the good times only to justify my stupid action. As Forrest Gump once so wisely stated: *"Stupid is as stupid does."*

I couldn't just sit back and enjoy my new-found carefree life in New York. I had everything going for me, Job to die for, much missed Korean food readily available on every corner. Yet, I was lonesome. I found myself longing for Hamid.

I made the one phone call I should not have made, the one my counselor had told me to *never, ever* make.

I nearly put the phone down several times before Hamid answered. My gut was telling me, "Don't do it, stupid."

I let my index finger do the talking. It dialed his number.

"Hamid, it's Jeanhee," I said almost shyly.

He was quiet for a few moments, mumbling to himself like he always did when he was either overjoyed or irate, but then he pulled himself together. "Jeanhee! I've missed you so much. I've been waiting to hear from you. Where are you?"

I started to cry. I wanted so badly to be needed and loved by someone with a familiar touch. When he asked if he could visit me in New York, I didn't even hesitate.

I said yes.

Within two days, Hamid was in New York City, ready to convince me he was a changed man. We went to the top of the Empire State Building, visited the Statue of Liberty, and walked around Times Square, all of the things I'd been too busy working to do. Our relationship felt as fresh and exciting as it had when we had first started dating.

"I miss you, Jeanhee," he said. "I've been a bad person and an idiot. Jeanhee. I've changed—I've been working on my temper, and I see now that how I treated you was wrong. I'll never lay a hand on you again if you'll just come home with me. We can attend the same university, and you can finish your four-year degree."

I believed every word that came out of his mouth, and my longing for him grew deep into place I couldn't fathom, so deep that it overrode all the bad memories. I agreed to move back to join him in Jackson, Mississippi. I gave two weeks' notice to my bosses, telling them I was going back to finish my degree and omitting the part about returning to Hamid. They were very disappointed, yet satisfied that I was leaving for education, and wished me the best.

Chapter 21

Mississippi

I HAD FORGOTTON ALL ABOUT the beatings, the twenty-three hours' bus ride with my boys dead broke after sharing three meals with $20.00, never mind the two black garbage bags of our life in tow. I was only thinking about missing a few good moments, and I wanted more of that. Blinded by flesh, the only thing that mattered to me were the promises he had made to me, "I have changed. I am not the same person anymore." Promises sure to be broken but my gut feelings were squashed and buried. Before I could begin to consider the ramifications of that phone call, I was on a plane to Jackson, Mississippi. The plane to Mississippi always stops at major hubs since Jackson is not a metropolitan city. I had two hours to kill in Atlanta.

It was noon and I was starving. I found a fine restaurant for lunch. I can't remember the name of restaurant, but I liked the solid mahogany beams, the wall and nice leather chairs. I found a perfect corner seat, and began looking through the menu. I heard man's deep southern accent from the next table asking me if he could join me. I glanced over to see a handsome, well-dressed man in his 60s. I was guarded at first, but then

I realized that we both were at the airport, waiting for our next flight. He would soon go on his way.

I said," Sure."

He said, "Hi, my name is Rock Truman."

"I am Jeanhee Kang,"

"Where are you going?"

"I am going to Jackson, Mississippi. What about you?"

"I am going to Dallas, coming back from Miami."

He said he was born in Dallas, divorced, and had a son who was in college at Southern Methodist University.

"Do you have children?"

"I do, two young boys age seven and eight. They are in South Korea attending math school, but they soon will be joining me in Jackson, Mississippi."

"I see," he said.

"What do you do in Dallas?"

"I am in the oil and gas business, been doing it since I was thirty years old. What do you do?"

The waitress interrupted to take a drink order. I ordered a glass of red wine, and he ordered Scotch and water.

"So what do you do?" I was hoping he had forgotten that he asked that question.

"I know I am not in the oil and gas business like you. Where I am from, we didn't have natural resources. If we didn't grow our food, we didn't get to eat."

"Aha... Really? Where are you from?"

"I am a run away from South Korea. I came to this country to find my childhood dream." I wasn't sure why I was telling a total stranger a part of my journey.

I continued, "I am in transition at this very moment, going from one life to the other. I wish I could tell you what I do. I am still looking for my childhood dream." I smiled sheepishly in fear he might catch on to my past.

The waitress came back with our drinks and took our lunch order. Suddenly, I was starving like I had been back when I was wishing for a bowl of white steamy rice to fill my starving belly. I ordered an 8-ounce filet medium rare with lobster, a baked potato with no butter, no sour cream, steamed broccoli and a spring mix salad with Tabasco hot sauce as dressing and an apple pie.

"I'll have exact same thing," he said to the wild-eyed waitress.

"Okkidokki!" she said. "Tabasco as dressing, as well?"

He nodded.

He said, "What do you like to do when you aren't transitioning from one life to another?"

I sipped red wine to wash down the hot sauce, and said, "I enjoy a daily run, would like to learn how to play tennis one day, even golf, and scuba diving too. I would like to see what is down under since I already know all about life here.

"And what about you?"

"I like to fly my own plane to see the land from the sky. I can see what people are dong from up there," he said, pointing at the sky with his index finger.

"Dang, you have you own air plane?"

"I sure do."

Then he looked at his watch and said, Can I tell you something before I go?

I thought he wanted my phone number or something after all.

He said, "I see you will be writing two books in the future."

"Me? Write a book? Nah… Impossible, "I said in disbelief. "I can't write. You know I wasn't born here"

He continued without skipping a beat, "Not only one book. I see two books." He looked at his watch again, "I got to go. It was my pleasure meeting you, Jeanhee Kang."

He shook my hand tightly and soon disappeared into the airport crowd. I still had thirty minutes left, but I decided to wait at the gate and asked for my check.

The waitress said, "Your lunch was paid by the gentlemen you were with, and he tipped me heavily. He just made my day." She smiled.

I arrived in Jackson, Mississippi, on a sweltering hot afternoon in July of 1986. The humidity drenched Mississippi sun smacked me like a wet brick as the double wide sliding door opened next to a large *Welcome to Mississippi* sign.

Things felt right between Hamid and me. Hamid made every effort to prove to me that he was a changed man. I had to enroll at Jackson State University, the school he attended so that he could keep his eyes on me. Soon, I brought my boys back from South Korea. I was so happy to have my boys back. I had missed them so much. As soon as I hugged them, all my doubts about Hamid disappeared. They had gotten taller. Both of them had earned a black belt in Taekwondo, and Jason had become a math wizard.

In our two room apartment, I fixed up bunk beds with Batman and Scooby-Doo pillowcases, and I had a little table and chair for them to study. Things went well for about three months, but then I found out I was two months pregnant, unwelcome news for me, a good news for Hamid. The last thing I wanted was to get pregnant, especially with Hamid. Hamid went back to his old self. As soon as Hamid found out I was pregnant, he knew he had me trapped. While I was contemplating an abortion as an option, he was after me day and night to marry him so he could extend his stay in America permanently.

"I just found you again, Jeanhee," he said. "I don't want to lose you *or* my son. If we get married, I can get my green card and stay here forever. We can be a family— for real this time. I can get a job and support both of us. Will you marry me? Please?"

"I don't *want* to marry you, Hamid, but I will, so you can stay in the U.S.," I said reluctantly. "But if you ever hit me again, I will divorce you in a heartbeat."

He agreed.

We exchanged vows in front of a Justice of the Peace in a simple, cold ceremony. Hamid never even put a ring on my finger. Although it was a legal marriage, the impersonal event did not seem any more real to me than my two previous failed marriages.

A fragile peace existed between us for a time. My pregnancy allowed Hamid to escape the suspicion that often arises whenever an American citizen marries a non-citizen, and he soon had his green card. He could stay in the country he despised.

Not long after Hamid received his green card, things grew worse than they had been in Baton Rouge. Now that I was the wife of a Muslim man, he suddenly demanded Muslim conduct. If I came out of the bedroom before his friends left, I embarrassed him by not acting like a proper submissive wife. I couldn't wear sheer fabric or makeup. My "can't-do" list grew daily. Hamid became irate every time he thought one of my outfits showed too much skin, so he cut up all of the designer clothes the New York investment firm had bought me and slashed my swimsuit to pieces. My girlfriends affronted him, and he denounced us for spending time together. I had to remain modest and soft-spoken and always be submissive—the latter requirement being non-negotiable.

If I talked on the phone, he was sure I was whispering to a secret lover.

"I'm pregnant, for God's sake!" I yelled back one time. "I'm not having an affair. No one wants to sleep with a fat pregnant woman."

Even going to the grocery store held potential upheaval. If a man looked at me too long in the freezer aisle, Hamid would dig his fingers into my arm, shove me forward, and whisper in my ear. "He'd like to have you. Keep moving, Jeanhee. Don't you dare smile at anyone else in this store."

I couldn't do anything right. Even the way I slept offended him. Under the strain of these restrictions and his suspicion, my third pregnancy became a nightmare. My body was racked with sorrow, and every movement I made felt labored. Hamid continued to physically and emotionally abuse me, calling me old and ugly, fat and worthless. He went out every night to gamble with his friends and smoke dope. I often wondered if he had another woman somewhere, maybe one he had dated while I was in New York. He denied it, of course. I was again reduced to a ghost of my mama, except she had at least found some escape in farm work. I could only pace through the apartment, my heart ripped apart with grief, regret, and anger at myself.

My pregnancy had inescapably bound me to a man I hated more with each passing day, and I was the only one to blame for my circumstances. I had come back to Hamid of my own accord and then forgotten to take my birth control pills. Hamid wouldn't listen to my pleas for a divorce.

He either ignored me or flew into a rage.

"Where you gonna go? Huh? You can't leave me when you're carrying my baby!"

Every time I brought it up, he got a little bit meaner. "You'll die as my wife, Jeanhee," he said one time. "That can be now or later. Your choice."

I couldn't bear to think that my life might end this way, with me afraid and lonely, the wife of a cruel man. I was sure I wanted to end the pregnancy. I made him drive me to an abortion clinic in New Orleans. He was against it, but he must have seen something in my eyes that made him back down. I told him that if he didn't take me, I would do it myself, either by throwing myself down a flight of stairs or smoking his dope until I miscarried.

When the doctor came in, I looked up from the sterile table. Seeing him and the nurses filled me with a wave of nausea, and horrible memories from the past returned to haunt me. I cried hysterically.

"Stop," I sobbed, motioning for them to go away. "I can't. I'm so sorry. I can't go through with it. I'm keeping my baby."

Hamid was overjoyed. I'd be stuck with him if I had his child. I had to drop out of Jackson State after two semesters. I was so filled with sorrow that I couldn't concentrate on boiling a pot of water, much less college studies.

I spent many of my days alone crying, trying to come up with a new run-away plan, always reassuring myself that my life would *not* end in misery. I reminded myself every chance I had that I would somehow find a way to *escape*.

Life was all about him. Whenever I craved simple things, like a can of 7-Up or mint ice cream in the middle of night, he yelled at me for disturbing his sleep.

The pain I endured during contractions annoyed him. He was not even remotely sympathetic. After the baby came, he didn't lift a finger to help me feed our tiny son or change his diapers. He constantly demanded things for himself. He stayed away most days, hanging out with his friends, living out his regular routine of dope and gambling. When he came home in the wee hours of the morning, I assumed he had been with his old flame. I finally understood how my own mother had become desperate enough to drink rat poison.

After our son Ahmad was born, I struggled with overwhelming waves of conflicting emotions instead of rejoicing the birth of my precious baby boy. My mistakes were piling on top of one another. I hated how my life had turned out. My childhood dreams were fading away right in front of my eyes. I wondered what had happened to that fearless girl in the muddy rice paddy who dared challenge to steal Dam Keeper's life. I asked myself, "Is it too late?" Doubts were creeping onto me as I looked at myself in ugly clothes in the mirror. I failed to find that girl I once was...I realized I had become my mama, unhappy—an ugly failure in life, for whom? My little tiny baby boy. I searched for the strength to make plans to escape. Soon those ideas fizzled whenever I looked at my helpless precious baby boy. While my childhood dreams were slipping away, I decided to tough it out and stay with the monster who called me an American infidel, at least for now. What else could I do? Ahmad was my son. I was his mama.

Then, one day after Hamid stormed off, I happened to turn on the radio to forget my sadness, I heard a powerful song that told of my tragic life. The song was Gloria Gaynor's "I Will Survive." The lyrics made all my hair stand up as if I was getting some kind of miraculous shock treatment. She was singing my life to me. I couldn't wait to buy the song. It was the first American song I had ever bought. I listened to that song over and over through my earphones, learning every word, every note. At first, I couldn't catch all the phrases, but the repetitive chorus stuck in my head and I knew that one day I would tell Hamid, *"Go on now go, walk out the door. I will survive!"*

That song became my religion. I felt as if every word had been written just for me, especially the part that said, "I've got all my life to live." Whenever Hamid wasn't around, I would blast the song, dance around the house with Ahmad, and sing in front of the mirror. I would pretend to tell Hamid to "walk out that door and never come back." I had given him five precious years of my life—and in the midst of it, I had also lost my childhood dream.

One afternoon in June of 1987, when Ahmad was only three months old, my favorite show, *The Oprah Winfrey Show,* came on TV. During the introduction, she said, "Today we're going to talk about domestic violence, and why women often remain in an abusive relationship. One in three women in America—about twenty women per minute—is physically abused by her partner." She paused, and then went on. "Why do women stay in these abusive relationships? Why can't they just pack up and leave?"

She got my attention. I was thinking the exact same thing, "Why can't I pick up and leave?"

Her angelic words got my full attention, as if she were talking directly to me. Her guests on the show were three women, one with her arm in a sling, and all three of them were in tears as they answered her questions. All of them said they were trapped, but kept hoping their men would change. One had a broken rib but stayed in the relationship for her children. Another had been knocked unconscious but stayed with her significant other after he promised to never hit her again. The woman with the sling came on the show with an assumed name wearing dark sunglasses. Supposedly, she was married to a powerful man who thirty years later was named to President Trump's cabinet. This story came out as scandal on Huffington Post, and he didn't make it to Trump's post. I hardly ever read Huffington Post. I had just happened to notice the story on Domestic Violence mentioned Oprah's show in the late 80s. Every question Oprah asked hit home with me. Why wouldn't you leave the man who beat you up?

Wanting to hear more, I turned up the volume, edged closer to the

TV and settled onto the couch. Oprah then said, "Domestic violence is the cycle of abuse— if kids grow up in an abusive home, they are likely to become abusers themselves."

Oprah asked the women who had managed to escape why they had returned to live with their abusers—and the women couldn't answer, except to say that the men always told them they were sorry, even though they most likely didn't mean it. They also swore they would never do it again, and the women would end up forgiving them because they wanted to believe the men would change. Oprah was talking about my life. Every word was describing my miserable life.

Each of the women had witnessed an abusive relationship between her parents and then fallen into the same role as her mother upon reaching adulthood. It was familiar to them. "Yes, that was my childhood."

"Men don't change. The cycle of domestic violence runs in family for generations," Oprah said.

Every word that was said made perfect sense to my thick skull, like someone had just hit me with a brick to wake me up from a coma.

"Thank you! Oprah! Thank you my angel!" Oprah's fifteen- minutes talk had convinced me that I was a victim of my childhood upbringing!

A guest psychologist on the Oprah show said, "You are the only one who can break the cycle. No one can do it for you." That was my Aha! moment. Now that I knew what was wrong with me, it was time to figure out how to break the heavy chain that had been on my neck for five long years, and soon.

That night, Hamid was nowhere to be found. It was already ten-thirty. I took a hammer and a handful of nails from the toolbox, studied the spot between the front door and the frame, and then quickly nailed the door shut, humming, *you are not welcome anymore… Go!*

Then I looked around and wondered if he might climb up onto the balcony and enter through *that* door—and sure enough, he did. He cursed at me, and called me crazy for nailing the door shut.

That was just the beginning.

I would kill him if I had to.

Chapter 22

Kill Him Dead

AFTER BEING TOLD SO MANY times that I was old, ugly, and worthless by Hamid, I was beginning to think maybe I really was old, ugly, and worthless until Oprah's talk. I remembered the adrenals I felt during my daily run when I was in college. I started running again every morning, listening to that one song, my anthem, all the way and back.

I had found my route in life again, and each step propelled me forward. My body had healed after Ahmad's birth, and now my battered soul began to heal. Hamid's physical and verbal assaults had wounded my soul, but I was still alive.

I started talking to myself, "It is not too late to start over, Jeanhee Kang.","" You can do it!" First and foremost, I had to get rid of the enemy who was holding me back.

How could I get rid of him? I didn't want to kill him outright, only because I didn't want to spend the rest of my life in prison. I toyed with the idea of shooting him, maybe in the knee cap, or better yet, in his balls.

I had never in my life touched a gun nor own one before. But, I felt like at the time, I was in need of a gun to assist me to set me free.

I needed a gun.

I wasted no time while Oprah's talk was ringing in my ears. I went straight to the flea market to purchase a gun the next day. Their shiny silver barrels glinted with the promise of freedom. Just looking at them made my heart race. I imagined the solid, reassuring weight of one of them in my hand. *That's it,* I thought. I picked out a small .22 caliber revolver. The seller, a fat, grizzled old man in late sixties breathing heavy, straightened in his chair and took notice of me.

I want this one.

I figured size wouldn't matter anyway, all I knew, gun kills people from what I have seen in the movies.

"Why are you buying a gun?" he asked.

"To kill my husband," I answered grimly.

He obviously thought I was joking. "He can't be that bad, honey. Just make him sleep on the couch for a few nights until you two make up." He chuckled at his own joke.

"Do you even know how to shoot?"

"No! I do not!", I answered.

Well, since you asked, "Can you teach me how to shoot my husband, Umm.. I meant, can you teach me how to shoot? ", "I had never shot anyone before...."

"Yeeh...."

In disbelief what he had just heard from 110 pounds, 5'1.5" tall Korean woman was telling him a point blank of her intended target. He gave me a quick two-minute drill about safety and showed me how to load and use the weapon.

"Now!" He said, "If you are going to shoot someone, you must be ready and intend to shoot and you must carry out, okay?"

"I know that part already...What I meant I shore will shoot him like you said."

"And here's the safety," he said, pointing it out. "Eight bullets fit in the cylinder. Don't point it at anyone unless you're ready to hurt them. And don't leave the gun where your kids can reach it. If you do, make sure you take out the bullets and hide them somewhere."

I paid him him forty-five dollars in cash.

And, I waited for my next fight with Hamid.

He finally picked the fight that would set me free. We were living in a two-bedroom apartment on E. County Line Road in Ridgeland. We had gone to the grocery store, and on the way home, I could see the rage building in him. Why, I didn't know. He didn't always need a reason to get angry.

We had barely walked through the door, situated Ahmad in a swing and set our meager bag of groceries onto the kitchen table when he grabbed my arm and dragged me into the bathroom.

"You, American infidel," he screamed as he smacked my face with his open hand. He grabbed my hair and shoved my stinging cheek against the bathroom mirror. "Look at the wrinkles under your eyes! Can't you see you're too old?"

He grabbed my face with his right hand and painfully turned my face to the right, then the left while pointing at my eyes with his left hand.

"Look, here! Look, there!" he yelled. "Look carefully. See how ugly you are?"

He literally foamed at the mouth. I recognized the signs. This was going to be another one of his frequent tirades about Muslims vs. the American infidels.

"Why did that man stare at you at the grocery store? Have you met him before? I saw how he looked at you! Why did you look at him?"

My mind raced. Man? What man? The only man I'd seen at the store was the kind cashier who gave me the receipt for our purchases. I remembered murmuring "Thank you" to him before we left. Is that what had brought on this attack?

"I know what that infidel wanted," Hamid spat. "He wanted to screw you! You knew that, didn't you? Didn't you?"

He loosened his grip on my face, and I took my chance and slipped away from him, racing upstairs before he could grab me again.

"Where do you think you're going?" he screamed in broken English as he raced after me.

I made it to the bedroom, but he grabbed the door before I could lock it and shoved his way in. My heart pounding, I raced around to the other side of the bed as he continued his rant.

A strange sense of calmness came over me, and I stopped crying. He never noticed.

His ranting never ceased as he lunged toward me across the bed and drew back to punch me in punishment for running away and trying to lock the door. That would have cost him money if he'd had to break it down—and not for the first time.

Thank goodness, I was on the opposite side of the queen-sized bed. I pushed the mattress up to block him and reeled backward to avoid the punch. The shiny handgun fell at my feet.

I snatched it up and backed into the corner. I had already rehearsed what to do.

I pointed the gun at his balls first, then aimed it at his chest, unsure what might happen when I pulled the trigger since I had never shot a gun before. My hands shook but I knew I would either kill him or hurt him bad if I shot him.

Then all at once, that odd sense of calmness returned, and I realized I held all the power now. From the stunned look on his face, I could tell he sensed it, too.

Thanks to the shiny gun clutched in my trembling hands, I had him by the balls.

The words of Gloria Gaynor's song *I Will Survive* rang through my head as he just stood there, too stunned to continue his tirade and unsure whether to be more afraid of my sudden tranquility or the gun in my hand.

I flipped off the safety, and his eyes widened.

In my mind's eye, I saw the monster who had terrorized me, brainwashed me until I was completely powerless, and taken five years of my life.

"What the hell?" he shouted, recognizing that I just might shoot him. "What is that?

"A gun?

"Are you crazy?"

"Yep! "I am crazy!" I said calmly, even though I was shaking inside. "I want you out of my life. If I you won't go, you'll die right here, right now. Today."

"He gaped at me.

194

"I'm done with you," I continued. "You will *never* hit me again."

At that moment, he knew it was all over.

Still angry and scared but holding his tongue, he quickly grabbed his clothes, and shoved them into a duffle bag. The devil was really leaving, and a sense of relief swept over me.

I lowered the gun.

He took advantage of my momentary lapse, raced into the next room, and grabbed three-month-old Ahmad—forcing me to make the most difficult decision of my life. I could either allow Hamid to stay, or I could let him walk out the door with our son.

Holding a screaming Ahmad, Hamid halted in the doorway and glared at me.

"If you *ever* try to take my son away from me," he said, issuing one final chilling threat, "I will come back and slash Josh and Jason's throats."

What else could I do but sacrifice Ahmad? I had to save Josh and Jason. So I let my little boy go, even though my heart ripped in two.

That day I ended the misery I had endured at Hamid's hand by holding him at gunpoint. I had gotten my life back, but at what cost?

I was thirty years old and now had to start a new life. A life without my infant son, who had been stolen by his insane father. I had no job, and only fifty dollars in the bank.

Too stunned to absorb what had just happened, I hurried into the bathroom and washed my face with cold water, then blotted my puffy eyes and took a long, hard look in the mirror.

Jeanhee stared back at me.

I attempted to feel something beyond my own heartbeat and the hum of adrenaline running through my body. I had been to hell and back, all one hundred pounds of me, and I had survived. Yet my head was still blank—I had no questions, no answers... only a deep spiritual emptiness I could not explain.

I had a void inside me, but did not know how to fill it. All the noises in my head went absolutely silent for once. Then, I remembered there was a world around me. A bird chirped on a branch outside the window, as if reminding me to snap out of it.

I stared d at Ahmad's baby swing, his diapers, and the half-empty bottle Hamid had left sitting on the counter. I walked over to the swing and gave it a wind just to hear it grind back and forth.

My God, what have I done? My baby boy is gone…he will be hungry soon…

If this was my punishment for having the abortion back in South Korea, for killing the helpless little baby inside me, then I deserved it.

Hamid took Ahmad away, the void inside me grew to mammoth proportions. My freedom and my worst nightmare had been born in the same moment.

Chapter 23

No Time to Cry

I NOT ONLY MOURNED FOR my three-month old baby in those moments after Hamid fled, but also for the girl who had strode boldly onto a bus after throwing her wig into a dumpster thirteen years ago, drunk on the dream of going to high school in America. I didn't sell my body for $20.00 bill to get here for nothing. I wanted to prove Koreans back home were wrong about me. More than anything, one day, I wanted to be accepted by Korean people as an equal, not as an outcast.

I must get my mojo back, the same bravery to survive the brothel to earn my chance to get here. I must get it back.

I must find a way to survive with my boys.

My gaze landed on a utility bill posted on the fridge, and my mind turned to survival. I was missing my God's face back home. If I could see His face, I would have asked him to feel sorry for me again.

All those years ago I had prayed to the God's face and begged him to help me, but, I had traveled too far.

Desperate in attempt to come up with a plan, I grabbed a pen and a yellow pad from beside the phone, went blank, it was hopeless doodles.

I crumpled the page into a ball, tossed it onto the floor, and started over. I decided to make a simple list of what I did have and didn't have.

On one side of the paper, I wrote first what I didn't' have. *No money, no car, no job,* and *no one to help me.* And, my boys and I will be kicked out of apartment in two weeks. What I did have side, I wrote list of failures since I agreed to give up OU scholarship.

I have wasted five years out of my life. I added one more to my failures in life list. I didn't' realized it until that moment, but all of my three marriages combined had lasted less than five years. Who does that?

But, in the midst of it all, I still believed I had a chance to restart my life. I still believed my childhood dream was valid and I wanted it.

My life was on the drawing board.

Jeanhee Kang, you are thirty-years-old. If you live to be ninety, you will have wasted one-third of your life—What about the hell you went through back in Osan? What happened to that five-year-old girl who begged to go to school to find the Dam Keeper's life and make it your own? Wake the hell up.

This moment of my self-realization was a turning point in my life. *"Thank you! Oprah! My angel!"* She might well be an angel even though she didn't' have white feathery wings on. Just imagine, if I hadn't watched Oprah's talk on her show that day, I would still be with Hamid.

The time had come for me to seize the momentum, my second chance, my everything.

I needed money to keep us alive—but how? I need to find a job.

I could return to New York and ask for my old job back since I had left on good terms, but I didn't have the money to move back there, besides I had never gotten used to the big city life. I was a country girl from Jolla Do at heart. I felt more at home in Mississippi than anywhere else I'd ever lived, and I wanted a safe place to raise my boys.

I was tired of running away. In this Bible Belt Southern state, I felt keen sense of security over us. Besides, how could I not like a place where everyone called me "Hun" or "Sweetie" and said "howdy" with beautiful, good-natured smiles? My kids had good friends here, and so did I. We were sick of being nomads.

I glanced at the clock again as I paced back and forth, clutching my to-do list. Not even an hour had passed, and I fought to keep the image of Ahmad's sweet face out of my mind.

To calm myself, I sang my favorite song inside my head,

"Go! Walk out the door… I will survive…"

I smiled. Hamid had *run* out the door. The energy of Gloria Gaynor's anthem flooded my body. *Go! Go out to the door!* No more fights, no more abuse—and no more Hamid. It was over.

A new worry came to hit me. Had Hamid cleaned out our bank account after he left? We didn't have much money, and most of that had come from his father.

My mind raced. *What are the chances he may have left some money? What if he didn't clean it out? What if he did? The odds were against me.*

It was time to pray to God's face for a miracle.

My hands shook as I opened the phone book and skimmed down the page to the number for Deposit Guaranty National Bank on County Line Road. A male teller answered my call, and I told him what had happened, leaving out the part about the gun.

I asked him if our account had any money left in it. He said there was only fifty dollars—a paltry sum—but a few seconds later continued with, "But ma'am, there is another account in your name, as guardian for a Jason Burch. Who is he?"

"My son." *Oh, my God.* A light came on in my head.

When my youngest boy was five-years-old, he had wandered off during Josh's school play. He had thought he could find his way home and had slipped away unnoticed. The whole school helped me look for him, and when we didn't find him right away, I called the police and learned he had been hit by a car. The impact had broken his pelvis, and the frantic driver had called 911. The insurance company had paid his medical bills and given us a small settlement, and since I was Jason's guardian, they had put the money in my name. I had always thought of it as Jason's money, so I had put it out of my mind.

"You can withdraw cash from that account as his guardian, ma'am," the teller said in a firm voice.

Still in shock, I asked, "How… how much is in there?"

"Twenty-two hundred dollars, ma'am."

I couldn't believe it. We were no longer destitute. I made him repeat the amount three times before I was satisfied he had gotten it right.

"Are you sure I can touch it?" I asked, thanking God even as I struggled to believe I had indeed gotten the miracle for which I had prayed. "I don't want to break the law."

"Yes, ma'am. You're his guardian," he said patiently. "Of course, you can withdraw the money. Any amount, at any time."

"Okay. What time do you close?"

"At three-thirty."

"I'll be right there. What's your name? Are you sure you'll be there?"

"My name is James. And yes, I'll be here, Ms. Kang."

"Oh, my God. Thank you so much. I'll be right there."

I wasn't sure if I said that thank you to the teller or to God, because I was sure God had sent James to be my guardian angel. How else could this have happened? He must have looked down from heaven and felt sorry for us. That one simple phone call—one I had almost been too hopeless to make—would help us start our new life.

I searched frantically for the car keys, then I realized I no longer had a car to drive. I quickly put on my running shoes, lacing them up sloppily in my haste, and grabbed my apartment key and my driver's license. I ran to the bank as fast I could, afraid the whole time the teller might have given me the wrong information or gotten my account mixed up with someone else's. I had to get there fast. Within minutes I was bathed in sweat and breathing heavily, but my years of daily jogging had served me well.

I found my stride as I sang, *"I will survive"*

I ran as fast as I could on Northpark Drive to avoid East County Line Road traffic, the same route I jogged every morning.

In ten minutes, I reached the bank's double glass doors across from Northpark Mall. I wiped the sweat from my brow and made a quick attempt to tidy myself up as I stepped into the bank and marched up to the teller's counter.

"I'm looking for James," I said. My words were thick and choppy because I was still gasping for air from running so fast. "I just spoke with him on the phone, and I got here as fast as I could."

Having overheard my request, a tall, young black man walked out from behind the teller counter and held out his hand. He was obviously surprised by how quickly I had made it. I shook his hand and got to the point.

"I just spoke with you about my son's money. I need to withdraw it right now."

"Certainly," he answered. "Have a seat, Ms. Kang. I'll be right with you. I just have to get the forms ready. Do you have your driver's license with you?"

"Yes, I do."

"Do you want to leave anything in the account?"

"No!" I almost yelled, before telling myself to calm down and doing my best to soften my voice. "No, I don't."

"So you want to close the account?"

"Yes. Empty it and close it, please."

"Okay. I need you to sign here and put down today's date," he answered.

I did everything he told me to do without reading the forms.

"How do you want it?" he asked.

"I frowned. What do mean, how do I want it?"

"Cash?"

"No, I mean what size bills do you want? Twenties, hundreds, or--"

"Hundreds," I broke in. Big bills would be easier to count and easier to hide if Hamid came back. I counted the money twice to make sure it was all there and then rolled the wad of bills tight. I ran back to the apartment, clutching cash in my right hand, my apartment key and my driver's license in the other. These twenty-two hundred dollars was the biggest wad of money I had ever held.

I ran back to my apartment and entered it carefully, looking behind every door to make sure Hamid wasn't hiding somewhere ready to attack me. Next, I was searching for a spot to hide a wad of cash as if it were my life. There was no secured spot I could think of. I opened the wash room and saw the heavy Kenmore washer sitting there. That was it. I threw my wad of cash behind it to keep it safe. He'd never look there. I jumped up to climb over to make sure it had landed safely and then took a deep breath.

As I was wiping the sweat off my forehead, it was time, my time to sort out how to put that money to use to turn my life around.

Instead of crying for my baby boy who was sleeping on his blanket a foot away less than an hour ago, I was writing my new beginning with $2,200.00 on a yellow pad.

I carefully made a list of the most immediate to at least important items. Every last penny was counted.

Total money on hand: $2,200.00
Rent: $320
Electric: $65
Gas: $20
Phone: $35
Groceries not covered by food stamps: $150
Unexpected expenses: $200

That left me $1,410.00 after this month's expenses. At that moment, all I could think of was how could I make money, and fast. Almost instantly, the smells and sights of Chinatown came to me. I had walked through there once while living in New York—taking in all the fake purses and watches, the throngs of tourists. I remembered Kim in New York sold fake watches at her store for $55.00 for which she paid only $8.00 in China town. I could rent a booth at the flea market where I had bought my shiny gun. That was it! I must go to China Town as soon as possible.

I dialed American Airlines to get the cheapest fare and added to my list, a *Round* trip ticket to New York *$460*. $1,410.00 – $460.00 = $950.00

I had $950, minus $60.00 round trip taxi fees to and from the LaGuardia airport and $20.00 each for my boys' presents. That left me $50.00 to eat two meals, including unforeseen expenses like cab fee from

Greenwich Village to China town.

I went over my list one more time just making sure because. I couldn't afford to make an accounting errors.

Exactly $800 was left free and clear—God given money. I was making a business plan for the first time in my life.

With my $800, I could buy one hundred fake Rolex's at $8.00 each. If I sold them for $55.00 each, my profit would be $47.00 per watch, for a profit of $4,700. After deducting the cost of my travel expenses, I would net $4,000 on my investment.

Holy smoke, I was seeing the shining lights at the end of dark tunnel. Just the idea that I could turn $800.00 into so much money and to turn my life around. In my mind, I was already counting $4,000.00.

Forget about breaking the law selling counterfeit goods. I wasn't hurting anyone. I wasn't out selling my body for $20.00 or robbing an innocent bystander. If I got caught I would deal with it then.

I glanced at the clock again. I had about thirty minutes before the boys arrived home from school. Eager to get started, I called my friend Kim in New York, who owned a boutique on the corner of Third and MacDougal in Greenwich Village, the same one where I had worked nights. My good nature and sunny smile had made me quite the saleswoman. I hadn't spoken with her since I'd left New York, mainly because she had made it no secret that she thought I was a fool to leave.

"New York is where all Koreans come to get rich," she had lectured me. "Don't be an idiot over a man, Jeanhee."

Kim was single-mindedly devoted to making money. She had no girlfriends to chat with because she had no time for anyone who wasn't going to help her turn a profit, but she did seem genuinely pleased to hear from me.

"Jeanhee ya!" she cried in a breathless voice. "Long time no see. How are you?"

"I'm great," I said, and in a way it was the truth. I might have lost my baby, but at least the devil was gone. "I'm coming to New York in a week. Can I stay with you for just one night?"

"You can stay as long as you want, Jeanhee," she answered, "but just a day?"

I replied, "Yeah…I must come right back."

"I want to start my own business," I said. "I am coming to buy merchandise. Can you tell me where I can buy fake watches in Chinatown?"

"Of course," she crowed. "Finally, you're making a good decision. It's about time you started getting rich like me."

At four feet tall, she was a tiny slip of a woman, but she was mean as a snake. She was the smartest, most cut-throat person I knew when it came to business. She saved all of her cash under her mattress and when she was ready to buy a condo in New York, she laundered it. She flew to Japan with the money tucked under her mink coat, deposited it in the nearest Japanese bank, wired it back to New York, and then flew back.

She loved retelling that story. "Ya! I never knew a hundred thousand dollars could be so heavy," she would say dramatically. "I swayed with exhaustion by the time I got off that plane."

She asked about Hamid with suspicion, and although I kept my story brief, she yelled across the phone line, "Ya! Babbo! Algo! Ya!"

Babbo means *stupid* in Korean. I was not offended because I knew I deserved her chastisement. Kim had no patience for men in general, much less for demons like Hamid. If a man had ever hit her, he probably wouldn't have lived long enough to watch the bruise rise on her face.

She ranted on, "I told you those curly haired sandbags are no good bastards, but you had to go back to him and ruin your life. Didn't I tell you that leaving New York was a mistake?"

By then, a groan had passed my lips. Talking to Kim was like being on the phone with my mother. She didn't need my answers.

"And everyone knows those sons of bitches take their kids when they go. At least, you finally decided to wake up. You should have stayed with John Durant. He came around asking for you a few times."

No way could I have stayed with John—the nonstop sex would have killed me.

"No more men," I said. "I'm done with them. I have eight hundred dollars to spend on purses and watches, and then I'll put all my energy into my business and my children."

"Eight hundred dollars?" That set her off again. "Algo! That is not money, Jeanhee ya. That is pocket change for Koreans in New York. When were you born? Let me guess, is it 1957?" I knew where she was going with this. I could almost see her tiny, short fingers adding up the years from 1957 to 1987, counting both forward and backward. Then she said, "You're thirty-years-old? Thirty-one, by the Korean calendar. You're getting old. I bet you're the poorest thirty-year-old Korean in America. Most Koreans are well off by your age and already have their businesses. Delis, dry cleaners, shops...."

"Okay, Kim. You're right, and I heard your every word. I was wrong for not listening to you. I should've stayed in New York. But better now than never, right? I'm ready to start fresh. Will you help me?"

"Hold on," she said, her voice softening. Maybe she felt bad for letting me have it, but she was justified in her frustration.

The ka-ching of her cash register carried over the line, and then she came back.

"You can buy watches for eight dollars' wholesale, Jeanhee ya," she confirmed. "You can find vendors at Canal and Broadway. I'll see you in a week."

"Mama! We're home!" the boys shouted when they entered the apartment.

Josh always looked for his baby brother to cuddle after school every day. I braced myself and held my breath until he called out, "Where is Ahmad? Where is he?"

My face grim. I was about to break their hearts.

"Why are you all sweaty?" Josh lifted a confused brow. "Did you go running?"

"Yes, Mama had to go for a very special run."

I gathered both of my boys into my arms and gave them a tight hug.

"Come on, you two." I tugged them toward the couch. "Sit down next to mommy. We need to talk." Both boys were worried and troubled because of the rare hugs they had just received.

Once they were settled, I looked at each of them in turn.

"Hamid moved out today. Because we fight all the time, we decided it was best for us not to be together anymore. He took Ahmad with him.

He wanted me to tell you because he had to leave in a hurry. He's sorry he couldn't say goodbye in person and that he had to take Ahmad with him."

"Baby is gone? I don't understand." Josh looked confused. "What if we miss Ahmad, Mama?"

"We will miss him every day and every night," I answered. How could I explain my agony to my young boys? Regardless of the abusive lives we had lived, I couldn't dare to tell my boys, Hamid would come back to cut their throat if I fought to keep Ahmad.

No way would I even consider telling my boys of a horrific threat, or how I had used a gun to run him out of our lives. Instead, I told my boys, "We had to make a trade. To have a better life, we had to let Hamid take Ahmad. I get to keep you two, and he gets to keep Ahmad. That is not a bad trade, is it?"

They looked at one another and said, "Yes, mama."

I held my boys tightly next to me and said, "From now on, until you both grow up to go to college, I'm going to be your mama and daddy all in one. I'm done with men. No man is coming into our lives to terrorize us ever again. I will not get married again. I will not allow any man to live with us again. It will be just the three of us. Okay?"

They both just looked at me solemnly, their dark eyes wide.

"Do you believe me?" I prompted them.

They both nodded and said, "Three of us!"

Jason and Josh turned to stare at the empty swing where they used to push Ahmad till he fell asleep, I turned my tearful face away. I had no time left to cry, especially in front of my boys. I had to show them that I was strong enough to move on with life. Who knows I may see my infant son again to explain what really happened between his father and me someday. I would tell him how I cried for him, and wished could have watched him growing up, his first walk, hearing his first word, "Mama!"

There would always be an empty gaping hole where Ahmad should be. Sadness had stolen too many years from me. Everything I did from this point on had to be worth the price I had paid for my independence and freedom.

Chapter 24

Word of Honor

I SPENT THE SEVEN DAYS prior to leaving for New York filled with anticipation. The airplane ticket price was too pricey for a last-minute ticket purchase. I drilled my boys who were nine and ten years old about their responsibilities while I was away. I couldn't afford baby sitter, so I depended on my neighbor Mary Ann to be there for them in case of an emergency.

"Don't go outside to play when you get home," I said, looking first at Jason who was more keen to get in trouble being younger than Josh, and then at Josh. "Make sure to leave the apartment key on your necklace, Josh, so you won't lose it .I bought a brand new alarm clock just for you." I showed them how to set the alarm. "Get up when your alarm goes off, eat all of your breakfast, and be sure to take your lunch bag with your name and Jason's name from the fridge."

"Yes! Mama, we know what to do."

"Don't miss the bus to school," I continued, "and if you do, call Mary Ann. Don't try to cook anything because you might forget to turn off the oven, and it will cause a fire. And be sure to drink a Coca Cola." They loved soda. I only bought it for special occasions and this was one. That was their incentives to be good boys while I was gone. My instructions sounded like a lot for two little boys to remember, but I said it to them so often they could sing it back on command.

"You must be responsible while I'm gone. I'll have things to sell that will make us rich, and, I will bring you each a present."

Their eyes brightened at that last promise, and I believed they finally recognized the urgency in my words and understood just how important this trip was to us.

"Don't forget to do your homework," I said again. "And don't forget to lock the door before you go to sleep. Don't tell anyone you're home alone, and only bother Mary Ann if you really need her. It's only one night, okay?"

"We can do it, Mama," they answered, no impatience in their voices even though I had lectured them endlessly. I hugged them and sent them to the bus stop, telling them again that I loved them.

I walked through the apartment one last time, making sure the windows were closed and that the stove was off. MaryAnn pulled up outside, and the click of her heels soon clacked against the pavement. I opened the door just as she raised her fist to knock.

We didn't talk on the way to the airport. We had already discussed my plan over and over again, and my sense of urgency was all-consuming, making words between us uncomfortable.

She didn't speak until she dropped me off at the terminal.

"Be careful, Jeanhee," she said. "I'll be here tomorrow night to pick you up."

"Thank you." I squared my shoulders and carried my small bag into the airport. The carry-on was almost empty because I was only staying for a short time and wanted to be able to carry some merchandise back rather than having to mail it all.

Despite my excitement and anxiety, I fell asleep as soon as the plane took off.

I looked out the window as the plane flew over Queens, and the view from the window seemed so desolate: a scattering of trees, tiny homes squeezed back-to-back like match boxes, and cars bumper-to-bumper on every street.

As soon as I picked up my baggage, I passed through the double exit doors at LaGuardia, the blare of horns and the smell of grime assaulted my senses. People were everywhere, and everyone was in a hurry. I already missed Mississippi with its green trees, fresh air, and friendly people who stopped to acknowledge each other's smile. Here everyone minded their own business and stared at the ground as they walked to avoid making eye contact with other human beings. A shrill whistle blew, alerting me that it was my turn to catch a cab. I told the cabbie I needed to go to Third and MacDougal.

"Up town or downtown?" he asked with a heavier accent than I had. He was testing my knowledge of the city to see if he could cheat me.

"I lived here until just two years ago," I said. "I remember exactly how to get there. Let's see if your way is better. I really don't want to see Queens Borough Bridge or Central Park on the way to 3rd and McDougal today, you know what I mean?"

"Really?" he answered in a dry tone, checking me out through the rearview mirror before pulling into traffic.

I was relieved when he didn't force me to tour the city I was dropped off in front of Kim's store on Third and MacDougal. I tipped him for taking me seriously.

Kim met me at the door, looking at her watch, and quickly stashed my bags behind the register, before assuming her business posture. "You'd better hurry if you want to beat rush hour," she said. "The Chinatown vendors close at four."

"Okay, I'll be back soon." I rushed out to China Town.

I was at the corner of Canal and Broadway, where the counterfeiters hawked their wares with hardly any fear of police interference. I walked around the block once, sizing up each vendor. I didn't want a small-timer who might vanish on me. I needed a big fish, someone who would be able to send a continuous supply of wares to me in Mississippi. Eventually, I wandered back to the corner of Canal and Broadway. The Vietnamese man who worked there seemed to be the busiest, and he certainly had the widest variety of goods. I waited my turn, examining his watches while some tourists paid for their items.

As soon as they cleared out, I strode up to him. "Hi! I just came to New York from Mississippi a few hours ago. I flew up here to make a business connection with someone like you, someone successful who can send me goods to sell back home."

I pulled out my carefully rolled up eight-hundred dollars and fanned it out before him. "I want to spend all of this with you today, but I can't afford to fly up here every time I need more merchandise. Can you send it to me every week? I will pay you back every week. I promise."

His small eyes widened, but his face stayed blank; his expression, inscrutable.

I continued, "There's no place like Chinatown in Jackson, Mississippi, where I live." I plunged ahead before he had a chance to say no. "I will be the only one selling these things there, and I can sell a lot of watches and purses. You'll make more money if you will trust me and send me merchandise. You are my only hope. My husband left me two weeks ago, and I need to start my life over with my two sons. I have no family to help me. Eight hundred dollars is all I have. Our life is depending on it."

I patted the money on the counter. He was probably thinking *what the hell? A chick I have never met asks me to trust her and send her merchandise all the way down to Mississippi? What if she doesn't pay me back? Where the heck is Mississippi, anyway?*

"It is next to Alabama and Louisiana.", I replied

Hoping to earn his trust, I looked him straight in the eye. Perhaps he could find that place of trust inside his heart, left over from his home country where people made deals with a handshake and a *word of honor.*

He thought for the longest one minute of my life, and then pulled a piece of wadded paper from his pocket. He unrolled the ball and tore off the corner.

"Here," he said. "Write down your address, and I will send them to you."

"Thank you!" I was shaking and nearly screamed with joy with this street vendor, an angel without visible white wings. I quickly wrote down my name and address before he changed his mind. I feared he'd lose the tiny slip of paper

"You promise you will send money back to me?"

"Yes, I promise I will pay you back. I give you my word," I said, still looking him square in the eye. "What's your name?"

"Call me Tony," he answered, jotting something on another piece of paper. "Here's my phone number. Call me every week with what you need, and I'll send it by the U.S. Post Office."

I chose $800.00 worth of watches and a few knock-off Louis Vuitton's he recommended as being good sellers.

"I have plenty," he said, "so let me know which ones sell the best, and I'll send you more of those."

"Okay," I said.

"You promise you'll send me money each week?" he asked for the third time. He apparently needed more reassurance.

"Yes, I will," I answered. "I give you my word. I promise I'll send you the money."

"Make sure you call me before eight in the morning, so I have enough time to go to the post office before I open for the day."

Another miracle, Tony was like an angel to me, perhaps sent by God. This Vietnamese man I had only known for a few minutes in the middle of China Town, New York City, had just agreed to give me a chance of my life time. My heart sang.

That night Kim and I ate Korean food—kimchi, goggitang, and steamy white rice—and it was so good. We watched Korean soap operas, yelling at the characters on the TV for the crazy things they did. Kim's husband—whom I jokingly called *Tulbbo*, or *hairy man*, because of his beard, a rarity for a Korean man—kept shushing us, but he didn't really seem to mind.

I had called my boys earlier in the evening before they went to sleep to make sure they were following my instructions.

"I'm going to call in the morning in case you don't hear the alarm clock, and I'll be home tomorrow. Sweet dreams, my sons. I love you, and I'm so proud of you for not worrying Mama. I have presents for you. Did you lock the door?"

I fell asleep as Kim stuffed wads of cash under her mattress. Sleeping among other Koreans gave me a sense of being at home. I slept like a baby that night.

I returned to Mississippi the next day. My sweet friend MaryAnn was waiting to pick me up at the airport. I told her about everything I had bought and how excited I was to see if the men and women of Jackson would love the items as much as I thought they would.

The one thing on my list I hadn't yet figured out was transportation. Thankfully, MaryAnn offered to loan me her car during the day while she was at her 8:00 to 5:00 job—another angel placed in my path.

When I arrived at my apartment, my boys were already back home, doing their homework. Their eyes lit up with excitement and they ran to me, asking what presents I had brought them. Josh wrapped his arms around my waist in a fierce hug. I reached into my carry-on bag and produced two "I Love New York" T-shirts with apple emblems—a black one for Josh, and a gray one for Jason. I also gave them two waterproof digital sport watches with glowing neon lights so they could tell the time in the dark. They immediately tried to figure out how to set the time and date, and of course, they couldn't wait to shower with them on to see if they really were waterproof.

Jason ran to his backpack and pulled out a test with a grade of *100* written on it in bold red numbers. He pressed the paper into my hand. "Look how smart I am, Mama."

"I beat all the other kids in a race," Josh interrupted, not to be outdone by his little brother. Even though Josh was older, he couldn't match Jason's exceptional IQ.

"Good for you, Josh. Jason will be a doctor, and you'll be a football player," I said to settle the brewing fight. "I'll be proud of both of you."

"Will you make money soon?" they asked as they pulled on their new shirts.

"Yes," I said, eager to get started. "We'll have money to buy good food and maybe even enough to buy you some new clothes. How about that?"

I could tell they wondered how this *rich mama* thing was going to happen, but I would just have to show them in time.

I threw myself into my new business as if there was no tomorrow. I had decided that instead of limiting my business to the flea market on weekend that I would become a mobile entrepreneur, peddling my wares from the trunk of Mary Ann's car. Every day after dropping Mary Ann off at work, I would create a plan, mapping out what shops and new locations to visit and about how much time I would spend per stop. To save gas, I stayed within a ten-mile radius of the North Jackson area. I ignored businesses' *No Solicitors* signs and waltzed right in, inviting the owners and their customers to visit the trunk of my borrowed blue Cavalier. Salesmen at car dealerships proved to be the easiest prey. They paid premium prices for fake Rolexes, as much as $150, even though I had only paid $8 to $15 for them. The solid gold watches, rimmed in rhinestones, were my best sellers at the highest price.

Beauty salons were also selling meccas. Entering a salon was like walking onto a movie set. All the ladies wore heavy makeup and red lipstick and had perfectly styled hair and flawless nails. They acted as if Christmas had come whenever I stopped by and would run out to my car and dive into the trunk, rummaging through purses and other goodies. My next stops were always at managers' offices at various apartment complexes, where I also did well. I was a born saleswoman. Within one week, I had sold every purse Tony had sent, and half of the watches. I couldn't wait to call Tony.

As soon as he answered, I burst out excitedly, "Hi, Tony, this is Jeanhee from Mississippi. I sold all the purses and watches in only one week."

I lied about the watches. Impressing him seemed like a good idea. I wanted to show him just how profitable a partnership with me would be.

"So I need more stuff. Can you send it today?"

He was surprised but happy he had made the choice to believe in me. He agreed to send me more merchandise. After all, when I made money, he did, too. I placed about five hundred dollars' worth of my stock in a word-of-honor credit account with him and repaid him every week. He sent me more goods, and soon the size of my orders grew.

My business gathered steam quickly. Before long, I was selling enough to pay my bills and pay back what I owed to Tony. Through a combination of my big smile I learned from Woojung, my natural sales ability, and my determination to survive, people were soon searching *me* out. Day to day events were never the same. I surprised my own self so many times listening to what I said to make a sale. To me, everybody was my customer, old, ugly, whoever had a purse, I viewed them first as prospects, soon to be my customers. They just didn't know it until they met me. Even out-of-towners started looking for me at the flea market. If I didn't have what they wanted, they would sketch the product and I would send the drawing to Tony so he could find it for me. I didn't' need to speak perfect English either. The thought of speaking perfect English while I was fast-talking to make a deal never crossed my mind.

Dam Keeper's dream was still at bay. I knew this was my last chance to find my childhood dream. I was going for it *at all cost*.

I loved being a businesswoman even if that business was peddling watches and purses from a borrowed car. So what if the void inside me grew a little more with each passing day?

Chapter 25

"I Will Survive!"

TWO MONTHS HAD PASSED SINCE my trip to New York. My heart no longer raced whenever a man's heavy footsteps walked past my door. I no longer feared that Hamid would come back. The dust had settled, and I had wrapped my heartache over the loss of my baby deep inside a secret place in my heart. I tried to keep my pain buried beneath a heavy load of work. Naturally, as soon as my fears eased, Hamid contacted me.

The phone rang, breaking the peaceful silence on a Sunday afternoon. I wasn't surprised to hear the hated tone of his evil voice on the other end of the line. I had known he'd contact me one day. It had only been a matter of time.

"Hi, Jeanhee, do you miss our son yet?" He stabbed my heart right away.

The last thing I wanted to give him was joy he was expecting, my pain and sorrow. I gathered my thoughts quickly, and said, "Yes. Of course, I do." My heart spasmed, the meanness in his voice sending an icy shiver all the way to my spine and back. "What kind of mother do you think I am?"

"Well, you know.... This is all your fault," he snapped. "You ran me off with a gun, you bitch. You're lucky I haven't come back and killed you and your kids while you were asleep. I've been thinking that I am the one who brought you here to Mississippi, and now it's time for you to leave. I can't stand having you in the same town, available to other men. You're still my wife."

"Leave?" I spat. "I don't think so. I happen to love Mississippi! If you can't stand me being here, you can leave, because am not leaving Mississippi. When he realized I was not going anywhere, he changed his demeanor. "Jeanhee," he wheedled. "Don't you want to come back to me? I changed, you know." He used the very words that had gotten me to Mississippi from New York. It had worked so many times in the past but not anymore, not ever again.

"No, I will never come back to you. It is over between you and me," I said again. "If you hadn't left that day, I would've killed you dead. And I still have that gun, in case you come back."

He drew in a sharp breath. I could tell he wanted to slap me around, then close his fingers around my neck. But those days were over.

"I'll kill you one day," he yelled.

"Oh, really?" I replied with a heavy question mark. If you dare try, I'll shoot you in the balls. What do you want? Tell me, or I'm hanging up"."

"If you want to see our son, I'll let you see him tomorrow. Here is my number." I could tell by the first three digits that he was somewhere in South Jackson. "Call me."

"Fine," I said. "I'll call you tomorrow."

"I'm not going to take my son away from his mother, no matter how terrible you think I am. But you have to come here," he said. Either he wanted to get on my good side, or he had something up his sleeve, but I couldn't resist seeing my baby. I wanted desperately to hold my little baby boy, smell his baby breath, feed him and change his diaper, how I have longed to see his dark almond eyes gazing up at me, his tiny baby fingers gripping my hand.

Several days passed before I could get enough courage to call and agree to go Hamid's apartment to see Ahmad.

The day I went to see my baby, I put the gun into my purse and then took it back out at least ten times. Should I take it with me? Should I leave it behind? If Hamid somehow managed to take it away from me, he just might kill me.

I tucked it back under the mattress and called Mary Ann to let her know where I was going in case I disappeared.

"Jeanhee, no," she said angrily. "Have him meet you somewhere in public. Don't you dare go to his apartment? He may kill you."

"Okay, MaryAnn."

I called Hamid to tell him that I wanted to see Ahmad at the park close to his apartment but he said, "Hell no. Take it or leave it. I am not bringing the baby outside."

I *had* to see Ahmad, so against MaryAnn's warning, I went to visit Hamid's apartment. His apartment was small and shabby with small TV, sofa, and dining room table with two chairs. Hamid's fake friendly smile when he greeted me sent chills all the way up my spine to the back of my head. I found it hard to believe that this was the same man who had beaten me so often. He tried to hug me, but I stepped back.

"No hug for your husband?"

His charm was as worthless as a moth-eaten garment. "You won't be my husband for long. I've already filed for a divorce from you," I said, punctuating every word. "You should receive the divorce papers any day now. Where is Ahmad?"

"What? You're really going to divorce me?"

"Yep."

He tried his hardest to look genuinely hurt, but I didn't buy it. He was wondering how I was making ends meet without his money. He had been certain I would crawl back to him, but now he realized that finances, or the lack thereof, wouldn't draw me back.

"Don't worry. I'll pay the attorney," I said. "You just sign on the dotted line."

I brushed past my shocked husband, who had never seen a Jeanhee like this—cold and harsh, every word from her mouth like the gun she'd pointed at him two months earlier.

Behind Hamid, Ahmad pulled himself up in his crib and tried to crawl, his chubby baby legs barely supporting his big Buddha belly. I was glad he hadn't lost any weight. His hair had grown longer and thicker. He grabbed his blanket with his little fat fingers as I scooped him up into my arms.

"Hi, my sweet baby," I murmured to him, lifting him out of his crib, hugging him tightly and smelling his sweet baby breath. I had missed his milky baby smell, and I rolled my nose over his cheeks. I wanted to let him know how much I had missed him. "I missed you, my pumpkin. Your brothers miss you, too."

I kissed him all over his face, tickling his belly with my nose while he giggled. He still liked belly tickles. I wished that for his sake, I could turn my cheek and somehow put up with his father. I hated myself for not being able to compromise, and tears trickled down my cheeks. I nuzzled him again. "Here are kisses from Josh and Jason."

I kissed his tiny fists and feet, and he gurgled happily. I wasn't sure if he actually remembered me. Did he even know Mama missed him day and night, wishing to feed him, give him a nightly bath, dress him in clean clothes, and rock him to sleep? I hated the fact that my baby boy had been without his mother for two months. Hamid left me alone and busied himself in the kitchen while I sat in the floor rocking and singing to Ahmad. Unfortunately, I had to go soon. I didn't see any sense in tempting the devil. After I played with the baby a little while longer, I changed his diaper, then kissed him on the forehead and tucked him back into his crib. Hamid snaked his strong arm around my waist as I straightened up, and I looked down at it in surprise.

The sight of his tanned skin and curls of black hair sent a shock through my body, and my breath came out in a hard gasp. I flashed back to that moment on the bus in South Korea, my nose full of the smell of kimchi and sweat, when the monster had groped me. Hamid's big hand inched toward my thigh, and I twisted around angrily.

"What are you doing?" I yelled. "Don't touch me! Don't you dare touch me."

He pulled my hair back with one hand and ground his lips into mine.

"Jeanhee, we can be a family," he panted when he finally lifted his head. "You can see our son all the time if you'll just come back to me. He needs his mama. Can't you see he missed you?"

"I'll never come back to you!" I shouted, shoving at him as terror and disgust filled my stomach. I swore at him in Korean, my whole body trembling. I had to get out.

But I'd waited too late. My nightmare with Hamid had not yet ended. I had called the police on him many times, but none of that mattered now. Within seconds, he had me cornered in the bedroom. He pinned me to the bed and fumbled with my pants, popping off the top button in his haste. I didn't bother to scream. If this was the price I had to pay to see my baby, I would pay it.

After a few minutes of labored thrusting, he gave a final grunt of satisfaction and rolled off of me. He pulled up his pants and walked out of the room without saying a word. I slipped off the bed and attempted to straighten my hair, then tugged the front of my shirt over my pants to hide the missing button. His warmth ran down my thigh.

Before I could escape, he walked back in.

"Don't even think about calling the police," he said. "We're still married. I'm still your husband. I didn't rape you."

I don't remember driving back to my apartment. I felt horribly violated, but I had gotten my tubes tied after I had Ahmad, so at least I didn't have to worry about having another baby with that devil. When Hamid called me a few weeks later, begging me to forgive him and promising not to touch me if I came back to visit the baby, my mother's heart overcame my good sense and I went again. He kept raping me until Ahmad was almost a year old. I couldn't do it anymore, not even to see my beloved little boy.

"I won't see my baby again if I have to be raped to do it," I told him over the phone after the last time. "I won't let you rape me anymore."

"What do you mean, you won't see our baby?" he asked incredulously. "You can't mean that."

He just didn't get it. I had to draw the line, so I said the unspeakable words, "I don't want to see my baby again."

"Do you hear me?" I screamed. "You will not touch me ever again."

Eventually, two months passed and he called again, but this time he agreed to meet in a public place. We met at the Ross Barnett Reservoir. The place was always filled with fisherman, so I felt somewhat safe. Ahmad was growing fast. I missed my baby so much. I cherished every second spent holding him again. As I sat in the front seat of the car, bouncing Ahmad on my knee, rocking my precious baby, I tried my best to ignore Hamid's dark presence.

Finally, he reached across the seat and grabbed my elbow.

"Jeanhee, I've changed," he said, tightening his grip on my arm.

Oh, God. Not this again. I refused to look at him. I pretended I didn't hear him.

"I know I've made lot of mistakes," he said. "But I'd like to start over. I *will* change. I'll do anything. We can even go to counseling. We can keep our own places for a while, but I want you to be Ahmad's mother. Babies need a mother. I want us to be in love again. I'll find a job. I'll even work for Americans." Shocking! He was bringing out even the kitchen sink to get me back to abuse me again.

"No, Hamid," I said without hesitation. "I am never coming back to you. I will not ever be your wife again. You need to go on with your life, find someone else your age."

Almost before the words were out of my mouth, he pulled a knife on me. The blade's dull gleam made me freeze as he pressed it against my inner thigh.

"You have an artery right here," he murmured, smiling so as not to alarm anyone who might walk by. "If I cut you, you'll bleed out. No one will be able to save you."

"No." I shook my head. I would not let him terrorize me. I couldn't.

We were there for hours. He cried like a baby, but his pleas, threats, even my blood on my leg didn't deter my decision not to go back to him. As Hamid yelled, at me Ahmad blinked at him and chattered to himself in his baby language, until he started wailing for milk in the back seat. I tried to reach him to give him his bottle, but Hamid waved the knife at me and said, "I won't let you touch him. I am going to kill you right now."

"Why won't you just let us be happy, Jeanhee?" he snapped. "I swear to God I have changed. We can be a family. Why won't you just listen to me?"

Ahmad's sobs increased in volume. People walking by the car turned to look, their attention caught by his wails and my swollen, tear-stained face.

"Let me change Ahmad," I begged. "He's wet, and he's going to get a rash. He's hungry! Can't you tell he is hungry?" I screamed my lungs out.

Hamid kept me in that car for nearly four hours, running the knife over my thigh. Finally, he popped the child locks he'd used to keep me inside and ordered me to get out.

He didn't have to tell me twice. Hamid sped off with my baby still crying.

I went straight to justice court to file a complaint against Hamid for holding me against my will at knife point for hours. The lady on duty at the desk was short, curly light brown hair about my height, and middle-aged, with curly light brown hair. Fay Smith I will never forget her name. I showed her where the knife went into my right thigh, which was still a little bloody. She entered my name into the system and stopped typing.

"How many times have you dropped charges against him?" she asked.

"I-I don't remember,"

I never heard back from the justice court.

I got an answering machine to screen Hamid's calls and decided to never see him again. I couldn't bear his threats or the grotesque weight of his body on top of me. The hours of joy I had received from holding Ahmad were overshadowed by my memory of hearing him cry for his bottle. I decided that it was best for Ahmad and me if let it all go. At least my baby didn't have to cry anymore.

My baby was sixteen months old before I heard back from Hamid again. "If you want to see your baby and if you want Josh and Jason to see him, this is your last chance. Because after this, you'll never see him again. So take it or leave it."

"What do you mean, never, Hamid?" I asked. Fear curdled my stomach. "Where are you going?"

"That's none of your business," he said. "You're lucky I'm letting you see him again at all. You can come by my apartment this afternoon."

"Oh, no, not again. I don't' think so. Your tricks don't work anymore."

After I pleaded with him, he agreed to let us meet him in the Wal-Mart parking lot on East County Line Road.

Josh and Jason chattered excitedly during the drive. "Mama, I thought you said Ahmad was gone. Is he coming back to live with us? Can he live with us again?"

"Ahmad can't live with us, remember?" I said. "Just can't…. boys, please understand. I can't take Hamid back. Not now, not ever." I thought about telling them what Hamid really said and did to me.

When we met Hamid, he managed to say, "Hi how are you?" to my boys and handed me Ahmad, saying brusquely that he expected him back in three hours.

I gathered the baby into my arms, and all of us took turns showering his face with kisses. Our little family of four squeezed into one side of a booth. Josh and Jason took turns holding Ahmad. I smiled as he gnawed fiercely on some chicken nuggets and French fries. He was old enough to eat table food, and Josh and Jason kept giving him their fries. After lunch, we decided to take our first and what would ultimately be the only photo of our family at JC Penney in North Park Mall.

If I could have looked into the future and known this picture would be the only one ever taken of me with all three of my sons, I might have lain down under the table and never gotten up.

After we had the photo taken,we had to give Ahmad back to Hamid. He was always full of lies, so I figured we would go through the same scene all over again in a few weeks. But two months went by, then a few more months went by and I never heard from Hamid.

No messages. No phone calls.

When I couldn't stand it anymore, I finally broke down and called Hamid. I just wanted to know how Ahmad was doing, even if I couldn't see him. I would just like to know.

"He's gone. I sent him to live with my father in Kuwait. It is all your fault!"

His words knocked the breath out of me, and I struggled to comprehend what he had just said.

"I told you to come back to me," Hamid continued. "I told you I've changed, but you wouldn't listen. You didn't want us to be together. It's your loss."

He laughed at me, knowing his derisive chuckle would wrench my already broken heart. His joy at my pain was more than I could bear.

I hung up, determined not to allow him any further satisfaction.

I had to tell Josh and Jason. We all cried together. We mourned the loss of a brother and a son and an amazing little life that should have been a part of us.

I decided right then and there that one day I would find Ahmad and bring him home, when I became rich enough to have a beautiful house, to be able to give him a good education, and to love him twice more to make up for lost time. The thought that it just might happen one day gave me hope and determination to chase my childhood dream. Now I had a more than childhood dreams to chase. I added my baby boy to my to-do-before-I die list.

The only photo with all my sons

Chapter 26

Street Peddler

IN ORDER TO TURN MY life around, I had to reinvent myself. But first, I had to let go of all of my past. There was no one to blame. It was all my own fault. I had wasted five years of my life with Hamid. I'd let him abuse me. I didn't have to come back to Mississippi, but I did of my own free will.

To start a new beginning, I had to start fresh. I had to believe thirty years old wasn't too old to start over. I said to myself, "Ages are just numbers." I decided that I was pretty. I pledge to myself that this time, no man was ever going to make me cry again. I counted the years I had lived in the land of opportunity— America, the country I always called *Meegook, the beautiful country, I* had been here for twelve years. My list of priorities now was simple and clear, stay away from men, get off welfare, and work day and night to become a financially independent woman. After all, I had been in this position before. The only differences now were that I was already in *Meegook*, so I didn't' have to sell sex to earn a second chance.

Once I had a clear goal, a talent I'd never known I possessed—as a saleswoman—flared to life like a match in a dark room. I *had* to be a likable person.

The first trick to being a great saleswoman? Smile all the time. My friendship with Woojung had taught me that a smile never hurt, and that if nothing else, it would leave a lasting impression. It was time to apply *smile more than yesterday* into a real life skill. Whenever my struggle with the English language caused a problem with a customer, I smiled. I became a quick thinker, a fast mover, and a faster talker. If I could have painted my face like an Indian warrior, I would have. For the past five years, I'd been blinded by the charm of a devil. Now I had to fight a demon—not Hamid, but the one inside of me. The demon that kept me from succeeding. With every passing sale, I became more confident. In my heart, I was convinced that all my customers *needed* my products even if *they* didn't know.

I had become a successful street peddler.

Mary Ann was the only real friend I had in Jackson, because Hamid's torment had made me forget the satisfaction of having a social life and kept me away from church. Now I had rediscovered the outgoing Jeanhee. For a while, I spent my evenings watching TV, mostly comedies, so I could mimic the most charming characters. Soon, I could speak Ebonics, ghetto, redneck, and Southern belle, always mixed with my inescapable Korean accent. I learned slang and laughed with my customers who got a kick out of hearing me use it. How many Koreans could boast having a Southern drawl?

One day, while testing a new sales route, I drove Mary Ann's car up Interstate 55, took the Northside Drive exit, and continued down one block to Old Canton Road, where I summoned all my courage and looked for a place to stop. I pulled into a strip mall called Colonial Mart on Old Canton Road and parked in front of MC's Beauty Box. I had to start somewhere if I wanted to increase my business, and I decided this was it. So I psyched myself up and went inside. The women in the salon all assumed I was a customer.

"Hi," I said with a smile. "I'm Jeanhee, your new street peddler. Would any of you like to buy something?"

"What are you selling, honey?" one of them asked.

"Earrings, watches, and bracelets. I've got 'em all." My enthusiasm piqued their interest. Mary Catherine, the owner of the place, said, "Bring 'em in, honey, and we'll see if you have anything we can't live without."

Tami, Nichole, and Dyanne rushed out to my borrowed car of the day like school girls. As I popped the trunk, I said "Welcome to my shop, Ta-da!" The three of us would soon become life-long friends, but at that moment they had no idea, neither did I. Offering the women no time to change their minds, I hauled my products into the salon and dumped them onto the counter. I was selling the earrings and bracelets for $4.99. I gave them the run-down on the rest of my prices. Nothing was organized or packaged in a pretty box. I'd dumped the jewelry into a laundry basket and kept the purses loose, grabbing what I could carry from the trunk—not the best system, but it worked.

That was the beginning of my expanded peddler business. My favorite stops were hair salons, In part because their peculiar names, Back Stage, Beverly Hills Salon, Spectacle, Salon Cosmo, Movie Stars. Their nonchalant carefree spirit caught my attention. I could just tell they could care less about my dark past. Their job was to make ugly people beautiful and they readily saw past my flaws.

My business was thriving. I couldn't believe I was having fun spending my days driving around in a blue Cavalier, selling out of anything and everything I could get from Tony in New York.

Some days, they bought things they didn't even want. They liked my gutsy attitude and wanted me to keep coming back. I learned that most hair dressers were movie star wannabes. They wore thick, heavy makeup, blood red lipstick, and bright fingernail polish, and they often sported wild hair styles and mixture of colors. One day a salon owner's hair might be fiery red, and the next she'd streak it with purple. They'd do anything to get noticed because they sold products meant to make women beautiful. They loved to flaunt their wares?

I never had to get a professional haircut from any of them during this time. I simply gathered all of my hair in one hand and sliced off the end of it with scissors. I always wore my hair in a ponytail anyway, so I saw no sense in paying thirty-five dollars to do it. I never revealed this style secret to my girlfriends though—they would have yelled at me.

I gave each of them an open credit line built on *word of honor.* I became a walking mannequin, always remembering to wear the outfit I wanted to sell that day, draped on all the jewelry, earrings, bracelets, rings, headbands, hairpins, scarves, necklaces, belts before I walked into their shops.

I would walk in carrying my bag and say, "Honey, you can buy whatever I've got on except my underwear and bra. I won't take those off."

They would burst out laughing at the Korean woman who was just as crazy as they were.

Car salesmen were the easiest preys. They liked to spend their money as soon as they made their commissions, and I was always there to harvest it.

A few of them asked me out on dates, but I always turned them down. One in particular was so full of himself he called me later in the day, after buying a wallet. For the second time, I said no. He went off on me for hurting his testosterone-filled ego.

"Who do you think you are?" he asked. "You're just a salesgirl, selling stuff out of the trunk of your girlfriend's car. You don't even have a car of your own."

I let him finish his tirade without interrupting. I had been here before and would not date a car salesman if he were the last man standing. I was turned off by their fast talk, slick hair, gleaming teeth, fake smiles and dressed-to-kill suits.

"Andy, that's just it," I said once he was done.

"I'm nobody!" *Nobody my ass, but I didn't say it loud.*

"Look, *I'm* just trying survive with my two young boys, struggling to pay my bills. I have no intention to go out on date with you or anyone else."

He calmed his ass down and said, *"Nobody, huh...."* I had shut him up and accomplished two things in the process: I had salvaged his ego, and I could now go back to his dealership without qualms. The men at that place of business would never pick on me again. I was just like they were, attempting to conduct business and make a sale.

I learned very quickly that every customer is different, talked different, too.

I finessed my skills as a saleswoman as time went on and soon became a good judge of body language and tone, knowing just what to say to close a deal. My English may have been scattered, but I calculated every word. Each customer was my best friend, no matter how little they spent nor how much or how little I liked them. I always remembered their names, their birthdays, what they bought, and which styles they preferred. And if I heard any gossip about them, I remembered that, too.

Making money became my obsession... my joy. I had no shame. I would stand on a corner near various festivals holding bags of watches without shame with my boys standing next to me. They knew the drills, Sale! Sale!

My boys would find a grocery cart from nearby grocery store to help me display my wares, yelling out, "Sale! Sale!" to everyone who passed by. Sometimes, we only sold one watch but it was worth the trying for us.

While working at the flea market, I spotted an advertisement seeking food vendors for Jubilee Jam, an annual music and arts festival in downtown Jackson. The organizer wanted fresh food ideas, so I skimmed through other vendors' food lists to see what I could propose that was different. I told them I could do a tempura tent, and I beat out the other applicants even though they were sponsored by restaurants. No one asked me if I knew how to make it nor if I had a restaurant. I guess they just assumed all Asians know how to make Tempura. I wasn't about to tell them the truth either. *Don't ask. Don't tell.*

I signed up for the two and a half days' event and paid the one-thousand-dollar booth fee. Now, I was in, no problem. All I had to do was find somebody who could teach me how to make tempura. *How hard could it be?* Tumbling a few vegetables to fry and sell to people who can care less about the fat content per serving.

I stopped at a local oriental grocery store on Highway 51 owned by a Vietnamese lady and asked her for some tips. She never stopped bagging groceries as she answered. "Always use Japanese tempura mix, *adda* mix no good. And make sure you mix the batter with ice cold water and keep the batter super-super *coldatthertimmess*—okay? She meant cold *all the time,* speaking in her Vietnamese accent mixed with a southern drawl.

I asked her why, and she told me so that the food would come out extra *crunchiii* and *yummiii.*

She said, "Heat the fryer to three-hundred-fifty degrees, and then pop in the vegetables one by one, never together, okay?"

I then went to Little Tokyo, my favorite sushi place, and asked the owner, Tommy sang, for a favor. I figured that since I was a regular customer, he would be obliged to order me six large bags of tempura mix from his vendor at the wholesale price. It just so happened that I already owned two deep fryers I had gotten at the flea market a while back. Who knew? I was actually going to use them. The only reason I had bought them was because it was too good of a price to turn it down.

Voila! I was ready for Tempura business.

I kid you not! My food booth had the longest line at the festival. I cut vegetables nonstop, my knife flying and catching everyone's attention. I threw sweet potatoes, zucchini, broccoli, and four jumbo shrimp into a basket for five dollars. My boys stirred the batter, I dropped the food into the fryer, and my girlfriends Tami, and Terrie fished it out, taking turns at the register, and handed out the steaming baskets.

One night after the festival, one of my friends called me, saying, "Jeanhee, I saw you on TV chopping vegetables at the festival. No man will mess with you after they saw your action with that big ass Chinese choppingknife!"

I had been so absorbed in cooking that day, I hadn't even noticed the camera on me. I wished I had known so I could have combed my pony tail instead of bunching it up with hand to tie it in a knot.

A hellacious heat rash around the seams of my underwear and bra, a small price to pay counting cash afterwards. Besides, the heat rash was nothing compared to the frost bite I used to battle during the winters back home. My medicine to cure all was green money. I made five thousand dollars in those two and a half days, and I ended up frying tempura in scorching one hundred-plus degree heat for the next three summers. The same cameraman filmed me every year.

"She's back," he'd say, "the lady with the chopping block." I was cutting vegetable so fast that I would have put a Chinese chef to shame.

I hadn't even known I had a hidden tempura-cooking talent. I fried those vegetables with merciless intensity. I never even took a bathroom break. I didn't dare leave, because I feared the impatient crowd around my tent might wander off.

Whenever a big box of purses and watches would arrive at my door, I'd slash through the thick packaging tape with trembling hands. Tony had kept his word, and I would keep mine—to him, to myself, and to my children.

What an amazing feeling, to forget the worry of how I would pay my bills each month. The second part of my dream, to be wealthy and live without worry, was slowly becoming a reality. Knowing that I was in control of my own destiny, independent from a man, gave me the motivation to wake up each morning, happy and full of energy. I dropped my welfare benefits in less than a year. I no longer needed assistance from the government.

My customer list grew longer. Many of them liked my ballsy bravery in selling goods to anybody, any place, and anywhere shamelessly. They all knew about my hard life with Hamid, how I had lost Ahmad, and that I was raising two boys on my own. But, I never told anyone about my prostitution days in Osan.

My customers admired how hard I hustled to make a buck. They wanted to help me succeed. I think a few of them wished they could get out there to hustle like me.

My customers were happy to purchase counterfeits which were the biggest ticket items. Once people told their friends, and their friends told their friends and my business thrived. Word of mouth in this town was like an underground newspaper. Back then cell phones were very expensive, and besides they were as big as a purse. I couldn't carry it even if I could have afforded one. I had to buy a beeper. My customers paged me constantly, and I wasted no time to call everyone back.

They would say, "Jeanhee, where are you? Has anything new come in yet? Don't sell to someone else before you see me. I'll pay you extra if I get first pick."

I had finally figured out how to create a loyal customer base, and that was by using the Korean way—my *Word of Honor*—the same reason Tony had trusted me. I never asked for money upfront, and that made it easier for me to sell larger quantities at one time. Customers love to be trusted.

Word of honor was the recipe for many life-long relationships, and soon my *black book* "was born—a notebook filled with the names of my clients and their work places, phone numbers, purchases, and debts. I listed them in alphabetical order and meticulously kept up with their preferred styles and little details about their personal lives. Before I met with a client, I would review their information and make sure to ask personal questions during our conversation. More often than not, this made them feel special. I'm not sure how I became so business savvy in sales. Perhaps I had inherited it from my mother, who had a natural knack for running a hotel, even though she had never done anything but farm work before. Maybe, it had been born of desperation and hunger. Hunger can make or break people. My hunger was very much responsible for making me

If I discovered a window of opportunity, I dove through it. I even opened a little lunch deli off Fortification Street once. How hard could it be? I didn't realize a person had to be eighteen or older to serve beer. A kind customer whispered in my ear one day that Josh was too young to be delivering beer, and that I could get in big trouble with the law. Anybody could buy and sell alcohol where I came from. I closed the deli within three months in fear of getting in trouble for selling alcohol without a license. Heck, I didn't' know I had to have one of those to sell beer. Besides, it was requiring too much work for too little return compared to selling counterfeits.

As time went by, I dated every now and then. I missed the companionship of a man. The first guy turned out to be like Hamid, obsessive and violent. I dropped him like a hot potato. He, begged and pleaded just like Hamid. Dejavu, right? Only this time, I didn't buy any of those stupid lies. It was time to hurt his manhood with my index finger wagging at his face, I said, "Hell No! I have been there and done that already." He was shaken and quick to realize that he was messing with the wrong chick. I never saw him again. I had no mercy left in my blood for any man who would even think he could hit me. I was a brand new

Jeanhee since I had heard Oprah's talk.

On my second try, I fell in love with a married man. Apparently, I was incapable of making good choices when it came to men. I needed to come up with Plan B.

I was still a young woman, and I struggled with sexual urges that sometimes overwhelmed me. I didn't want to meet men only for sex, but at the same time, I craved physical intimacy. I wished I could lose this desire. My life would have been different if I didn't have sex period. I came to realize, all my troubles in life began with sex. It had taken me how many years to figure this out? Sex was the cause of my misery. I could only imagine what my life would have been like if I hadn't had sex with Heechang. My girlfriends once suggested I buy some sex toys, but that didn't sound satisfying and I was horrified at the thought of explaining what they were to my boys should they come across them, especially my Jason. If I had anything hidden, Jason could find it. He had proven that to me every Christmas

I poked my inner thigh closed to you know where with a steak knife hoping the pain would make my urges go away. Finally, I decided upon a genius solution to this problem. I went to see my doctor for my annual check-up to pursue my plan B. When Dr. Russell asked me if I had any questions after exams, I don't think the one I asked was what he had in mind.

"Do what?" he responded, wide-eyed.

"Could I… have my clitoris removed?" I repeated.

He continued to gape at me. "Why would you even consider that?"

"Because sex gets in my way," I said. I'd read that clitoris removal was a common practice in some cultures. "I don't have time for sex. It always gets me into trouble with men. It ruined my life. I had to poke myself in the leg with a knife a few weeks ago so I wouldn't run out and fall into bed with the first man I met."

"Mutilating yourself won't stop your desire for sex, Jeanhee," he replied, looking at me as if I'd just made the most peculiar request he'd ever had. "Removing your clitoris will just keep you from ever having any satisfaction. That's the worst of both worlds. You are a young woman. It's natural for you to want sex. Besides, that's a barbaric practice. It's not anything we would do in America."

I ignored my sexual urges as best as I could. I worked long hours and was too tired to think about it anymore. I sometimes went out with my friend Laura. She was single, with no kids. I had met her at the beauty shop she owned. We hit it off when we first met, and she often loaned me her car whenever Mary Ann was out of town. But I just couldn't bring myself to have one-night stands like Laura often did. I was too afraid I would catch some kind of disease. Some of those girls were worse than the whores back in Osan, taking any able man home every time they went out. At least whores in Osan got paid to get laid, but not in this free country, they were giving it away for free every night.

Except for my nights out with Laura or an occasional date, I buried myself in work, focusing on street peddling by day, and the flea market on weekends. At night, I focused on my boys. I had little time to spare beyond that. And of course, I spent a lot of time collecting what people owed me. Almost everyone paid me in full and on time. A few girls lost their jobs and had to choose to either pay me or the rent, and I didn't hold that against them. What I made off of them overall was more than what they owed me, and I figured they needed the money more than I did.

As my weekend-flea market business boomed, many of my customers opened their beautiful homes to me and invited friends over to buy my goods on week days. One of my sweet customers even ran an advertisement in the paper that read, *Jeanhee is setting up her fashion purses on Thursday 9:00 to 2:00. Please come by.*

I never forget one guy's name, Alvin Douglas. He was twice taller than me, a skinny black guy, and he was one of my best customer at the flea market. He would buy 10 watches every weekend.

One Sunday afternoon, he approached me with an idea. "Jeanhee, I can sell fifty watches per month for you. I don't have money to pay upfront. If you trust me, I promise I will pay you back every week.". "At that time, $1,000.00 was a lot but I decided to trust him.

Two weeks passed, and there was no sign of Alvin.

What had happened to his word of honor? The thought of giving up my $1,000.00 never crossed my mind. I decided to teach him a lesson he would never forget.

After the flea market closed on Sunday at 6:00, I dropped off my boys at home. I normally would take them with me, but I had a gut feeling that my boys should not go with me. I had looked up Alvin's address in the phone book from a payphone booth. I headed toward his apartment on Robinson Road in South Jackson. It was in a rough neighborhood with sagging front porches and rusted cars. A few children played ball beneath a hoop nailed to the side of a shed.

By the time I reached the apartment complex on the edge of the neighborhood, it was getting dark. I parked as close to Alvin's Apartment door as I could in case I had to run. His light was on. Before I got out of the car, I tucked the .22 into my back blue jean pocket. Even though I had never shot anyone yet, I figured it might come in handy. I wanted to teach this guy a lesson about the word of honor system. I was calculating how much more I must sell to fill $1,000.00 void if I didn't get it back although there was no way I was going to let him off the hook.

"Alvin!" I yelled, angrily pounding on his door. "I know you are in there."

I could see him peering through the peephole, but I was so short he probably couldn't tell it was me.

"Open up, Alvin! This is Jeanhee from the flea market, and you owe me money!"

He opened the door slowly, his eyes wild. He was twice my size, but he was still afraid of this tiny Korean woman who was yelling like a crazy person on his doorstep.

"You are a liar and a thief!" I berated him in a loud voice. "I trusted you and gave you a chance, and you cheated me."

"Ms. Jeanhee, please!" All of a sudden, I am "Ms. Jeanhee" to him. He raised both hands. "I was going to pay you. Don't yell, because the neighbors will call the cops. I really was going to come find you tomorrow, I swear."

"Well, I came to you instead," I said. "You'd better give me back those watches."

"I don't have them anymore," he said. "I can pay you tomorrow."

"Oh, no. I'm not leaving until you give me something to take back," I said, lifting my chin and standing my ground.

He eyed me warily. "What do you want?"

"Let me in so I can look around," I said. "And don't try anything funny."

As I walked past him into the apartment, he drew in a sharp breath. I figured he had seen the gun sticking out of my pocket.

The first thing I spotted was a brand new Hitachi color TV, still in the box. I pointed at it and hissed, "Did you take that and not pay for it, either?"

"No, I paid for it," he answered.

"With the money you owe me?" I asked. Then, not waiting for an answer, I said, "I'll take the TV, and you are going to carry it to my car, please."

He did so, without saying a word. His girlfriend didn't say anything, either. She was apparently amazed that her big boyfriend was following directions given by a short Asian women yelling in broken English.

When I got home with the television, my boys were over the moon.

"Mommy, Mommy, is that for us? So we can watch cartoons in color T.V.? Thank you, Mama!" At first they thought I had bought it, but when I told them I took it from a big black man, I became their hero. "Wow, Mommy, you did that? Really?"

Twenty-five years later, I still have that TV in my garage, and the remote, too. I won't get rid of it. That TV was my reward for standing up to a big man who owed me money, a reward for not backing down. That event set the tone for my stand against injustice. I never did like liars and cheaters. I may have made my share of mistakes, but I would never steal from anybody, especially from a single mom.

I was lucky during my street peddling days, other than the Alvin episode and one person who wrote me a bad check. The culprit was a lady name Tina from Forest, Mississippi—and the check was for one hundred and seventy-five dollars. She had seemed so nice with a deep country southern accent, calling me honey as she bought two watches and a purse.

Her address was written on the check. I tried to call her at home, but she never answered. One afternoon I told my kids, we were going for a ride to Forest. I had never been there, but I wanted to find that lady who gave me a bad check. The town was about an hour drive from home. Back then, there was no Google map I pulled into a gas station and found an old man drinking coffee in the little snack bar.

"Howdy! I came all the way here from Jackson to find an old friend of mine," I lied. "Her name is Tina Story. She told me how to get to her house, and Dang it, I can't remember it if my life is depended on it? Uh… You don't happen to know her by any chance, would you?"

"I shore do know Tina Story" She went to school with my daughter all the way from 1st grade to High school down yonder. The old man more than ready showed me some old-fashioned Southern hospitality. He didn't' only tell me how to get to her house, he drew a map to her house for me.

"Thank you! Sir, Have Yosef a Blessed day."

"Yo do the same.", he said.

In less than five minutes, I pulled up in front of Tina's place and knocked on her door.

She found me standing at her door, my kids behind me. She just about peed her pants.

"Hi, Tina," I said, kindly, pretending she had no idea the check was bad. "I went to the bank yesterday to cash your check, but they said, I should better find you to get cash in person" I didn't' want to embarrass her by saying BAD CHECK front of my kids.

"Oh, my goodness, I am so-sorry, Honey."

"Did you have to drive all-the way from Jackson?

"Yes, I did."

"I honestly don't know what happened with dat. I'll bring you the cash tomorrow," she said, nervously gnawing her lip. "I don't know what happened to my bank account. I am fixing to find out when I get there tomorrow" "I shore will get yo money, Honey."

"Okay, where in Jackson do we meet tomorrow?"

"How-about if I meet you at the Waffle House on McDowell Road off I-55 tomorrow at four-thirty."

"All right," I said. What else could I do? She knew I would drive back to Forest to find her again if she didn't show up. "You also owe me thirty dollars for the insufficient fund charge. So you need to bring me two hundred and five dollars."

With a swift bob of her head, she said, "I shore will."

I couldn't believe it, but she actually did show up the next day and gave me the money. Tina became one of my favorite customers. I let her write checks again, too.

My quest for a four-year college had now been replaced by dollar signs. I didn't need an education anymore. Well, not really…what I meant was that I would get 4 year college degree after I made a plenty of money.

I kicked that uneasy feeling to the curb and continued peddling counterfeit purses and watches, putting my heart and soul into it. Unlike New York, Mississippi had no good jobs for Koreans who spoke only broken English. I knew selling knock-off goods was against the law, but I figured that if I made sure my customers knew my merchandise wasn't real, they weren't being cheated.

My life and that of my sons was on the line in this foreign country. *Do or die* was left for me to choose. We needed money to survive and I had every intention of making it happen.

I was shamelessly happy in street peddling and making door-to-door and business-to-business sales. One day at a time! There was no sense worrying about what I couldn't have nor what I didn't have.

The greatest indication of my success was that Hamid was eliminated from my body and my soul forever.

Chapter 27

Independence

I NEEDED A CAR OF my own. My girlfriends had been so gracious to lend me their vehicles, but I could tell the wear and tear I had inflicted on them had put my friends' kindness to the test. It took me almost a year to save enough for a down payment. I drove MaryAnn's blue Cavalier one last time to Herrin-Gear Chevrolet on I-55 off High Street—this time as a customer—and marched right in. My purse, heavy with cash, hung on my shoulder.

"May I see Buck?" I asked the receptionist. She probably thought I was trying to sell him another fake Rolex watch. Buck overheard me and came into the office.

"Hi, Jannghhe," he said. This Mississippi home boy could never get my name right. "Did you get some more watches in?"

"Guess what? Buck, I'm here on different business today," I answered.

"Oh really now?" he asked.

"Yes! Buck, I am going to make your day. I want that car right out there in red," I said, pointing at a brand new Z28.

"You said you'd sell me a car for three thousand dollars down, remember? I bet you thought I was kidding when I said I'd be back."

"Oh, nah, I knew you weren't kidding, Ms. Kang." I was upgraded to Ms. Kang when Buck smelled my cash. "I shore-doo remember loud and clear," he chuckled as his double tummy wiggled up and down.

"You're one of the most determined people I've ever met. No, I didn't think you were kidding. No, Sirree."

He took me outside to see the brand-new red Z-28 I had been eyeing since the first day I had visited the dealership.

He quickly copied the vehicle number from the windshield and led me back inside. I pulled out three thousand dollars, all in twenty dollar bills, as soon as I sat down in his office.

Buck was already tasting his commission check, and I was seeing a brand new Camaro to take home, my first brand new car.

"Do you want to test drive the car to see if you really like it?" he asked.

"No, I'll drive it when it's mine," I said. While he was doing paper work, I started to count the money the Korean way, rubbing every single bill with my thumb and index finger, quickly flipping one after another like an automated machine. I counted money so fast and so often that I had developed a callous on my right index finger. Buck interrupted when I was almost finish counting and I started over. By then, the other salesmen stopped what they were doing to stare at me and watch my fingers in action.

"Dang! Did that Korean street peddler woman really come in to buy a car from Buck?" they whispered.

"Jeanhee," Buck said, shaking his head at me and smiling. "You really shouldn't carry that much cash in your purse. It's not safe."

I just looked at him.

When he wrote the sticker price on my contract, I shook my head and jabbed the paper with my finger. "That's not a good enough price," I said. "I can either buy it from you today for two-thousand less than that, or I take all my cash money back in my purse."

"Don't be doing that, Ms. Kang." Buck wagged his head, "I

thought you might say that, but I've got a deal for you. Today is your lucky day, I will give you the best discount ever, just for you.

He gave me his business card. The fine print on the back read, *bring a customer to me today or any day and get $50 cash on me.*

Bursting with pride, I drove my brand spanking new car straight home to show my boys. We wouldn't have to beg for rides or borrow a car from my friends anymore. Josh and Jason checked out the car, inside and out, smiling as they inhaled the new car smell. They jumped in, and we drove around town for hours, stopping at Burger King to celebrate our new car.

My business was thriving. While peddling one day, I happened to see a sign that read *Lease to purchase* next to a beautiful condo on the Ross Barnett Reservoir. The asking price was $65,000. I stopped and wrote down the real estate agent's name and number. I wasn't sure what *lease to purchase* meant, but I hoped I would qualify because I loved the home on the waterfront.

Living at the reservoir would be great for my boys, and with 1,200 square feet, all of us would have plenty of room. This place felt right, and I believed it was time for us to have a home of our own.

I had never borrowed money before. I called the bank to ask how a loan of this type worked. They told me to bring in my tax returns for the past three years, along with my pay stubs and information about my assets. I had never had a credit card, but I had managed to buy a car, so how hard could it be?

All I had to prove my income was my green budget book, the records I'd kept since day one of my business that included every expense—down to the fifty cents I had spent for every Diet Coke. I also brought my black book that contained my list of receivables from all of my customers as proof of income.

I walked into the banker's office just as confidently as I had walked into that car dealership. After I filled out the loan application, I met with the banker and his assistant. I pulled out my green and black books, and a short older man hurried in and peered at me over his gold wire-rimmed glasses. His assistant appeared to be fresh out of college. They examined my tattered books with skepticism as I explained what they contained.

"Well, I don't really know what to think," the older banker huffed.

"This is the most peculiar loan process I've ever seen." His thin eye glasses were doing their best to understand my green book.

I didn't miss a beat, "I'm a hard worker," I said. "I know every penny I have made and how much I spent EVERY single day, and I know exactly how much I have in inventory every single day." I continued, "I'll never miss a payment." I felt like that banker with thin gold rimmed glass was liking my way of doing business. It was all recorded. I was making money daily seven days a week, saving money and spending very little.

"I still say it's peculiar," he said. "But I like how detailed and responsible you've been with your income and expense records for the past two and half years. I believe we can make this work, Ms. Kang."

I was silently screaming with joy Yay!!

With the banker's approval, I signed a lease-to-purchase agreement, and in six months, if I didn't miss a payment, the brand new condo on the water would be all mine. We moved in that week with our meager belongings with no man hovering around my life, just my boys and me.

I had been roaming around Jackson as a street peddler for three years while still running my flea market booth on the weekends. As I became financially independent, I became more nervous about making my living selling counterfeit goods. Whenever a police car drove by or an officer strolled past my booth in the flea market, my heart pounded. If I went to jail, who would look after my boys? I needed an exit plan.

I *had* to stop selling counterfeit merchandise before I got into trouble. I wasn't sure how to stop ordering goods from Tony, when he had been willing to take a chance on me, so I started making up excuses whenever he called to get my orders.

"These things just aren't selling as well as they were," I would say. "My clients aren't as interested as they used to be."

I didn't tell him I was afraid of getting in trouble with the law. I didn't want to offend him or make him angry in case I did need to order from him again in the future. I did tell Kim the truth, though, and she helped me contact various vendors in the Broadway wholesale district. If

I had been in New York, I don't think she would have been so generous. She hated competition, and that had become a sore subject for her after her husband's friend opened a business next door to hers, selling merchandise like hers. I told her not to worry. I wasn't coming back to New York to open a shop next to her...

"I am going to die right here in Mississippi," I said to seal her trust.

At the time, inexpensive fashion watches were very popular among women—with bands in all colors and faces in different shapes and sizes. I could buy them for five dollars apiece, sell them for twenty, and still make an excellent profit. Most of the vendors in the wholesale market were Korean, so we spoke the same universal discount language. I was able to get rock-bottom prices on earrings, sunglasses, and accessories and sell them at three-hundred percent markup.

Thanks to my contacts in New York, no stores in Mississippi could beat my prices. I hired employees and sent them out to survey competitors around town, so I could keep my prices lower than theirs. With Kim's help, I had the latest trends before they even hit the magazines. If something was hot in New York, I was selling it in Mississippi before anyone even knew about it.

It was January of 1990. I had been a street peddler for two and a half years. I had to purchase school supplies for Jason at Northpark Mall in Ridgeland, the biggest mall in the state of Mississippi at the time. I strolled from one end of the mall to the other end, day dreaming. Every store had beautiful store fronts, all glass doors, gleaming marble columns, bustling anchor stores, and specialty stores with high-priced, perfectly arranged merchandise. Tall, slim, size-zero mannequins posed in nearly every window, displaying the latest fashion. I could only imagine how expensive renting one of those stores would be, not to mention buying enough merchandise to fill it.

The marble floors looked too expensive for a peddler like me to even walk on. I could only imagine what the shop owners had done to own such beautiful stores. How did they get the money? Did they have rich parents? Or had they had a dream like mine and worked their way up? *"I want to own one of these stores!"* *I said* to myself. Owning a store here seemed like an impossible goal, but I couldn't help wishing that maybe one day....

I shook my head and continued walking, and as I did, I kept noticing empty kiosks in the middle of the corridor. I had to start somewhere, so maybe I could start with one of those. I passed at least seven empty kiosks before I finished my tour of the mall, each with a display sign that read *This could be yours. See the mall manager today.*

It suddenly occurred to me that all those little kiosk wagons looked very attractive, and I wondered if they might be within my budget. and They were all empty. But which location was the best? I picked out one near the main entrance, because it would receive more foot traffic. I wanted to get walk-ins as soon as they entered the mall because my street peddling wasn't going to stop anytime soon.

I found the mall office in minutes then ran to my car, my feet flying in excitement. I grabbed the laundry basket half-filled with jumbled fashion watches and arranged them as nicely as I could before be heading back into the mall and walking through the heavy double-doors into the leasing office.

A secretary sat typing at the front desk. I glanced at her nameplate and said, "Hi, Sharon. May I talk with the manager?"

I noticed that she stared at me as I sat my basket on an adjacent chair, her eyes moving back and forth from the basket to me. She picked up the phone, pressed a few buttons, and said, "PJ, there's someone here to speak with you." He must have asked who it was, because she turned away, covered her mouth with her right hand, and whispered in a loud tone, "An Asian lady with a basket full of watches."

She thought my basket was tacky, but I didn't care. Using it was easier than hauling the watches around in their original cardboard shipping box. She looked at me strangely while I waited. I didn't think that I looked that *weird*, but maybe she had never seen an Asian woman before. Jackson wasn't exactly a diverse city.

When the weight of the moment finally hit me, I got nervous. Here I was, eager to convince the mall manager of the newest, nicest mall in the state of Mississippi that my little watches would sell well in their main entry way—the mall's best location.

When PJ came out of his office a few minutes later, I got up and shook his hand.

"Hi, PJ," I said. "I'm Jeanhee Kang. I'd like to sell watches at one of your carts."

"I see." He gave me the same peculiar look Sharon had given me, then stared at my basket. Curiosity filled his gaze. Perhaps he wondered if he should pity me, or if he could actually get some money out of this crazy Asian lady.

While he was deep in thought, I anticipated his first question, looked him straight in the eye, and burst out with, "Yes, I can," using the same sincerity I had shown Tony at Canal and Broadway. "I can make the rent and still make a profit. I just need you to give me a chance."

"I can only rent it to you if you promise not to sell those watches out of that laundry basket," he said gruffly.

Growing more hopeful, I nodded. "I can buy a better basket."

"No baskets in my mall." I was clueless why he hated my basket so much. I had just bought it from Walmart a few weeks before then,

"Okay, no basket," I repeated after him. I would toss that five-dollar basket into a dumpster as long as I could have a kiosk." I had to jump on this opportunity. I wasn't about to question issues with my almost brand new laundry basket.

"How much is the rent?"

"Eight hundred a month for a six-month lease," he said, his tone growing amused as he picked up on my excitement. He had probably never had anyone so thrilled about possibly renting one of the little wagons in the mall.

My face fell in disappointment when I considered the price. That was more than my mortgage. "Eight hundred dollars?"

"Tell you what. I'll give you a short-term lease so if you can't make it, you can leave. But you've gotta give me a thirty-day notice before you go. Can you do that?"

"Yes, sir," I said, grasping his hand and shaking it again.

"When do you want to start?" he asked, motioning for me to go into his office.

I followed him in and sat in a chair across from his desk. "Can you give me a few days? I need to call my mama's fortune teller for the best opening date."

Though I had embraced my life in America, I still held on to some basic Korean traditions, and one of those included consulting a fortune teller before making any major life decision. Knowing the best day to open a business determined success?

The secretary twirled around in her chair to look at me, and PJ's mouth fell open.

"I can wait for that," he finally said, "but only if you ask your fortune teller about my future. Will I be rich one day?"

"I'll ask her if you give me the date and time of your birth," I said, rummaging in my purse to find a scrap of paper.

He chuckled. "I was just kidding, Jeanhee. You can have a few days. Just call me when you're ready to come in and sign the lease."

I couldn't wait to call my mama and tell her I was opening my very first business in the most beautiful mall in Mississippi. I still wanted her to be proud of me. I waited for nighttime in South Korea and dialed her number with trembling hands. I hadn't talked to her in months because my shame still weighed on me so heavily for being unable to send her money. The last thing I had done worth bragging about was getting my associate's degree a few years before.

She could tell by the tone of my voice that I had good news.

"My Jeanhee is finally going to be rich in America," she said with pride. She had no idea my store was just a little ten-by-three kiosk. I didn't' want to burst her bubble, so I kept my mouth shut about the size of my business. To her, opening a business in America was a million-dollar dream. She was imagining a beautiful store filled with pretty fixtures, a full line of merchandise, and lots of employees to boss around. I decided to let her revel in her own dream.

On February 2, 1990, I had the most beautiful dream. It wasn't a dream like Jesus and the angel dream or other strange dreams, like the one I'd been having for years about a large white bird with humongous feathery wings. Nobody was telling me to go to church or it wasn't my time to die, nothing like that this time. Instead, I dreamed of beautiful gold fishes swimming in a clear pond, and to my surprise, every time I blinked my eyes, they got bigger and bigger and the size of pond enlarged to accommodate those bigger gold fishes.

It was the day to open my very first legitimate business in a kiosk in the aisle of Northpark Mall. I called my business the *Time Machine*. Kathy, another staffer in the office, had reminded me to make my display pretty, as if it belonged in a high class mall rather than a flea market. I had no idea how to imitate other beautiful stores around me. However, I was willing to try. I spent hours arranging my watches until they were perfect. I couldn't afford fancy risers like the other stores, so I covered small cardboard boxes in pretty fabric I bought from Hancock fabric store and pinned the back, making it look as if I had covered the entire box.

I opened a business account from the same bank teller who had helped me that day. I installed a phone, applied for a Mississippi sales tax number, and bought an inexpensive cash register from Sam's Wholesale. I made sure I had absolutely everything I needed to open shop that first day. I worked eleven hours a day Monday through Saturday, and seven hours on Sunday. I couldn't' afford baby sitters so my friends took turns to bring my boys to the mall after school. I would help them with homework, and they would study underneath the cart until the mall closed.

Working long hours in the mall was never a problem for me. I didn't consider it as work at all. I was working to earn my own money to in a beautiful mall. My leech days were over. Why would anyone call what I did "work" when she had clean clothes and plenty of steamy rice to eat, especially when butterflies tingled in my stomach every single time the cash register rang with the sound of money? I was earning my own money at a 4 feet by 10 feet kiosk, selling watches for $10.00 to $20.00 each

As I was beginning to taste my sweet independence, a setback was waiting at bay...

Chapter 28

Consequences

LATE ONE AFTERNOON IN MAY of 1990, two U.S. Customs and Border Patrol officers found me. My heart raced I was scared to death. I instantly knew I was in deep trouble.

"Are you Ms. Jeanhee Kang?" one of the officers asked.

"Yes, I am," I answered, my voice quivering.

"We have a search warrant for your home," another officer said. "We have reason to believe you've been trafficking in counterfeit goods."

He rattled off a long list of things I'd never heard of and had certainly never sold, but I was too shocked to even try to correct him. I had just started down my path to success. How could this be happening to me now? I had *just* made a plan to become an honest business woman.

"We'd appreciate it if you'd come back to your home with us," he said. "We'll need to go through your things."

The other agent asked for my car keys and said I should ride with the first agent and that he would follow us in my car. Enrooted to my condo, we stopped at the Harbor Pine Storage on Spillway Road, where I had stored mostly broken or outdated merchandise.

The officers placed some of the goods on top of my car and took pictures of them. Cops were everywhere on the road in front of the storage facility, and I figured they were waiting to chase me if I decided to run.

The boys were at home when we arrived in an investigator's car, and I hugged my boys, urging them to stay close to me.

"Mommy is in trouble," I said. "These officers have to search our home."

Josh nervously eyed the beloved San Francisco 49er memorabilia he had arranged for display on one of our bookcases. The tears in his eyes broadcast the truth of what he was feeling. He and Jason were frightened of what I might have done to cause these officers to dig through our home.

"Mommy, will they take away my Joe Montana and Jerry Rice cards?" Josh asked, crying.

One agent, who was kinder than the others, stopped his search and said, "No, son, we're not going to take your football cards."

"Thank you, sir," Josh quickly answered, wiping his eyes on his shirt sleeve. He ran over to his cards and clutched them to his chest, then returned to my side. We sat quietly at our kitchen table while the officers went through everything we owned, opening cabinets, rummaging through drawers, overturning the toy chest, even going through our trash cans. They didn't find a single thing and were forced to leave, frustrated.

Suddenly, I became notorious. This went far beyond the article in my high school newspaper or my story on the evening news talking about me chopping vegetables at Jubilee Jam. My face was plastered on the T.V. screen during the primetime news and in the *Clarion Ledger*, the leading newspaper in Jackson, Mississippi.

People who walked by my kiosk in the mall gave me a second look, trying to figure out if I was that Asian lady they'd seen in the paper.

I got calls from customers and friends. They were concerned, asking how I was doing and telling me I had been on the WLBT news as the biggest counterfeiter in the state. The agents had taken my black book and had everyone's phone numbers. My life was in a tailspin. I had just bought a car and given the bank the down payment on our condo, and I only had $3,300 left in the bank.

MaryAnn said, 'Jeanhee, go and get that money out of the bank before they take it away from you right now."

I did that and took the money to MaryAnn to hold it for me. When I read the newspaper article and learned that I might be facing five years in jail and a $250,000 fine, my terror grew tenfold. That is when I realized I was in a deep trouble. Hearing that I was in trouble and reading it in the newspaper were two completely different things.

What would happen to my boys? When would I see them again? I could send them to live with their dad in Missouri, but then I might not get them back. And how in the world could I afford a lawyer? Mary Ann's boyfriend was an attorney, so I called him first. Richard informed me that he didn't practice criminal law.

"Legal fees are steep, Jeanhee," he said. "You can try J. C. Crook. He might be your best bet."

I found J. C. Crook's name and number in big, bold letters in the Yellow Pages. I called and made an appointment to meet him.

His receptionist led me through a pair of heavy double doors and into his office, lined with wall to wall books. When I saw him sitting behind a big, impressive desk smoking a cigar, I thought he must be the most powerful defense lawyer in the world.

I handed him the newspaper article about me.

"How do you pronounce your name?" he asked.

"You can call me Jeanhee," I said.

He leaned back in his chair and stared at me.

"Well, hon. I normally charge $5,000 upfront and up to $10,000 after the case is settled, depending on how hard I have to work." The intense way he looked at me made me uncomfortable.

"I don't have that kind of money," I said.

With a glint in his eye, he sat up straight. At first I thought he was looking for a soft spot, maybe even feeling sorry for me—enough so that he was considering discounting his fee.

I was wrong.

"I tell you what, Jeanhee. Did I say your name right?"

I nodded.

"Let's get to know each other a little better. I think it's necessary if I'm going to keep you out of jail."

A sick feeling in the pit of my stomach told me where this was going. What a slime ball. No. Way.

"If you come to my house tonight, we can eat dinner together, drink a little wine, and just relax. The amount of your fee will depend on how well we get along."

I don't drink, I thought to myself, and quickly tired of seeing myself through his slimy eyes. So I got up and snatched my newspaper article away from him.

"No, thank you," I snapped. "I won't be that hungry by tonight."

As I walked out the door with my head held high, I forgot to tell him that my prostitution days had ended a long time ago.

I turned again to the Yellow Pages from a pay phone booth and found James Bell's phone number. He was a former Hinds County judge and his office was off Fortification Street near the location my short-lived deli. I remembered him paying special attention to me whenever he came in for lunch, and he always asked for me at the kiosk whenever I was out peddling. He recognized the desperation in my voice and agreed to set up a consultation with me as soon as possible. Since I no longer had a car, he agreed to come to the mall.

We met at Ruby Tuesday's.

James could have easily passed as a preacher. He had a certain peace about him, and his kind, soft voice instantly earned my trust in him. The more I told him about my situation, the more I believed that he saw *me,* not just a case or a situation. He reminded me a lot of Robert, and that left me with a strange sense of longing, a longing I quickly pushed aside, because James was a married man. We agreed on a payment plan, and I left the restaurant with the first spark of hope I'd felt since the customs officers had shown up.

Luckily, my cart business made enough profit for me to pay my rent and restock my merchandise. I was, however, forced to file for chapter eleven bankruptcy to protect my condo. I tried not to lose heart, even though I felt as if I were back at square one, broke and alone in America once again. Yet I had no time to be sad. The difference this time was that I had learned how to make money and was determined to believe I could do it again. And after meeting with James, I *knew* I could.

I told the boys over and over that things would be okay and that we would get through this trial. But kids at school taunted them. Rumors flew, and one of the bullies in Josh's class told him that his mother was a cocaine dealer. That was the last time he bullied Josh. He clearly crossed the line when he started bad mouthing his mother. Josh got on top of him and applied his black belt Taekwondo skills he learned while he was in Korea and nailed him with a bloody nose and a black eye in the hallway front of the principal. Nobody knew Josh was black belt in Taekwondo until that day. Josh never told me about the fight, but Jason did. Jason could never keep secrets longer than two minutes. Jason, also told me that Josh was never reprimanded for beating up the bully that day.

I distracted myself from worry by working seven days a week. I didn't have much choice if I wanted to keep a roof over our heads and food on the table. I needed to make every penny I could, especially with my lawyer's fees piling up.

My boys were exceptionally athletic, they both started playing soccer, flag football, and baseball. Instead of asking me to take them to practice and games, they asked other kids' moms for ride. Some days, if they didn't have ride, they would walk five miles home instead of calling me at work. They understood I was working to make our life better, their duties were to cause the least disruption while I was at work, and to always remember my promise I have made to them.

All the notes I had written to their teachers about them freely giving them corporal punishment worked. My boys always knew where they stood if they got in trouble at school. I wasn't one of those mothers who turned against teachers and defended their children's rotten, spoiled, and bad behaviors. I was still a Korean at heart. No way would I allow my own kids to be disrespectful to teachers, and, my boys always knew better than to ever bring complaints about their teachers to me.

I was always proud when a few of their friends' parents would beg to have my kids come over, in hope that some of my boys' respectful behavior and love of their mother would rub off on their children.

They would ask, "What is your secret?"

I replied, "I kept my promises I made when they were little. "They didn't' ask what those promises were, and I didn't' divulge stories like... a bag of condom my boys got on their 15th birthday in a brown bag. I swung by Health Department on their birthdays and picked up free condoms in a brown bag. I told my boys just like it is written…. "Use this if you ever have an urge to have sex with girl. And I further stated "Hear me clearly! If you ever get a girl pregnant, firstly, you will break my heart in pieces, secondly, *I WILL NOT take care those babies!* No sir, I won't do it. I am done being momma after you all."

Do you understand me? My boys nodded their heads at their mama respectfully. That was my one-minute sex education, my parenting as a single mom. I was not going to let my boys be teen fathers, not while I was breathing. Another rule was that if they ever got in trouble with the law, if they ever ended up in jail, they should not waste their time calling me because I would not bail them out. One year, Jason, begged to go to Florida with his best friend David to visit his real mom. I knew David was bad news from day one. Jason managed to convince me that he would not get into any trouble while he was with David.

At 200 A.M. the next morning, I received a call from the Pensacola Police Department. The officer on the phone said that he had Jason in his custody, I jumped out bed, terrified and angry at Jason. After I calmed down a bit, I told the officer, "You can keep him. I am not coming to bail him out."

He said, "I t already knew you would say that. Jason had begged me not to call you and told me you would say that."

He continued, "I have been on the police force for fifteen years and arrested a lot of young teen boys, but I got to tell you, I have never met a fine young man love and respect his mother like Jason and behaved respectfully to us while in our custody. You have raised your boy very well, Ma'am. you should be proud of this young man.

What? I was trying to grasp what I was hearing… I didn't' know what to say. I was pinching myself. I had received a call call at 2:00 AM, telling me that my son had been arrested for having beer in his possession on a public beach. At the same time, he was giving me thumbs up on raising my boy as a fine young man.

Jason made it home safe the next day, tired and scared. Jason knew he was in big trouble with me, and he went straight to his room got into his bed, rolled a blanket over his body to avoid getting a whipping from me, and said, "Mama, I am sorry, I know you are very angry at me. I should have listened to you about David. I promise, I won't see him again.

And, Mama," he said in tears please don't whip me anymore. I am fifteen years old now. I somehow dropped my whip right then, I realized what he must have gone through during the last 48 hours, scared to death thinking I may disown him while being locked up in jail.

I said, "Okay, son… I believe you." I never had to whip Jason again. Jason gave me piece of paper with his court date, and I called to find out when I needed to get Jason back to Pensacola to face charges. I found out that, not only had that police man let my son out of jail, there was no record Jason ever was arrested that night.

I needed a vehicle desperately. In two months, I had saved enough for a down payment on another car. I went to Blackwell Chevrolet on I-55. I couldn't exactly return to Herrin Gear since I assumed that Buck had found out Z-28 was confiscated. I spotted a red Geo Tracker in the showroom as soon as I had walked in. I liked the price rather than the car. I didn't need a fancy sports car. I just needed one that would give me no trouble on the road. The only problem was that it was a 3Stick shift. I had no earthly idea how to drive a stick shift, but figured I could learn.

The salesman had barely introduced himself before I pointed at the red Geo.

"You came to the right man! I can make that happen in two minutes." He smiled. "Are you ready to take it home today?"

"On one condition. You have to teach me how to drive a stick shift."

"Not a problem," he said, talking even faster than I was by then. I was probably the easiest sale he had ever made. "I used to run a driving school. You'll be a pro in no time."

I figured he was lying, but so what? Ten minutes later, I had signed all the paperwork and we were out in the parking lot. He gripped the passenger dash handle as the car lurched forward and backward. He showed me how to maneuver the clutch and release the brake while switching gears. I was sure I could get the hang of it.

"Ms. Kang!" he shouted at one point. "Watch out! Don't hit those other cars!"

"Okay." I barely squeezed by one and squealed to a stop. "That's good enough. I think I can make it home. I'll just stay off the highway and away from hills."

"You are one crazy lady, Ms. Kang. Good luck."

We shook hands, and I drove my brand new car to the Beauty Box about five miles across the I-55 overpass, where Tami, who would become my best friend for life, worked. Tami could pass for Nicole Kidman's sister. Her skin was pure white, but her eyesight wasn't worth a plug nickel. So everybody had to drive her around. I knew she'd love to make fun of me for buying a car with a stick shift when I had no idea how to drive it. She thought I was crazy half the time anyway because of my wild sales tactics.

I veered into a parking spot and strode inside. The sharp scent of hair dye filled my nose. "Hey Tami," I called, "Come outside for a minute! I got something to show you."

"I'll be right back," she said to the lady in her chair. "You've got another twenty minutes until your color is done to make you beautiful again"

She followed me out the door, slipping on her black sunglasses to protect her eyes from the bright sun. "Oh, my gosh, is that your new car?"

"Yes, it is. Get in!" I answered. "I'm going to take you for a ride. Better put on your seatbelt."

She climbed into the Geo. I didn't want my inexperienced gear shifting to throw her into the floorboard, so I waited before starting off.

"Are you ready, Tami?"

"Yes, let's go." She apparently hadn't noticed the stick shift. I smiled, as if we were both about to go on an adventure.

"Here we go," I said. Unfortunately, the salesman hadn't warned me about going uphill. I couldn't get out of the parking lot to the main road. Coordinating the shifting of gears, pressing the gas, and pushing the clutch was much harder on an incline. After three or four tries, my car went dead. Tami hooted with laughter.

"You bought a car you can't even drive, Jeanhee?" she asked. "You're still going to be walking everywhere."

"Shut up, Tami. I can drive this stupid car if you'll just give me a minute. Do you want to try?"

"Nope, Honey" she said, sitting back with a devilish grin. She pushed up her glasses and wiped the tears from her eyes, still laughing. "I'll wait for you to figure it out all yo'self, honey. I can't drive, remember?" she said as she made sure her seat belts were buckled ever tightly.

My heart nearly gave out during the ten tries it took me to get up that one-foot high hill, but I still gave Tami the ride of her life. She laughed the whole time. I laughed too but not as hard she did.

"I love your car, darling," she said when she got out.

As I drove away, she called, "Watch for that hill on your way out!"

Moments like that kept my spirit from dying during my legal trouble. My friends and customers treated me with compassion throughout the process. Their way of helping me out was buying unneeded products to help me pay my attorney.

It had been four months in waiting for trial. My defense was that, although I knew it was illegal to sell counterfeit goods, I was only trying to make a living and provide for my boys. I could not help but think of the worst scenarios. I rehearsed what I wanted to say to the judge over and over, "I had to survive with my boys. I needed the money."

The fear of the unknown outcome weighed on me constantly. What would happen if I went to prison? My boys wouldn't get to see me. They would be orphans. Where would they go? Who would raise them? Their own daddy wouldn't even want them. Even if their father wanted them back, I didn't want my boys to live out my childhood. There was no way I was going to let my boys grow up in that trailer park back in Missouri. More than anything, I wanted to witness my boys graduate high school with the same friends, attend college together, and experience college life freely with no baggage and financially free. If they needed anything, all they had to do was to make that one call to mama.

One Saturday night while my boys spent the night with their best friends, I went out with Lauran. She likes to drink and likes men more than men like her. We went bar hopping a few places before we ended up at On the Rocks at the reservoir. She was drunk as always, or was on one of the strange looking pills she always offered me and I always refused. Laura wasted no time picking a drunk she would take home with her, and an ugly drunk closed in on me thinking I was an easy prey like Laura. When I refused to dance with him, he called me names I had never heard even back in Osan. I smiled back, but what I wanted to yelled back was you will never touch me, not in this life or the next. The music was getting louder by the minute while dark and nasty smoke similar to the Lucky Club back in Osan filled the club, and drunks and whores who looked like devils busy trying to match up one night stands. I knew many of them. I swear, they didn't look like devils with horns on their head until that night.

The time came for me to leave that dark place. I waved at Laura who was beyond drunk by then. I had escaped, but I was afraid those devils would catch up with me any minute if I didn't walk to my car as fast as I could. I drove straight home, went to bed knowing exactly what I was going to do when I woke up.

I felt as if I were sinking in quicksand and that if I breathed or moved too fast, I would drown in my misery. The possibility of going to jail was tearing my life away. I needed—urgently—to talk to Jesus. I didn't have a Bible and probably wouldn't have read it if I had. I normally would have driven straight to the Flea Market to work my booth, but on that Sunday, I needed to go to church. I remembered seeing a big church on top of a hill on Old Fannin Road called Family Life. A banner on the side of the building read *Jesus Lives Here.*

I hit the brakes and turned my wheel 90 degree left into the church's parking lot and found a space among hundreds of other cars. The service had already started as I slipped in and sat in the back so no one would notice me with my unwashed smoke-filled hair from the night before. I didn't know it then, but my life was about to change forever.

I was about to be saved—renewed as a person—and I would soon leave my sinful life behind. Pastor Mark introduced a visiting pastor from Oklahoma. I was thinking strangely, Oklahoma? That is where Jesus came to visit me in my dream seven years ago.

During his sermon, visiting pastor Hagin from Oklahoma spoke straight to my heart about being in trouble with the law and turning one's face away from sin.

"Give your burden to God He will take away from you," he said. I felt as if he were talking directly to me. I was ready to hand over all my troubles in exchange to receive Jesus as my savior.

Unlike my brief church experience back in Baton Rouge, no one dragged me in, or enticed me with sweet rice cake, I wanted to be there.

The longer he spoke, the lighter my heavy heart grew. For the first time in my life, I was listening about Jesus. Right there, on the spot, I was ready to accept Jesus as my Savior who died to save me.

I was ready answer the "Why aren't you going to church?" a question he had asked me in my dream eight years before.

My church attendance in Baton Rouge five years before had prompted my most vicious fight with Hamid, the violent altercation that had sent me and my boys running away to New York. This time, a devil wasn't around to stop me. It was between Jesus and me.

At the end of the sermon, Pastor Kenneth Hagin stepped up to the pulpit and said, "If any of you would like to be saved by the blood of Jesus Christ, please come forward during the final hymn."

By then I was in tears and ready to ask for my sins to be wiped away. I walked down that aisle and knelt in front of him, then confessed my sins to God and asked Jesus for forgiveness.

This was my prayer.

"Jesus, I am at your church. Here I am. I'm here for a reason.
Please don't let them send me to jail.
Please give me peace in my heart, so I will stop hurting.
And while you are busy forgiving my sins, Lord,
Please give me lots of money.
I really could use it to live a good life with my boys."

My prayer might not have been conventional, but Jesus saved me that day in front of the church's three-thousand-member congregation. I relinquished all my troubles to God. Amazingly, I felt lighter than a feather.

That night, Pastor Hagin and his wife came to visit me in my dream. Both stood tall in the front of my living room, both of their right hands motioning at dark shadows while chanting, More lights! More lights!" until all the shadows of darkness in my home disappeared and instantly were replaced with beams of bright light from sparkling chandeliers everywhere. By the time they had finished, my home didn't contain even one particle of dark shadow. I floated around my house on a blanket of absolute peace. I had never been in a place where my heart felt so right.

After that Sunday, I attended services twice a week. And each time, the pastor reminded me to be good and stay away from temptation. I never saw Laura again. I had attained a new ability to distinguish right from wrong with such clarity, I knew where to draw the line and left the sinners to do their things.

The truth was, I was afraid God was watching my every move.

Chapter 29

Mississippi Girlfriends

MY COURT DATE WAS SET for November of 1990. When the day finally arrived—the day on which my faith, my future, and my boys' futures hinged—I was a nervous wreck.

Federal Judge Henry Wingate, the man scheduled to preside over my case in United States District Court, was known for his tough sentences and emotionless verdicts. I had never been inside an American courtroom before and had only seen them on television. I was scared to death.

I didn't want to be a crybaby, but I certainly *felt* like crying. I had nobody else to blame for what I had done. I knew there were consequences for breaking the law, but I had been left with little choice. I had struggled to feed and house my boys.

I had no one to call for moral support and no way to get out of my current situation. The only thing I could do was to pray, wait for the verdict, and take responsibility for my wrongdoings. For the first time ever, I was glad my mama didn't live close to me. If the court found me guilty, I would be too ashamed to tell her that *Meegook* had decided I was a criminal. I didn't want to fill her days with more hardship.

That morning we followed our normal routine. I made my boys go to school just like always so as not to worry them. They didn't even know about the trial—I dared not tell them. I didn't believe the authorities would take me to jail right after the trial. Surely they would let me say goodbye to my boys if I was convicted. Wouldn't they?

The air was cool, but not too cold for me to go running. As I ran across the trestle bridge on Lakeshore Drive, I did my best to shake off my worries while remembering another unusual dream. I was in a dark, muddy black hole about six feet deep, crying because I couldn't get out no matter how I tried to climb out. The mud was soft, and there was nothing to hold on to climb. I fell back and cried hopelessly. Suddenly, a man's right hand reached down to pull me out of that dark muddy hole. There was no conversation, no time to say thank you. He was gone as I woke up.

My biggest worries were my boys' wellbeing. What would have happened to Josh and Jason if I went to prison? How would they live? What would they say to their friends?

The possibility that I might go to prison burdened my feet with extra physical weight. Rather than giving in and quitting, however, I sped up, running as if an unknown being were chasing me. I'd had no contact with Josh and Jason's dad for many years, and I hated the thought of having to call him. He had seen the boys once when they were four and five years old. I had no idea what he might be doing, whom he might have married, or what his financial situation might be. The last communication I had with him was that he would not pay child support because he didn't believe the boys were his. That was okay with me because, I didn't want my kids to grow up poor like me in Missouri with him. What goes around comes around. One day he would wish he knew his own kids, but by then it would be too late for him. My boys would never forget who was there for them and loved them unconditionally. I wanted to instill in my boys the importance of getting education and to graduate college with their friends. I could care less if they read Shakespeare or Tolstoy's *War and Peace*. More than anything, I wanted to be at their college graduation witnessing my college dream at their hands.

"Please, God, I'm all they have. Please don't let me go to jail."

No matter what the outcome of the trial might be, I wasn't ashamed of myself. If I hadn't become a street peddler to do what I did, I would still be on welfare enduring Hamid's abuse. Or I might even be dead. I had no doubt he would have killed me sooner or later. If not physically, then spiritually, as he slowly sucked the life out of me.

After my sweaty adrenal run, I took a luxurious hot shower, finishing it off with a quick five seconds of ice cold water.

"Okay, Jeanhee, are you ready?" I asked myself in the mirror. I slipped into the clothes James had recommended—a dark navy suit with a skirt that hit just below the knee, low heels, no jewelry, and no nail polish. I needed to look conservative and respectable without heavy makeup. I'd never liked makeup anyway. As I pulled my hair into my trademark ponytail, I said a silent prayer.

God, this is the time I need you the most. Please walk beside me today. If you can't forgive my sins for my sake, please do it for my boys. They need me. I'm all they have.

Before we walked into the courtroom, James attempted to soothe my nerves.

"You will have another hearing after today," he murmured as we entered the courtroom. "Even if the judge decides to send you to jail, it won't happen right away."

I released a huge sigh of relief at that small reprieve.

I took my place on that hard wooden bench as I worked to hide my trembling knees. Finally, I looked behind me and discovered that the benches behind me were filled with rows and rows of familiar faces.

My Mississippi friends and customers had come to show me their love when I needed them. They came to plead with the judge to have mercy on me. My heart melted, tracing back to those unforgettable moments I was all alone to decide do or die. This time I was not all alone. I had friends who were there to stand by me. I was no longer a lone soldier at war to take on the world all alone. I shed tears of joy, tears of relief, knowing that I was no longer fighting the war alone. I knew at that moment that I was going to be alright. Emotions I had held together in an icy cold pack in fear of being turned away by society melted away forever. What a beautiful country it is, my *Meegook*.

My eyes welled up with tears. With this kind of love and support, what could be against me? The fear of the unknown was replaced with peace while waiting for the judge's instructions.

In America, making a mistake didn't matter. My friends stood by me. Something else about my friends, no one, not a single one had ever asked about my dark secrets or wondered why I couldn't go home to the country. That day, I became one of them, a Mississippian.

The bailiff said, "All rise."

Seconds later, the judge strode in. I stood up with everyone else. The judge was a tall black man whose heavy robe flowed around him as he walked. He settled into his seat, adjusted the microphone, and shuffled the case files before him. He appeared to be even more surprised by the turnout than I had been.

After the bailiff allowed us to sit back down, Judge Wingate peered over his glasses and cleared his throat. "Who are all these people? Is this a trial or a block party?"

"They're the defendant's friends, Your Honor," James said as he came to his feet. "The community holds Ms. Kang in high regard."

"I don't care what the community thinks," the judge answered. "Right and wrong are what matters. If anyone disrupts this trial, I will throw them out or charge them with contempt. Is that clear?"

Silence filled the courtroom.

The judge nodded at the government prosecutors. "Counsel, you may proceed."

My dearest customer, Ms. Sandra, who must not have heard the judge's instructions, stood up fearlessly, before the prosecutor began his opening argument.

"Your Honor, Jeanhee was just trying to survive and take care of her little boys. She never told us those bags and watches were real. We all knew they were fakes when we bought them."

Of all my customers, Ms. Sandra, an Executive Director at a posh retirement home in Ridgeland had always believed in me the most. She was in her late 50s about 5'7", beautifully aged in perfect size 4 figure with thick silver hair pulled back in a ponytail, always dressed in designer's clothes. I never forgot the day she told me that I would be a millionaire someday. There I was a peddler, and Ms. Sandra was seeing an incredible future for me, and when I heard the word *Millionaire*. All I could say was "Thank you! Ms. Sandra." After she was finished shopping with me, she allowed me to walk right past the *No Solicitors* sign in front of the retirement home and sell to her employees.

Tears flowed down her face as she pleaded with Judge Wingate. The judge didn't seem as annoyed by her interruption as everyone had thought he would be.

"Sit down!" he said tiredly. "No more of that."

He motioned for James to give his opening statement.

"Jeanhee Kang is a law abiding citizen, has never been in trouble until now and is a good mom," he said. "She got off welfare two years ago and has been paying her bills all on her own ever since. She has never even gotten a speeding ticket. The way she saw it, if she could make enough money to survive, she wouldn't have to go back to her abusive husband. She doesn't receive child support from her ex-husband. She has no family in this country to help her.

The prosecutor, on the other hand, did everything he could to send me to jail. The government had a long list of brands I had supposedly sold, as well as the amounts I'd made, but they didn't have any proof except what they'd found in the storage room. And they couldn't find a single person willing to testify against me.

In the end, Judge Wingate found me guilty. He gave me three years' probation and no fine, sparing me from a jail term.

My friends in the courtroom went crazy, jumping up and down and hugging one another as they celebrated the outcome with me. Some of them called out loudly, "Thank you, Judge Wingate. Thank you! You're a good judge."

I silently thanked God for staying with me during the trial, and then I hugged James, wetting his suit with the tears streaming down my face.

I dropped by the mall to tell my part-time worker that afternoon, Kristin, that I didn't have to go to jail. She was happy both for me and for her future employment.

I needed time to calm down. All the worries I had lived with for the last six months came crashing down at once. I took the afternoon off and went home to cook my sons' favorite meal—tuna casserole with no onions. On the way, I stopped to get a Coca-Cola and a Hershey bar.

My boys were surprised to find me home so early waiting for them when they got off the school bus. "Mama! Are you sick?"

No, I'm not sick, son" I said with a smile. "I'm just so happy today, and I stayed home to tell you all how much I love being your mama." They both were puzzled by the strange emotional love talk from their Mama. Koreans don't praise their children in fear they won't be humbled, and they never say how much they love their children in words so common in *Meegook*. I don't recall if I ever said to my boys those simple words, *"I love you!" I love you!* terms were used only among lovers in Korea. Instead, I showed my love for my boys by my actions, being a good provider, keeping them safe, making sure they went to school to get an education, having enough money to take care of them until they finished college. I would pay for tuition, books, spending money. They wouldn't have to worry financially until they finished college and got a paying job. That was my duty as their mom and that was how I showed my love for them.

My nerves were too frazzled for me to work over the next few days, so I took a rare break and spent the time visiting all of my old customers and friends. My friends took turns in giving me long hugs and said, "Jeanhee, go and make lots of money and remember us when you become rich, okay?"

Chapter 30

How Could He Dream of His Own Death?

ONE AUGUST 15, 1994, I got a phone call no mother ever should receive.

Jason was talking frantically in a tearful voice, "Mama! You must sit down first. I got to tell you, something happened to Josh. Are you sitting down, Mama?"

Startled by the urgency in his voice, I quickly sank into a chair near the cash register. .

"Mama, Josh is hurt bad. Really bad," he said, his voice cracking. "You need to hurry up to go to the hospital—UMC, Mama. Right now. Hurry! The ambulance took him just a minute ago."

My head was spinning in shock. I dropped everything and headed out, running to my car as fast as my legs would carry me. I rushed to the hospital as fast as I could, expecting to see my boy when I got there, ignoring what Jason had told me about how badly his brother was hurt.

Josh was a dreamer just like me. He had a childhood dream planned out, even as young child. He dreamt of becoming a pro football quarterback one day. He used to tell me, "Mama, I'm going to take care of you one day. I'll buy you a beautiful home and give you so much money, you'll never have to work another day in your life." I wasn't sure about all that not working another day of my life but my heart melted.

Josh would get Jason ready for school every morning, even though Jason would always ignore his first wakeup call. Josh would badger his brother until he finally crawled out of bed. Then they would both take turns showering and tiptoe past my bedroom to slip into the kitchen and eat breakfast. If Jason dropped something on the floor, Josh would reprimand him in a whisper, "Quiet! You're gonna wake Mama up."

Once they finished breakfast, I would get up to give each boy lunch money for the day. If I didn't have exact change, $1.25 for lunch, I would pull out a twenty-dollar bill. Jason would grab his quickly and promise to bring me the change, but Josh would never accept it.

"No, Mama," he would say with a shake of his head. "I don't need it today. I'm not taking your twenty dollars. I may lose the change in the locker room after football practice."

Later, I learned that he would ask his friends for their leftovers in order to save my money. He hated to ask me to buy him anything. He would wear tennis shoes until his big toe poked through. Whenever I told him he needed a new pair, he would assure me that he could wear them for another month—that only the left shoe had a hole in it.

By the time I got home from working at the mall each day, I was exhausted. The house would always be clean, and my bed made, Josh placed all the stuffed toys I had given him over the years against my headboard in rows, from the smallest to the largest. If he was awake when I got home, he would hug me and lift me into the air.

"How was your day, Mama?" he would ask. "Did you have a good day?"

If he hadn't yet eaten, a can of tuna, a package of macaroni noodles, and a can of cream of mushroom soup would be on the counter. He would salivate as I made his favorite dish—tuna noodle casserole. I would smile as he devoured every creamy morsel.

I was finally able to buy Josh's dream car, a brand new Toyota truck. I wrapped it in the biggest red bow I could find and had it delivered to his school during football practice.

You can imagine the happiest boy coming off the football field, Oh! Boy, was he ever happy…

How surprised he was. His joy was priceless.

"Mama, am I dreaming?" he said in awe. "Or is this for real? Mama, pinch me?" he said, sticking his handsome face to my hand to be pinched.

I wanted to spoil my boys, to give them what I didn't and couldn't have while growing up.

Josh would always tell me that he loved me. I could never say it back, instead, I said, "Me too, son." A few times though, I reminded myself that I was no longer in Korea and managed to say it back, "I love you too, son."

Like me, Josh was driven. Rain or shine, he was outside throwing a football, often by himself. Sometimes, he begged me to find him a daddy who could practice drills with him. I had to reason with him.

"Josh, do you remember Hamid? What he did to your mama? Remember me promising that no man will ever come into our lives and terrorize us again?"

"Yes, Mama, I remember."

"I'm so sorry, son." I cried, then he cried and we both cried some more.

I said to him, "I have a great idea, how about if I find you a private football coach?"

"You will, Mama?"

"Yes, I can afford to pay him."

Josh's football idols were Joe Montana of the San Francisco 49ers and Jerry Rice. My son knew every winning throw Joe Montana had ever made and every route and catch Jerry Rice completed. He lived and breathed his dream of becoming a pro football player like Montana. His wall was filled with posters, articles about the 49ers, and even his own drawings of team members.

"Mama," Josh said one day, "I was the fastest in the hurdle race competition, and I was invited to try out for the Junior Olympics in

Singapore, but I turned it down because I was afraid I'd miss football practice."

I am not sure exactly when Josh began to talk to God. I believe it was when he made it to become a quarterback in the 7th grade. Josh prayed to God every single night before he went to sleep. He would kneel by his bed with the lights off, his palms together, his head bowed, and his forehead touching the ends of both index fingers. *"Dear Lord, remember me? I'm Josh. You remember me, don't you? I have been good all day, and I practiced my routes really hard. I didn't do so well on my midterm test, but I think I passed. My mama is still working. Please help her to get home safe. Dear Lord, I know I ask every night, but I'm going to ask you again. Will you please make me taller and stronger? In return, I promise to be a good son to my mama and work hard to be the best quarterback my school has ever had. Thank you, God!"*

After his nightly prayer, he would tuck himself between his 49ers sheets without causing a wrinkle, center himself in the bed, take one last look at the posters on his wall, grab his football, and place it in the center of his belly—on top of his navel, to be exact. As he fell asleep, he would hold that football with both hands and dream about the pro football team he would play for when he grew up. He would often wake from his nightly dreams with visions of throws he would make to Terry Wray, the fastest running back on his team He truly believed that if he kept his promises to God and lived by His words, God would honor his prayer request, so he stayed away from friends who drank or did drugs. He was very selective in choosing his friends and always hung out with team mates who loved football as much as he did. Besides, he needed them to practice with him since he didn't have a daddy to practice with him.

Josh knew he needed to be bigger and taller to play pro football, but he was at a disadvantage. His mother stood a mere five-two and weighed only a hundred pounds. He needed divine intervention to ever grow big enough to play pro ball, so he turned to God for help. He attended twice on Sunday and Wednesday night services and prayed daily. He knew exactly how tall Joe Montana was and how much he weighed. He also knew that he needed to be stronger and taller in order to beat out his competition for first string quarterback in August of 1994.

The new school year had begun, and soon the boys would find out who would play first string for the varsity team. Josh had not missed a single practice, and he had worked out all summer to impress Coach Coats, his head coach. After practice every day, he would come home and practice some more in an open field near our house. Even on rainy days, he was out there, looking for someone to catch his passes. Often, he would throw the football and chase the pass down himself. Almost daily he begged his best friend, Wes Bell, to come catch the ball. *His* black book was filled with daily squat and pushup counts, lists of detailed workouts, and the number of wind sprints he had run.

Josh had been en-route to football practice with his girlfriend, Kristine, in her dad's navy blue Mercedes. His best friend, Wes, was in the back seat. Kristine ran the red light at the intersection of Old Canton Road and County Line Road and slammed into the back of a school bus. The side where Josh sat slid beneath the back of the bus, and his head hit the bumper.

I can't remember how I drove to UMC without wrecking the car. The hospital was only about ten minutes from Northpark Mall, but the trip seemed to take forever. My heartbeat skittered frantically as I whipped into the parking lot.

"Oh, my baby boy," I cried out in fear. "God, please keep him safe!"

When I dashed into the hospital, the emergency room waiting area was filled with Josh's friends, teammates, and teachers. Ms. Jan Hughes and Coach White greeted me with hugs. They told the nurse I was there and asked the doctors to come talk to me. The doctors told me their titles, but I couldn't remember their names. They said, "Ms. Kang, we're doing everything we can while we wait for Dr. Das, the plastic surgeon."

I was in denial. I failed to hear the words, a *serious head injury* and *unconscious.* Still in shock, I was unable to understand of the seriousness of the head injury Josh had sustained. It was incomprehensible to my world. My boys and I, just the three of us were supposed to live happily ever after. It all just seemed like one of my incredible dreams, impossible to accept, it all seem unreal I was confident that the doctors would bring him back to life soon and tell us to take him home with us.

I wanted to see him, but the doctor said that I couldn't until Dr. Das, the plastic surgeon, had repaired my son's jaw.

"Oh, no!" I screamed. "Not my son! Please, I beg you. Let me see my son!" I pleaded with Dr. Das, "Please bring him back to me. Please."

After what seemed like hours, they finally let me see my boy. Josh had tubes and cords attached to his body, helping him to breathe, giving him medicine, and checking his heart rate. His handsome face was so swollen he was almost unrecognizable.

"Josh?" I reached out my trembling hand to touch him. "Can you hear me? Can you hear Mama? I need you. Come back to mama?"

"I love you!! Josh! I need you to come back to me. Can you hear Mama? Did you hear me?"

I was torn to pieces, as if a sharp arrow pierced through my heart. I begged another doctor this time, "Please bring my boy back. Please... I need my boy back, please..."

The doctor ordered the nurse to give me a sedative to calm my torn heart. I felt as if a piece of my heart had been ripped away—leaving a hole in my heart and filling it with a piercing pain. Part of me said this wasn't happening, that this is one bad nightmare and I longed to myself wake up...

During the final stretch, I grabbed Coach Coats, Josh's football coach from Northwest Rankin, who'd come to the hospital to tell Josh he'd been chosen as the team's first string quarterback.

"Please tell him," I begged him. "He needs to know he made first string."

"Josh, can you hear me?" he said to my son. "This is Coach Coats. You're my first string quarterback. You made it, boy."

If it were possible, Josh would have gotten up and jumped around the room.

As I took in his injuries, I knew he wouldn't want to come back like that, unable to play football, unable to fulfill his lifelong dreams. He would rather not live if he couldn't play football again.

Pastor Mark from my church stepped into the room and walked up beside me. I assumed that he was there to offer comfort, to help me pray to Jesus to save my son. Instead, however, he said the strangest thing I'd ever heard.

"I've come to rescue Josh," he said, taking my hand in his.

What did he mean? Didn't he have eyes? Couldn't he see how badly my son was injured?

"I'm going to lay my hands on Josh, and he will come back to life. I've done it before a few years ago."

"Yes!!!" I screamed, desperate to have Josh live. "Lay hands on my son right now"

He did so, but laying his hands on my son didn't work. The pastor was a man of God, so why didn't God hear his prayers and bring Josh back to life?

Within twelve hours, I lost my son forever. I didn't quite understand what had happened to my son until the doctor deliberately said the unspeakable. "Your son had died." It was only then that I realized my Josh was really gone.

If I had just been able to say goodbye…and tell him how much I loved him…. If I could just see his handsome smile one more time….

I would give my life in a heartbeat to hear, just one more time," I love you, Mama!"

I clutched my aching heart, suffocated by regrets for working so much instead of give him more love. I came face to face with reality that I had lost my son. I began to get angry at God. If He couldn't save my Josh for me, how could I expect Him to save me? God had let me down and taken my beloved son away from me.

Three months earlier, in May of 1994, Josh had told me that he had dreamed of his own death. On a few previous occasions, he had shared dreams that had actually come to pass. Many of those dreams were about football. In one of them, he had thrown a touchdown pass, and that dream came true the very next day *exactly* as he had seen it in his dream.

On that Sunday in May, Josh had just gotten out of the shower and was getting ready to go to church. Water still dripped from his hair as he came into the kitchen wearing only his favorite black gym shorts, and I noticed that my boy had grown into a handsome young man with perfect six pack abs.

"Mama, I think I am going to die in a car accident before the summer is over," he said, his lips pouting with sadness. "I saw it in my dream, Mama."

"No, son," I told him as a chill rolled through me. "You just had a nightmare. I have had many strange dreams ever since I was eight years old. You're not going to die, son. You can't die before me."

Three days later, Josh came to me in a dream. The same Josh I remembered from that morning back in May when he told me he was going to die. He was standing in his favorite black gym shorts in the same spot, water dripping from his hair, his lips pouting with sadness. He didn't speak to me, but I could read the message he sought to convey just by looking at him.

"Mama, I was trying to warn you. God was ready to take me away from you."

If I had believed his dream might come true, maybe I could have prepared myself, but I *hadn't* seen it coming. I didn't know my son could dream about his death. How could I? How could I ever imagine my son was going to die before me?

Had he—or God—tried to warn me that Josh's short stay on this earth was near its end?

Josh at Northwest Rankin High School

Chapter 31

She Didn't Mean To Kill My Son

AS OUR HEARTS WERE TORN in pieces, a fragile girl was blaming herself for Josh's death. Jason and I had talked about our broken hearts and how there was another soul with a broken heart. We agreed to forgive her for my son, his brother's death. Kristine had been under suicide watch since the accident. She had cried for days, refusing to come out of her room, unable to eat or get up and go to school.

We wanted to stop by her home in North Jackson to comfort her. On our way, we stopped by Greenbrook Floral Shop on Old Canton Road and bought two dozen yellow roses for Kristine.

Her mom came to the door in tears, surprised and somewhat fearful to find us on her doorstep. Apologizing to us for Josh's death instantly, she told us Kristine wasn't feeling well enough to see us. Jason told her, "It is okay, we understand." I asked her if we could take Kristine to dinner at Amerigo's when she felt better. She agreed.

Kristine's mother called us the next day to say Kristine wanted to see us, so Jason and I met her at the restaurant that night. As we sat down,

I could tell she was in a fragile state and was scared to death of us. She was a skinny girl of about five three, with long blonde hair, a freckled face, and blue eyes—bloodshot from crying over Josh. The poor thing had been unable to cope with having been the one behind the wheel that day.

She told me she wished she had stopped at that red light at the corner of Old Canton and County Line Road, instead of hurrying to beat it. She searched for words to express her sorrow, but she couldn't find them. So we just hugged each other and cried. Jason and I knew how much Kristine loved Josh.

We ordered cheese fritters as an appetizer, pasta with shrimp for me, a salad for Kristine, and steak for Jason. Kristine had trouble maintaining her composure in front of us, but finally managed to say, "Thank you for the yellow roses. I liked them a lot."

"We both know you feel responsible for our Josh's death," I told her on behalf of Jason and me, "and we want to let you know we forgive you. Josh would want you to live a happy life. He wouldn't want you to be sad. We want you to go on, too. Accidents happen, Kristine. And unfortunately, life is full of them. I've made too many to count. You have to move forward. You have to forgive yourself. Will you do that for us? Will you do that for Josh?"

"I'm so sorry, Ms. Jeanhee," Kristine said, crying profusely, "I'm so sorry, Jason. I am so, so sorry. I didn't mean to run the light and cause that wreck. I promise. I didn't mean to kill Josh."

"We know, Kristine. We know. Let's have dinner together and call this a celebration of the new life ahead of us. Josh is in heaven, looking down on us, happy we are going on with our lives instead of crying all the time."

Kristine finally calmed down and accepted our forgiveness, and that put her at ease. I think she was astonished that we had extended our love to her at a time when most people would seek revenge.

After our somber dinner, we consoled each other. Then Jason and I gave her one final hug before her mom picked her up. My son and I cried together on the way home, our hearts aching from a Josh-sized hole. How we wished he was still with us. Even so, we were happy we had been able to help Kristine forgive herself.

We had buried Josh only eleven days earlier.

Losing Josh was like having my still-beating heart right ripped out of my chest. The pain I felt would never go away.

Looking back, how I wished I had more time to enjoy life with Josh, to attend his football games and tell him how much more I loved him but it was too late to realize it.

Jason once asked me if I could be a *Brady Bunch* mom. He'd seen her on TV as the mom he wished he'd had. How could I be like that, though? Even if I tried, I couldn't, how could I? I wasn't raised here in American. Saying *I love you*, hugging each other, constant complimenting was never part of their Korean-born mama's lifestyle. I was so deep into survival mode, too busy making money. I thought if I could just make enough money for us, everything would be alright.

A few years before the accident, Josh had given me a note he'd found at the flea market featuring a poem titled *Climb 'til Your Dream Comes True* by Helen Steiner Rice. He said to me, "Mama, you must keep this and read it when you're sad. Okay, Mama?"

Had he always known he was going to die? I think so. But if not, God knew. Just as He had given Josh a dream to prepare me—a true miracle in my eyes—He gave me this note to help me understand how to continue living without my son.

After Josh died, I came to accept unfair life as a part of my life. I had experienced so much pain. I had literally gone to hell and back. Every moment, every breath I took became precious, but looking at the world around me, I saw nothing perfect about it. I had no second thoughts about forgiving another human being who caused my Josh's death, Jason's brother. Kristine was the same age as I was when I broke taboo. No one would give me a second chance for the crime I had committed against tradition. When I had cried out begging for a second chance, no one was willing to give it to me. I was happy to give this girl a second chance.

Heartbreak helped me to become a better human being and taught me to have empathy for others, to feel their pain as my own. Losing Josh

276

was another turning point in my life, one that changed me as a person and made life all the more precious.

Even so, the void inside my chest only grew deeper from missing my son.

Notwithstanding that yawning chasm, I learned to love life as it is, no matter what it might bring me. What other choice did I have?

I also learned that I can't force anything because life can't be forced. Every precious breath I would take from now on was a blessing, and I vowed to live my life more fully despite the emptiness inside me.

A month passed, and as often I do, I stopped by Josh's grave site, to tell him how much I missed him, *"Josh, I wish you were with me."* I cried all the way home.

I had a dream that night.... Josh was riding the most beautiful silver bicycle. Even the wheels were silver, and on the back seat, a baby boy was holding onto Josh's back. Josh soon pulled over and set the little boy off in the center of a fully lighted, perfect circle surrounded by a dark circle. A little boy with a white t-shirt and blue jean overalls, about 16 months old, ran around playing in the lighted circle, but when the little boy got too close to the dark outside of rim of lighted circle, Josh ran quickly to pick him up gently, by the back of his overalls and placed him back in the center of lighted circle.

I shared this dream with my best friend Tami the next morning, and Tami told me about her own dream.

Tami said," I saw Josh in heaven with countless baby angels, and Josh was babysitting those angels. That was his job."

Several Sundays after Jason and I gave Kristine our forgiveness, I realized there was still someone I wasn't able to forgive.

While sitting in church listening to a sermon by Pastor Mark, I glanced at the empty seat next to me, broken-hearted, and begged God for an answer.

Why me? Why my son?

As Pastor Mark continued to speak, I couldn't take it anymore.

I couldn't accept that the same pastor who only a few weeks before had tried bring my son back to life by laying hands on him was behind the podium spouting the Gospel. He had lied to me.

I got up and headed for the exit door of the church. I didn't notice that my friend Suzie Conner also got up and followed me. She had tears on her cheeks when she stopped me at the top of the steps outside.

"Jeanhee, where are you going? Are you okay?"

The minute she looked into my eyes, she knew I was leaving God and leaving Family Life Church for good.

"I'm done, Suzie. I am done…."

"Will you please call me?" she asked. "You know my mother and I love you so much."

"I know, Suzie. I'm just having a hard time believing in God right now."

"I'll pray every day that you'll return, okay, Jeanhee?"

We hugged and said goodbye. As I pulled out of the parking lot, I glimpsed at her in the rearview mirror and realized that she and I both knew I was leaving her church.

I ran away from God, never intending to believe in Him again.

I left church!

Chapter 32

Rags to Riches

THE FOLLOWING YEAR, A WINDOW of opportunity opened up for me. Christine, my part time help was to work at my kiosk that day so I could make my rounds collecting money owed by my customers. She called to tell me about a commotion two stores down, at *Accessory Accents*. The store was going out of business, and people were walking out with bags full of discounted merchandise. That particular shop was called a *forty-yard-line store* by retailers because it was next to the center court—one of the mall's most expensive spaces.

I instantly envisioned myself in that store. Why couldn't it be mine? Sensing urgency, I wasted no time to get to the mall. and literally ran to the mall office to talk to PJ.

Filled with the buoyant possibility of owning that beautiful glass-front store, I bounced in without even knocking. PJ was usually too busy for a small fish like me, and he didn't stop flipping through his files. I hadn't noticed until then that he was missing half of his right index finger, but I tried not to stare. I could probe deeper into that story later. He was a short man, about five-foot-four, but he still managed to intimidate me—perhaps because of his icy blue eyes or maybe because of his brisk, business-like northern accent Even more likely it was because he held the power to say *yes* or *no* to my dreams.

Catching my breath quickly, I said, "Hi, PJ!" I continued, "Is Accessory Accents' space available to rent?"

"Who wants to know?" he asked absentmindedly.

I lifted my chin. *"Me,"* I said, pointing my index finger toward my chest.

"You?"

He raised his eyebrows, no doubt remembering that I was the lady with the laundry basket full of watches—and surprised by the fact that I now wanted store space forty yards from center court. "Really?"

"Yes, me!" I said, putting on my most winning smile. PJ could not deny my smile.

He looked at me. "Well, I don't have a tenant for it yet, so I guess you can have it. But it's only temporary. We don't rent forty-yard line space to locals."

I nodded, knowing that he meant he didn't usually rent to a little fish like me.

"I'll move out whenever you tell me to go. How much is the space?"

"Eight hundred dollars a month."

I blinked. Eight hundred dollars was what it had cost me to start my business with Tony from Chinatown, to rent my own kiosk, and now about to rent an eight hundred square feet size store? I decided that *eight hundred* must be my lucky number.

"When can I move in?" I asked.

"Tomorrow," he said. "But if a national chain notifies me that they want it, you'll have to move within a week."

"Within *one* week? How about thirty days?"

"Jeanhee, you're just--" he broke off, and I could tell he was losing patience with me. Then he huffed and said, "Okay, fine. Thirty days."

"Okay," I said, backing out of the office as fast as I could before he changed his mind. I didn't care that he was only allowing me to rent the space on a contingency basis. In fact, I decided that our arrangement might actually work better for me than having to sign a long-term lease.

PJ rounded his desk, hurried up to the door, and called after me, "You know, Jeanhee, that if you don't pay the rent, I'll keep all your merchandise and kick you out. You remember that, right?"

"Thank you, PJ!" I hollered back with a grin. "Thirty days." I could only think about the fact that it was now my chance to be a big fish.

The store I had rented gave me about eight hundred square feet in the center of the mall—and the best part was that the previous tenant had left behind all of his racks and glass display cases. My only problem was that I didn't have enough merchandise to fill eight hundred square feet... I couldn't exactly fill it with hair clips and watches, so for the time being, I spread out my merchandise and spaced it as far apart as I could without being too obvious.

To help fill the blank walls, I ordered some purses, sunglasses, costume jewelry, and a lot of cheap printed T-shirts from New York. I scattered the sunglasses and jewelry along the counters and hung up the T-shirts, then hired two teenagers as part time employees. I kept a mental inventory of every shirt, every watch, and every pair of sunglasses, down to the color and size.

I memorized every customer's name and what they bought. My black-book customers came by the shop every week. Their peddler Jeanhee now had her own store, and that fact alone made their eyes tear up. Their stopping by to just say hello and congratulate me melted my heart.

The T-shirts I had ordered proved to be more popular than I could have ever imagined, so I ventured out into more types of clothing. I had no idea what was popular among teenagers, what kind of music they listened to. I never understood their head-banging lyrics. While American kids were chanting, no more wars, asking for more freedom to smoke pots, and people of color were fighting for equal rights, I was a honey badger. I just wanted to get enough food to fill my starving belly. I had absolutely no idea about American cultures. I needed some feedback from cool teenagers. I ask them about the products that interested them and added different items to my inventory every week. I developed a list of teenagers to call whenever new merchandise arrived—and this not only guaranteed me some sales, but also made them feel special. They liked that I had remembered to call them and almost all of them became regular customers.

Within two months, I had transformed my store into the most popular store in the mall by adding music posters, lava lamps, black lights, black light posters, body jewelry, skateboards, more T-shirts, and a variety of grunge clothing—all booming trends among teenagers—to my inventory. This was before national chain stores caught onto the booming T-shirt business, and I cornered the market in Central Mississippi.

***

I could do no wrong when it came to making money, just about everything I touched turned into gold.

I did remember bargaining with Jesus to save me that day in church back in November 1990. I vividly remembered asking Him from the bottom of my heart, *"Please give me lots of money. I really need it to live and take care of my boys. Then I am all yours."* I thought that if He was God Almighty and could save someone like me that I might as well ask for what I really wanted. Had I known to ask God for lots of money, I would have asked during my welfare days.

I couldn't believe the speed of success of my business. The time had come to have my own store inside the mall.

I planned out every detail and managed construction of my new twenty-four-hundred square foot store as the general contractor, hiring subs to cut costs. My security guards who were moonlighting on weekends, Assistant DA, John Kitchen from Madison County and his chief investigator Carol Phelps showed up with tool box and carpentry machine every night and weekends to help me out.

I designed my store using the latest trendy themes with high-powered lights on eight feet long metal beams every eight feet apart,

282

galvanized metal interior walls, and a wooden floor with an exposed black ceiling. To rock every teenager's mood, I installed Bose speakers everywhere to blast music as the teens walked in. I called the store *Underground,* after a popular bar in New York City.

I was the last person you'd think would own such a store. I had been starving in the rice paddies of South Korea while Jimmy Hendrix wooed America with his guitar, and I had been too busy trying to get to America to pay attention to *Stairway to Heaven* in the seventies. I had never watched MTV. I couldn't even begin to relate to what fascinated most teenagers, but I knew what sold—and I sold it. During Christmas, the store was filled with mothers and grandmothers with page-long lists to be filled, and I was there to harvest every bit of it. I even flew one of my brothers in during the Christmas madness season to help me. Underground became teenagers' shopping central.

After the fiftieth customer asked about navel piercings all in one week, I sent one of my employee to a piercing shop in South Jackson to find out about pricing and techniques. She reported that most shops were charging $50.00 for every piercing. After discovering how lucrative the practice could be, I wanted to learn how to do it myself. The cost for the needle and navel ring was $2.00, leaving net profit of $48.00. Two-minutes of labor for $48.00. I was adding it all up in my head. If I could make $48.00 every two minutes, it added up to $1,440.00 per hour. I could be a millionaire at that rate in no time as Ms. Sandra had predicted.

One day, a guy in early twenties about 5'7", dressed in blue jean and t-shirt walked in and asked for his nipples to be pierced. I had never done it but I wasn't going to turn down a $100.00 bill. The first nipple went without incident, but as the 14 gauge needle went through the second nipple, one side to the other, he passed out right front of my eyes. I could see his face turning pale white, his face soaked in heavy sweat. Holy smoke! I had no idea what to do. No one had ever passed out on me before. I was no healer. I couldn't' even save myself if that happened to me. I still don't know where it came from. In my panic, I just hit his forehead with my right palm, and said, "Heal!" I kid you not. He came back to me, just like that. His face went white as chalk and his whole body was soaked in cold sweat. I hit his sweaty forehead with my palm one more time and held his head so he wouldn't fall over. After that scary healing incident, I never touched another man's nipple. The last thing I needed was somebody dropping dead on me. Saving somebody's life wasn't exactly on my to-do list on my dream plan. Besides, I was too busy saving my own life.

Work wasn't all about making money. I had fun doing crazy things from time to time. I had just returned to the store after chasing shoplifters all the way to parking lot one day when an overweight lady came to get her navel pierced. When I said overweight, I mean she was no less than 250 pounds. I almost said, "Lady, no one is ever going to see that ring on your fat belly," but I bit my tongue. I wanted her money more than I wanted to speak my mind. Fifty dollars was more than enough to keep my big mouth shut?

"Can you come over here?" I asked as I walked toward an empty wall.

She followed me. "Sure."

"Raise both of your arms, stand tall, and lean against the wall, and don't' move," I said. She had no idea she had a triple layer of belly fat. When I finally found her navel, I cleaned the area with Betadine and dug until I found her belly button. Then I stuck the needle through her skin and followed it with a 16-gauge ring. I was fifty dollars richer, and she was proud to have her ring somewhere under there.

The days weren't long enough. I wished my store could open the store around the clock. Why sleep when making money was so much fun? I could bring my fold-up bed and take a nap, then work some more. The only thing that kept me from doing so was that I needed to be at home for my boys.

I kept my kiosk business, a money-making machine, especially during the Christmas season. Impulsive shoppers were perfect preys, and I had the perfect price range—under twenty dollars. Believe it or not, annual sales at that tiny kiosk were $250,000.00. I had three to four kiosks during Christmas season.

I kept the promise I had made to my mother before I left Korea. I set up an auto draft monthly to her account. On her birthday and my dad's birthday and on New Year's, I sent them twice the usual amount. I showered my mama with fancy reading glasses she didn't need but wanted because she believed they made her look distinguished. I bought her two pairs in different colors. I gave her a custom made necklace with an eight-hundred-year-old Spanish coin surrounded by sapphires and diamonds, coral rings for luck, and a diamond bracelet for bragging rights. I wiped out my dad's gambling debts and bought my mama her own house with a rose garden, where she could live peacefully and worry-free for the rest of her life. For her retirement money, I sent her my Josh's life insurance policy check. I couldn't dare to spend my son's death money. Instead, I gave it to my mother to save for a rainy day.

In South Korea, parents earn bragging rights from the success of their children and the gifts they received. I made sure nothing was left to speculation.

I soon added more stores, one at a time—in Ridgeland, Meridian, Hattiesburg, Vicksburg, and Jackson, Mississippi. Then I added some out of state, beginning with Monroe, Louisiana and Atlanta, Georgia, then adding two more stores in Charleston, South Carolina. I worked fourteen hours a day, seven days a week.

I was tireless. Counting mountains of cash gave me all the relief my swollen feet and tired body needed.

My success didn't go unnoticed by the community. In August 1998, Newscaster Sherri Hilton from WLBT, Jackson's NBC affiliate, called to ask if I would be interested in telling my story on the air.

"What story?" I asked, suspicious of her motives. I was proud of my success, but certain parts of my history weren't anyone's business.

"We plan to call the series *Rags to Riches,*" she said. "And we plan to focus on successful business men and women in Mississippi. You're one of those people."

The title of the feature confused me—*Rags to Riches*. I wondered how in the world they knew I had gone from pushing dirty rags across a mud floor to living out my childhood dream in America. Who had told this woman about me?

"Jeanhee, several people mentioned you when they found out I was looking for candidates to interview," she continued.

Her proposition caught me completely off guard. I'd been so busy working, I didn't even know how much money I had made. I never even knew I was rich until my accountant finally pointed out the numbers on my tax return.

I reluctantly agreed to allow Sherri to interview me, after remembering that a few years earlier the same TV station had smeared my name by saying I was the state's leading seller of counterfeit goods. Now, they wanted to put me on a pedestal and broadcast my success to the entire Jackson, Mississippi, viewing area.

"That might be all right," I reluctantly agreed and said, "but I'm not a millionaire. I was only trying to survive, be independent and take care of my boys, you know? I had no idea anyone even noticed about my success."

"Don't worry about a thing, Jeanhee, just tell your story briefly, and I'll do most of the talking on camera and will guide you through the interview."

The next day, she and a burly cameraman came into my store and taped an interview with me for the six o'clock news. I pretended the camera was a person and tried to talk as naturally I could. Why not? This would be great publicity for my store. I gave them my best smile, the one I'd learned from Woojung a hundred years before.

The feature was so successful that the news station repeated it the next day. My phone rang off the hook with customers calling to tell me they'd seen me on TV. I was their gutsy Jeanhee who had gone after her dream.

The story came on right after the six o'clock news and was introduced by longtime WLBT TV newscaster Maggie Wade.

"And tonight our business segment features Jeanhee Kang, who has truly gone from rags to riches," she said in her smooth newscaster's voice. "Jeanhee Kang was born in South Korea and came to America to live the American dream. She spent time as a street peddler while raising her sons as a single mom. She started her business with only eight-hundred dollars, worked at the flea market on weekends, and made door-to-door sales on weekdays from cars borrowed from her girlfriends. And now, only five years later, she's a millionaire with her own chain of stores.

When Sherri asked me to tell her the driving force behind my success, I proudly replied, "Have a dream! Everyone should have a dream—and as long as you believe in it, it will come."

My proud smile and words echoed in the hearts of viewers all over Mississippi. I forgot to be humbled for a short minute... I liked the sound of the segment's title— "Rags to Riches"—that was my story.

Chapter 33

Getting My Boy Out of the Middle East

ON JUNE 10, 1995, I received a phone call I'd dreamed of for six and a half years. One call was about to change our lives forever. The possibility that I might someday reconnect with Hamid was the sole reason I had never changed my cell phone number. That number was my lifeline, my only hope of ever seeing Ahmed again. My heart leaped inside my chest when I heard Hamid's voice.

"Hi, Jeanhee, It's Hamid." Dead silence followed his greeting for several long seconds. "How are you?"

Goosebumps ran from the top of my head to my tail bone, and then back right back to where they started. My hair stood on end, anticipating what was he up to, why he was calling me, what he might want from me. The silence chilled me, but I figured he had called to tell me either something was wrong with my baby, or that he wanted to beg me to come back to him. Either way, I knew he would only have called me for a reason.

"How are Josh and Jason?" he asked in falsely cheerful tone.

"They are fine," I replied. At first I wasn't even going to tell him about Josh. I was infuriated that he had even dared ask about the boys, seeing as how the last time he had said their names, he had promised to cut their throats if I tried to get Ahmad back. I would never forget his terrifying threat. Well, I decided to stab him to see if he was a human and might even bleed. I quickly changed my mind and decided to tell him the truth, snapping out a fiery, "Josh is dead. Are you happy?"

"Stop it," he said. "I was asking nicely."

"Josh is dead!" I told him with a clenched fist. *"Dead!"*

Another long silence followed my shout. I drew satisfaction from having shocked him. I'd never known that evil man to be at a loss for words before.

"Dead?" he finally asked, stumbling over the word. "What? He is really dead?"

I wasn't about to share the events surrounding my boy's death with such an undeserving person. So I gave him the short version of the story.

"He died in a car accident last year," I said, still fuming about Hamid's death threats against Josh and Jason as he stole my baby boy from us. I cried in silence and bit my tongue to keep from letting him know just how much he had hurt me. I wanted to jab an invisible knife into his *heart.*

"I'm sorry about Josh, Jeanhee," he finally said. "Really."

"Cut the bullshit," I replied. "How is my baby? Where is he?"

"He is doing well, he is with my family."

"What in the hell do you want?"

"I need to borrow eleven thousand dollars.

"Excuse me?" I barked a laugh. "You must be kidding."

"I'm not. I've been working hard ever since you loaned me the money for truck driving school," he said, reminding me of yet another mistake I had made. "I've been working for Warner Trucking, driving all over the country. But if I could buy my own truck, I could make more money."

I didn't say a word.

"I-I got married and have another son now," he said after a brief hesitation. "We're struggling to make ends meet. I need eleven thousand for a down payment. Can you loan it to me? I promise to pay you back in just a few months."

He had never paid me back for the first loan, and I was certain he never intended to do so.

"So you remarried," I retorted. "Do you beat her and rape her, too? Are you going to steal her baby and send him to another country?"

He didn't say anything, but, amazingly, he was still on the line. I decided he must be pretty desperate if he was willing to endure my taunts. So maybe…

"I want my baby back," I said. "I want Ahmad to come home."

"I still love you, Jeanhee."

"You have a funny way of showing it." *I couldn't believe he was still up to his old tricks. He had no idea he's dealing with a changed woman— the tough, no-nonsense woman he's forced me to become.* I scoffed at him. "I'll just bet you still love me."

Out of desperation, he remained calm. He had never controlled his temper like this before. I swiped angry tears from my face and again gathered my composure. He didn't know it, but bargaining had become my forte. Dealing with angry customers and making them believe they were getting the better end of the deal had become as much a part of my life as sleeping. Maybe even more so. I prepared to make the deal of my life.

"Why should I loan you any more money?" I asked him in an unruffled tone. "You never paid me back from the last time."

I wanted him to beg, but the fact that he was reacting in a rational manner told me that he already believed I would say no. His Muslim beliefs would normally never have allowed him to accept this kind of questioning from a woman.

"Please, Jeanhee," he begged. "I just want to start a new life."

Had he just said *please?* I'd spent years with him and never heard the word *please* come from his mouth. Not once. That told me I had him by the balls.

"Since you have a new baby," I said, "then give mine back. If you have any heart left, give me my son back. I have lost Josh forever. I don't want to lose Ahmad, too."

Hamid went silent. I figured he was mulling over my proposition.

To keep him off balance, I asked, "Where is he?"

"In Jordan."

Relying on my years as a street peddler, my wheels were turning, trying to think of a way to get my back boy back.

"With your parents?"

He said, "Yes."

"Didn't they live in Kuwait?"

"Yeah, but they had to move to Jordan after the war in Kuwait. My father and all the Palestinians got kicked out of Kuwait for helping Saddam Hussein. My father lost everything. My father lost his business. They were only allowed to take what they could carry when they left Kuwait." he offered, surprising me with his candor. "The Palestinians thought Saddam was going to win the war."

"My baby was living in a war refugee camp?" I gasped.

Hamid told me that Ahmad was living in a refugee camp when they first got to Jordan, but he was no longer there, that they now had a little house.

My heart sank imagining my baby's suffering in the Middle East with no food.

I wanted to say something derogatory about his new life, but I decided to save it because I heard the desperation in his voice. I realized that his father was in no position to support Hamid's lifestyle anymore.

I suddenly realized that Hamid and his father's misfortunes might provide a tremendous opportunity for me.

"Okay, then... I'll tell you what," I said once I digested that information. "Give me my baby back, and you can have the money and never repay me."

He said, "What? It's not up to me," he said. "My father has custody of Ahmad. It is Arabic law. And my father will never let you have him. Never mind about the money."

He hung up.

The click of the line haunted me, but I knew by the tone of his voice that he would call back. An eternity of angst-ridden hours passed before he finally did.

He wanted to negotiate, but I stood firm.

"I only have one condition, Hamid. I want my baby back. Give him to me, and I'll give you the money right this minute, and you never have to pay me back"

I was fully aware of his fears and had rehearsed the words he needed to hear. Like most Muslims, Hamid held a deep hatred for Americans, a hatred he'd become expert at hiding. This abhorrence of American culture is what had prompted him to send Ahmad to live with his father in the first place. So I decided to make the vow he needed to hear.

"I will never get married," I assured him. *"I will never bring an American man into my home. Ahmad will never call an American man Daddy.* You will always be his father. And I promise I will never force him to convert to Christianity."

"Jeanhee…" He let my name trail away. Then he said the magic words. "Fine, you can have him back… but it's for Josh, not for you."

He'd needed to stab me one last time. I didn't care. I ignored his jab.

"Okay," I replied, my excitement rising. "For Josh, then."

"I will call you tomorrow after I speak with my father."

That evening, I paced back and forth breathlessly, my eyes on the phone as I waited for the most important call of my life. I had forgotten to ask when Hamid might call, but it didn't matter. I had waited six and a half years—what was another twenty-four hours? I already dreamed about holding my baby in my arms.

I can wait, I told myself, trying to slow my heart rate.

The next morning, Hamid finally called. He gave me his father's neighbor's phone number in Jordan.

"My father doesn't have a phone," he said. "You can call him at ten o'clock tonight. He will be waiting to hear from you."

"Thank you, Hamid." My heart skipped a beat at the thought of holding my baby boy again. I nearly fainted.

No matter the cost, I would find a way to bring Ahmad back to America.

My phone call to Hamid's father was brief and went surprisingly well, without any yelling or accusations. He spoke in broken English but well enough to understand our mutual interest, Ahmad, my son, his grandson. I told him I was coming to talk to him about Ahmad's future. He invited me to visit Amman so we could talk face to face. During our brief phone conversation, I made sure that I used carefully chosen words to avoid hostility, but I wanted to make sure that he understood that the intent of my visit was to bring Ahmad back to America.

I couldn't wait to call my attorney, James Bell, the next day and share the happy news with him. He was thrilled and took immediate action. Senator Thad Cochran wrote a letter to the American Embassy in Amman asking for their assistance. The embassy warned James that no American woman had ever successfully left an Arab country with one of her sons, that they all returned empty handed and heartbroken in the past.

I said to James, "Not me! I will come back with my baby boy, even if it cost me my life" The Korean girl from a muddy rice paddy was not even considering failure.

Mississippi's longest serving Senator Thad Cochran had discovered that under The Hague Convention on the Civil Aspects of International Child Abduction, I could retrieve my boy without the consent of either Hamid or his father. On June 8, my attorney obtained a court order from a Chancery Court Judge Stuart Robinson and granted me full custody based on a handwritten promissory note I'd made Hamid give me before I released his money.

The Department of Justice issued me an emergency passport within ten days.

On June 28, 1995, I left for Amman, Jordan. Before I left, I filled Ahmad's room with new furniture, a TV, a stereo system, a Mickey Mouse lamp, and a framed picture of him with both of his brothers, the only photo of all my sons together. A brand new backpack filled with school supplies sat on his bed.

On June 28, 1995, I took one last look at Ahmad's room, then removed the cross necklace I had worn since I became a Christian in 1990. Even though I had stopped going to church and was still somewhat angry at God, I considered myself a Christian, and I was smart enough to know that I must hide my true beliefs until I got my baby back onto American soil.

During my flight to Amman, surreal anticipation to see my long-lost baby boy was killing me. Tingling waves of tightly wrapped emotion I had kept deep in my heart overwhelmed me. Just thinking about holding my boy made my heart race I rehearsed what I would say to my baby using the few Arabic words I knew. In my mind, Ahmad was still the little baby I had held in my arms. I had trouble imagining him in a boy's body. The years I had missed weighed heavily on me. What would he be like? What color was his hair? His eyes? How tall was he? Did he have enough food to eat? I was his mother—and regardless of how much time had passed, I was sure he would know that. As the plane descended onto the runway at Queen Noor International Airport, an endless, sandy desert filled the small oval window below me.

The airport waiting area was hot and humid. It had no air-conditioning. As soon as I came out of customs, I began searching for my boy, and quickly noticed a heavy set old man with gray hair waving at me—Hamid's father, Ahmad Sr. Beside him stood a little boy in a white shirt and black pants. He was the spitting image of Josh, with a slightly larger nose. The moment I saw him, I knew he was my boy, Ahmad.

My baby.

In that instant, I forgot the words I had rehearsed. I knelt in front of him and hugged him tightly. I ran my hands all over his body, making sure all his limbs and fingers were there, hugging him again and again. A bewildered look came over his precious little face when I hugged him. I kissed his cheeks and forehead, then placed my hands over my heart and said, "I'm your mama."

"Mama?" he replied timidly.

Hearing that endearment slip from his tongue allowed my heart to come to life for the first time since I had lost Josh.

"Mama," Ahmad said again, using his small hands to wipe the tears of joy from my face. Then he smiled.

I melted.

Finally, after I got over the shock of seeing my son again, I took in Ahmad Sr.'s reaction. He did not seem upset. Surprisingly, he came forward to give me a welcome hug.

"Welcome," he said in his heavy accent English, kissing me first on the right cheek, and then the left.

I said, *"Keef Hatlak!"* In Arabic how are you?

He said, *"Hamdula!" Thanks to Allah. "Keef Hatlick"*

I said, "Ana Bikhayr. Shorcran!"

I thanked him for allowing me to come to Jordan.

"Come." He motioned toward the baggage claim, and within seconds Ahmad held my hand tightly as we walked toward the parking lot.

Now that my baby knew I was his mama, I no longer needed words. I merely held him tightly and stroked his hair as we rode in Ahmad Sr.'s older model red Toyota. My baby Ahmad was perfect—his limbs were intact, he had all of his fingers and perfectly seated eyebrows, and that handsome nose was centered just right. A sheepish grin curved his lips.

Deciding that experiencing heaven must feel a lot like that moment, I looked toward the sky and secretly thanked God for keeping my boy safe.

Ahmad drove the Toyota along a bumpy dirt road amidst endless miles of red desert until we reached a heavily populated Palestinian refugee neighborhood on the outskirts of Amman. My senses were assaulted with a kaleidoscope -- Tin roofs in many different colors, red, blue, natural colors, soaring metal antennas in various heights, street vendors pushing their cars around to attract pedestrians, people everywhere wearing mixed shabby looking clothes. As we neared our destination, we drove up in what it looked like circles until we finally reached the top of the hill overlooking the village full of tin buildings. The place reminded me of my childhood village, except there were tin roofs instead of thatched roof made of rice shoots, and there were no rice paddies. Instead of rice paddies, there was a lot of red dirt. It was about 85 degrees but not humid as a Mississippi summer.

Even though the American Embassy was well aware of my arrival to take my boy back to the U.S., getting into a car with Ahmad Sr. was going to unknown war territory. As we drove away from the airport, I was unsure that I would live to come back, but I pushed my fears away. With my baby tow in my arms, what could hurt me? I had to believe in the humanity of his grandparents.

A final jerk accompanied by squealing brakes landed us in front of a small concrete house with a rusted tin roof. Nahol, Palestinian, a village on the outskirts of Amman was filled with rundown houses with sagging tin roofs, clothes pinned to the lines outside, and skewed TV antennas on top leaning toward an outhouse. The entire family greeted us when we arrived, including my Ahmad's grandmother, his uncle Tariq, and his aunt Hanna. They each offered me an Arabian hug and kisses on my cheeks, but I could read the mistrust in their eyes. We all understood why I was there—to take away their beloved Ahmad. One side would be left with a broken heart, and I was determined that this time it wouldn't be mine.

Ahmad pulled me into the room he shared with the rest of the family. The place was dilapidated, containing two small chests and an old mirror, and had piles of clothes lining the bare concrete walls. The floor was also concrete, with only one dingy rug in the center of the room. The entire family shared two rooms—a kitchen and a living room. They had no refrigerator but did have a small kitchen sink with a bucket to catch the nasty brown water from the faucet. Both electricity and water were rationed daily. Despite the dirty conditions, the family didn't wear shoes inside the house.

"Thank you for inviting me into your home," I said. The mistrust grew in their eyes when Ahmad took my hand again and pulled me away from them.

That evening, while Ahmad's grandmother was cooking dinner, I produced a large bag of gifts I had brought for everyone. The bag contained new clothes for Ahmad, a remote control car, and a box of Hershey bars. Ahmad was so excited that he ran off to show his best friend his new toy car. Before he left, I stopped him and placed two squares of chocolate into his mouth. Once he tasted it, he stopped and opened his mouth wide open for more. I dropped several more squares into his mouth.

"Ummm," he murmured in delight.

"That is from *Meegook,*" I told him, remembering how incredible my first taste of chocolate had been when I was his age.

"Yummy, Mama," he said the heavenly words. He called me Mama.

Everyone tasted the Hershey bars. They seemed to enjoy the treat and offered their thanks in Arabic while they opened their other gifts. Hanna thanked me in English—she was an English teacher at a local middle school and was my link to the rest of her family. Everyone's eyes were watching the interaction between Ahmad and me.

After they finished opening their presents, we sat on the floor around a large pan of Mansaf—salad—and homemade pita bread that we ate by hand. We washed the meal down with heavily sugared tea.

They questioned me about Josh's death, paid me sincere sympathy, and then Hanna asked about my life in America and about Jason.

When she asked if I was married, I replied, "No. I will never marry again. I work seven days a week and have no time for a relationship." I passed the first test.

Apparently satisfied with my answer, she shared it with the rest of the family.

Before bedtime, Ahmad allowed me to bathe him and wash his hair with soap and shampoo I had brought with me. His grandmother mixed just enough stove-heated water with some of the cold, brown tap water. He was fascinated with the shampoo, soap, and tooth brush. While I was giving him his bath as if he was my tiny baby way back when, I made sure to wash every inch of his small body and was satisfied all his limbs and bones were attached perfectly to his body. Ahmad took my tooth brush to brush yellow teeth that looked like they had never been brushed before. I noticed Ahmad's peculiar interest in the tooth brush. He kept brushing his teeth as if it was a new toy. I squeezed toothpaste onto the bristles and brushed his teeth with it and noticed a mouth full of decayed teeth. He must not have a tooth brush of his own. There was only one brush which was very worn out. I must take him to the dentist as soon as we went home to *Meegook*.

The family allowed me to sleep with Ahmad in one room while the rest of them crammed into the other room. Ahmad's grandmother brought in a blue plastic pad, and I quickly realized Ahmad needed it in case he had an accident during his sleep. I stroked his face as he fell asleep in my arms. He had grown so much. I wished that Josh could have seen him. I silently thanked God again for answering my prayers, then fell asleep with a full heart and joyful tears on my cheeks. My baby boy was back in my arms.

The following morning, I awoke before anyone else, carefully rolled off the pallet without waking Ahmad, and put on my running clothes. I had been careful to select clothing that wouldn't offend the Muslim culture. I doubted any women in this part of the world dared to run—for exercise, anyway—but I wasn't about to break the daily routine that had allowed me to finally take control of my life.

After my run, we ate a breakfast of scrambled eggs, hummus on pita bread, and hot tea. I helped Ahmad put on his school uniform, a white shirt and black pants. After noticing that his shoes were completely worn out, barely wearable, I sent him on his way, waving until he disappeared from sight. Shortly after that, Hanna and Tariq both left for work, leaving me alone with Hamid's parents.

"Come," Ahmad's grandmother said, waving me outside and over to a neighbor's house.

I was surprised to find a brood of ladies with covered heads inside waiting to check me out. None of them spoke English. We had tea, and I listened to their warbling Arabic gossip. All I learned from that meeting was that their neighbor was close friends with Ahmad's family, and their son was Ahmad's best friend.

My boy in the middle, his best friend and his cousin in Nahol

During the seemingly friendly gathering, I couldn't help but wonder what stories Hamid had told his family about me. Did they think I had abandoned my son? Did they believe I was an unfit mother? I am certain all were horrible stories.

After sharing tasty kunafeh and sugared tea with the ladies, we returned to the house. For lunch, Grandmother prepared a salad and an odd mixture of rice and yogurt. Ahmad Senior motioned for me to join him for tea on the living room floor. I figured he was ready to grill me about the Koran and how I might raise Ahmad should he allow me to take my son back to America. He was extremely skeptical.

"So...Jeanhee!! Come!" Waving his right hand toward his mid-body back and forth. "Come, come! Sit down. Ahhm. I want to speak with you about Ahmad!" His wife stared at me with concerned eyes. I was sensing his deep emotion, both of his eye brows lifted up and down searching for words to come out in English.

I beat him to it, hoping to lighten the tension a little bit. .

"I know you have raised him," I explained, "but don't you think Ahmad deserves to know his mother?"

He didn't respond immediately, but I could tell he was thinking about my question because he furrowed his brow.

"Will you take him to church?" he finally asked. "Will he forget the Koran?"

"No," I replied. "I won't force him to go to church or to read the Bible."

"Do *you* believe in Bible?" he asked in a cutting tone.

I didn't want to answer him, because my true beliefs, even though I stopped going to church after Josh's death, would only make him angry. I was relieved I had left my cross pendant at home. After a moment, I said, "I don't know much about the Bible, not enough to argue what is wrong and what is right. But I have been told it is the Word of God."

"But, I want to know if you will take Ahmad to church?"

"I will not take him to church to become a Christian."

"Will you ever marry again?"

I said, "Never. I will not marry again. Ahmad will not call another man, father. All I am interested in right now is to give Ahmad a life with Jason and me, and give him an opportunity to get an education in America. Wouldn't you all like to see Ahmad know his mother, living a deserved the good life I can give him?"

"I am not here to hurt any of you. I am only here as Ahmad's mother, and mostly importantly, his isn't about being Muslim or Christian," I continued. "We are talking about a little boy's life and his future."

I could sense that my argument tormented Ahmad Senior. Ahmad's grandmother's eyes were saddened by thought of losing her grandson, her facial wrinkles were shrinking as she tried to read our tone. This was my chance to convince Ahmad Senior, and l wanted to let him know that Ahmad needed his mother, and I wanted my son more than anything. I showed them photos of my beautifully furnished home, and Ahmad's own room. Ahmad's grandmother pointed at the white baby grand piano in my foyer and motioned with her fingers, asking if I played with finger motion. I don't, but I nodded anyway. For two seconds, I remembered that hateful music teacher when I was in middle school. I never did learn to play the piano because of her.

They saw my brand new Mercedes parked next to the boat in the garage, and the whole family turned their head to each other.

Ahmad ran into the house when he came home from school. "Mama!" he exclaimed, hugging me tightly.

I pointed at his feet. "Let's go shopping for shoes."

Tariq drove us into Amman to shop for Ahmad a brand new pair of shoes and new clothes. . I told him he could have another pair, but he said no in Arabic with a glance at his uncle, who observed us with watchful eyes.

On the way home, I noticed a grocery store where only rich Jordanians shopped. I let Ahmad get whatever he wanted and assumed he would pick candy, but instead he ran to the tomatoes first. Soon, Ahmad had filled our cart with things he had never had. He was especially thrilled to get his very first toothbrush and tube of Colgate toothpaste. Ahmad was a bundle of joy, chattering all the way home. Seeing him so happy made my heart sing.

That night, Hala, Hamid's eldest sister, and her family arrived for Hanna's impending wedding from Jerusalem. I connected with her instantly. After the entire clan ate dinner, Hala held my hand to her heart and said, "You are Ahmad's mother, and you should raise him. Don't let them keep him. I asked my mother to explain this to my father. I never believed you were a crack addict and whore. Here is my address. Please write to me and let me know how Ahmad is doing in America."

"Thank you," I replied in relief. "Thank you so much, Hala. You are my angel. I promise I will write and send pictures."

We hugged and exchanged kisses as she and her family left.

Before we went to sleep, Ahmad looked through my photo albums and stumbled across a picture of Jason riding a jet ski. His jaw dropped. He said, "Jason?"

"Yes, this is your brother," I replied. Then I showed him the family photo we had taken the day he was kidnapped. His eyes grew bright at the discovery that he had a family he hadn't known about. I kissed his forehead while he thumbed through more photos. He pointed at Josh. My face crumbled, and I cried. Reading the anguish in my tears, Ahmad guessed that Josh died. He mimed Josh sleeping with his eyes closed.

I hugged him tight," Yes, he went to sleep, "I said, pointing at the sky.

I told Ahmad, by motioning, together, "We are going to *Meegook* soon."

He asked in Arabic, "Shoo *Meegook?*"

"Yes," I replied. "*Meegook*, America."

Too many words for Ahmad, *"Meegook,"* he repeated.

I wasn't sure he understood what I meant, but he liked the sound of the word. So did I when I was his age, eight.

The next morning, I awoke to find Ahmad Sr. pacing back and forth by the kitchen area.

As soon as he saw me finishing up a quick breakfast, he said, "Come, Jeanhee. We must go to Amman to get Ahmad's papers." He had said the magic words. I jumped up, grabbed my purse and ran to his car.

We went to the Civic office in Amman to get Ahmad's residency verification to leave Jordan. When an official learned Ahmad was an American citizen and had been living in Amman as a Palestinian war refugee, he began counting Ahmad's illegal days in Jordan. To them, Ahmad was an illegal alien, and they were counting every day since Ahmad's grandparents were forced to flee Kuwait. Ahmad would have been four years old. At three Dinars per day for 4 years to July 16, 1995, it totaled 4,380 Dinars.

I was shocked and angry at their demand. I asked, "Do you speak English?"

He said, "No."

I told Ahmad Sr. to interpret. "My son is an American citizen. He was born in Jackson, Mississippi, and was brought here against my will. His father stole him from me. I will not pay. Let me see your phone, and I'll call the American embassy."

My mentioning the American embassy changed everything. The official changed his tune and informed us that he would waive the fee—just this time.

It was almost 12:00 by the time we got out of the Civic office. As the time progressed, my heart raced as I sensed Ahmad Sr.'s uneasiness, knowing he could still change his mind any moment about letting Ahmad to leave Amman. I called the American Embassy to inform them that we were coming in to get Ahmad's passport. Torah Cottrill, Vice Consul of the American Embassy said that they were ready. I told her that I only had Ahmad's baby photo and didn't have time to get a current photo. She told me that it would not be a problem.

Ahmad Sr. drove us to the embassy to get Ahmad's passport. His eyes grew sad as he pulled up to the gate. I told the guard to inform Torah Cottrill, that I was looking for her. She met me at the front office immediately. I gave her the Jordanian document clearing Ahmad to leave and Ahmad's baby photo.

I asked her again if his baby picture was sufficient.

She said, "That doesn't matter." She went on to explain, "His passport is Red Tape Status. You won't have to go through customs. When you reach the U.S. with this passport, no one will question, you will be escorted straight to baggage claim."

The whole process took less than thirty minutes. We were literally walking through the passport process like a grocery checkout. While we waited for the ambassador's signature, an Arabic-speaking employee told Ahmad Senior that under Arabic law, he didn't have to let Ahmad go.

"Don't let infidel have your son," she urged him.

Little did she know that I understood every word she'd said

"If you don't shut the hell up," I whispered in her ear as a wave of fury washed over me, "I'll go straight to the ambassador and get your ass fired for calling Americans infidels."

Her face turned white as a ghost and she hurried away, terrified by the possibility of losing a prestigious job.

We drove back to the house without a word. Ahmad Senior was heartbroken. I didn't want to say anything because I was afraid I might anger him.

When we arrived, Ahmad ran outside and hugged me.

"Mama!" he cried, asking where I had been in Arabic.

"Let's go for a walk," I said, taking his hand and leading him through the neighborhood.

Word had gotten out that Ahmad was leaving. His best friend Mohammed approached us and asked if it were true. Ahmad started to answer, but I nudged him and motioned for him to remain silent. Ahmad understood and never mentioned America to anyone else while we were in Jordan.

That evening, we packed our suitcases. Ahmad attempted to pack his worn clothing and old shoes but I kept pushing it away.

"You don't need those anymore."

He insisted, however, so I let him pack whatever he wanted.

On July 16, 1995, we loaded baggage into Ahmad Sr.'s Toyota and said goodbye to Ahmad's grandmother, Hanna. Tariq was clearly disturbed and refused to hug me goodbye, but he did hug Ahmad.

Once we checked our bags and the men at the gate checked our passports, we paused to say goodbye to Ahmad Sr. before moving into a more secure area.

Ahmad and Ahmad Sr. shared a long tight hug.

"Goodbye," I said, "and thank you. And thank you for letting me have my son."

By now the older man was weeping. I wept for his pain.

I said, "This is for Ahmad. You are letting him go because you love him."

He nodded. "Yes. We are doing this for Ahmad."

As we were getting close to the secured area to board the plane, I felt like someone was going to grab my neck from behind any second, and I kept looking back over my shoulder to make sure no one was chasing us. I was sure that at any moment someone would try to snatch my baby from me. I counted the seconds until the plane finally began to roll. Come on.... Come on... I said to myself, holding my last breath, helping the plane to lift up in the air. With my help, at last, the plane lifted into the air, and right before Amman began shrinking beneath us, I was surprised to see Tariq,

Hamid's angry brother, and several policemen on the tarmac, arriving too late to arrest me for kidnapping my son.

Thrilled by the excitement on Ahmad's face, I released a long-held breath and pulled out a Hershey bar. I would never tell Ahmad that I had kidnapped him from Amman, Jordan. For Arabs, my son may be theirs, but Ahmad is my son, I had him, and he was born in United States of America.

My fingers shook as I broke off a square and placed a piece into his mouth and into my mouth, just as I was dreaming of *Meegook* when I was his age…. I was taking my boy to give him the life I had prepared for him.

"We're going to *Meegook,*" I said.

"Meegook!" he repeated. I remembered the very first time I had said, *Meegook,* "*I am going to Meegook when I grow up, Mama*" … I was Ahmad's age, eight years old, thirty years ago.

Meegook. One of the most beautiful words I've ever heard. A beautiful country, the land of second chances. I was bringing my baby boy home.

It was along flight. We stopped one night in Rome, and then on to New York, Atlanta, and, finally, to Jackson. Looking down on the Ross Barnett Reservoir from the air, I had never been so relieved to be back in my home state, Mississippi.

Jason and my attorney James met us with colorful balloons at the airport.

"Hi, Ahmad!" both yelled out, handing over the balloons. "Welcome home!"

Ahmad leapt into Jason's arms.

"Hi, Hamada – Ahmad's nick name! My brother!" Jason said, hugging his brother once James let go. "I'm Jason, I am your brother."

Ahmad replied, "Ana Ahmad!" They instantly bonded, "I will never let you go again," Jason said hugging his little brother tightly.

They'd even brought our dog, Yellow Dog, who was as almost excited to greet Ahmad as Jason was. *Yellow Dog* jumped up to lick

Ahmad's face.

I'm still Korean and believe that we should respect the dead. On our way home from the airport, we stopped at the cemetery to allow Ahmad to meet Josh.

Once we reached his grave, I knelt and brushed the dirt and leaves from his tombstone because Josh liked it that way.

"Hi, Josh," I said.

"Look, look, Josh," Jason said. "Our little brother is here to see you."

Ahmad knelt and touched the Bible verse etched onto the tombstone next to Josh's name. "Hi, Josh," said Ahmad.

I wrapped my arms around Ahmad, and we cried. I wondered if he remembered Josh changing his diapers, bottle feeding him, and rocking him to sleep while he rubbed his brother's tiny belly.

When we finally drove up to our home-sweet-home, Ahmad's eyes filled with fascination. I couldn't quite explain to him why it took me six and a half years to bring him back home.

Our five-bedroom house with the back deck facing the Castlewoods Country Club Golf Course must have seemed like a castle to him. The white baby grand piano that I'd bought with the intention of learning to play sat in the foyer, and our large living room was filled with white couches, photos of our family, and a handmade wooden cross hanging over the fireplace. When we walked into the kitchen, Ahmed couldn't wait to check out the refrigerator filled with food.

Jason took his brother by the hand and led him upstairs to his new bedroom. Ahmad gawked at the TV, then turned to check out the stereo, the desk and chair, and the only photo of us together that I had hung on the wall. Overwhelmed, he looked around in bewilderment and ran his hands over everything, including the bed.

Then he turned to me.

"Ana?" he asked, pointing at his chest with his little index finger, in Arabic *"Me?"* He said, obviously thinking of his thin pad and sharing a room with his entire family in a small home built with mud infused cement.

I smiled at him and nodded.

"Anta, yes. For you."

His eyes sparkled with excitement, and he gave us the biggest smile.

"Mama!" Ahmad said. I knew what he meant.

I hugged my baby boy, kissed his sweet cheek, and said, "This is your home! I knew I was going to find you! I love you!"

Ahmad didn't' understand a word I said to him, but it didn't' matter. I was going to learn to say *I love you* more often, and give him hugs and kisses like American mothers. Rarely had I shown any of these emotions to Josh and Jason. Just because my mama never taught me, didn't mean I had to follow her tradition. It is never too late. I still had a whole life time to make up for those lost years. I would also shower Ahmad with the love I had saved just for him and show him how much I loved him for the rest of his life. I would make sure he would never be hungry. I would make sure he would graduate from a four- year college with his high school friends, and I would see him at his graduation as a proud mama.

My little baby boy came home, and while his little fingers were bigger than I remembered, in my eyes, he was my baby boy still wearing a diaper, waiting for his mama to feed him and rock him to sleep.

Jeanhee Kang

Ahmad's first day of school as a 3rd Grader at Vine Street Elementary School

Ahmad's high school senior portrait at Northwest Rankin High School

Chapter 34

I Am Still Hungry

I COULD NEVER AGAIN BE accepted in South Korea, but I now had a country of my own. *Meegook,* the beautiful nation. America had offered me a second chance with no questions asked and allowed me to live out my childhood dream.

In Mississippi, my home state since 1986, I had bonded with life-long friends who could care less about my dark past. They have accepted me as I am. MaryAnn, Dyanne, Jane, Nichole, Terrie, Jamie and Tami live a few minutes away. Tami, my best friend, placed her only son in my arms at his birth and said, "Jeanhee, this is your godson. He will grow up to play football just like Josh did. He'll be a quarterback."

Ahmad graduated from Northwest Rankin High School in Brandon, Mississippi. with the friends he had had since the 3rd grade He followed his brother Jason to graduate as a die-hard Ole Miss Rebel at the University of Mississippi in Oxford, Mississippi.

"I kept my *I will never remarry promise to my boys.*" I had remained a single mom for twenty years, had showered them luxuries I couldn't have, and paid for college educations, fancy cars, books, clothes, and plenty of spending money. In return, I was rewarded by witnessing their graduation ceremonies, memorizing every step as if it were mine.

In time, I no longer felt driven to earn every penny I could. Sure, making all that money was fun while I was doing it, but not anymore. I no longer needed money as I once had so direly. Once my boys graduated from college, I was done. My job as their mama was over. I sold all my stores and intended to retire… perhaps to enjoy time off doing nothing for a while.

On September 11, 2005, as an avid tennis player, I was honed into the final match between Roger Federer and Andre Agassi in the U.S. Open Tennis matches on TV. Between sets, there was an advertisement about Match.com, *"You can secretly check them out… meet a man of your dreams…"*

Hmm… I was home alone, my kids were gone, and I had been feeling an empty nest... I hated the dating scene. Dating? Tennis match? I had always chosen tennis over dating men. Still, the Match.com commercial was ringing in my ear. I was still single and young at heart. Maybe, I should give marriage another try. I didn't' trust myself to pick a man. My past history proved it. Well, what the heck. I signed up on Match. com and explicitly described what kind of man I would like to meet. It was like a grocery list to cook a fine meal, but I was making a list of both what I hated and what I wanted instead. My list grew to a page long: I did not want man with kids still living at home, still married, someone with a violent temper, nor a woman beater, drug user, alcoholic, gambler, bi-polar bi-sexual, ex-convict or swinger. I did want a tall, nonsmoker with lots of patience, a self-made man with a beautiful house with lots of windows and plenty of money, and someone who loved golf, tennis or both. Furthermore, he had to be willing to live in Mississippi because I was not leaving the state that was my home.

Why beat around the bush? I knew what I wanted. I told them not to contact me if they were on the "what I don't want list" because I would run an extensive background check.

It was a genius solution to weed out the ones that I did not want. One man stood out after a month of message exchanges with an assumed name, I finally agreed to meet him. We met at Amerigo's for lunch. He showed up in blue jeans, a plain shirt, and no gold chain on his neck. He had grown up in Union, Mississippi. He was the only man that I met who didn't fall into the *I don't want* category. Somehow, we both knew almost immediately that we would be together forever. When he invited me to his beautiful home for the first time, I didn't' tell him that I had already been to his beautiful home in my dream. His beautiful home, built with real wood and glistening glass windows was exactly what I had dreamed of when I was a hungry child standing in a muddy rice paddy

I decided to give it one more try. I married for the fourth time. For the first time ever, I had a wedding ceremony and wore wedding dress for the special occasion, a celebration with my friends and all my family from Korea. My daddy on one arm and my mama on the other delivered me to my husband, thanking him for accepting their daughter. Although I was fifty years old by then, I felt like a virgin bride. As we exchanged wedding rings, I promised to my new husband and myself that this one would last.

"Why am I still hungry?"

Chapter 35

51 Hours

WHY NOT? AGE IS JUST a number, right?

It was time to finish what I had set out to do fifty years before, time to finish my "high school" education like Dam Keeper.

In November 2013, unlike the ten mile walk with my mother to register me to "high school" fifty years earlier, I drove myself in a brand new white Mercedes to the University of Mississippi.

I met with my advisor, Beth at Ventura, the Liberal Arts Office by the Grove. She pulled out an inch-thick folder of transcripts including credits from overseas college hours from 1981.

Beth said, "You need *51 hours* to graduate from Ole Miss."

"How long would it take to graduate?" I asked.

She said, "It will take you two years if you start this coming semester."

"Two years? I don't' have two years." I mumbled.

I had to think quickly how I was going to execute *51 hours*. I had no intention of spending two years in Oxford. Besides, I had a husband back home three hours away who had no clue why all of the sudden his wife—the wife of Castlewoods Country Club's owner—was in need of a college degree. He thought that I should enjoy playing golf and tennis and baby sit my grandbabies.

At this time, it was no longer about living out what I had missed in high school. I was there for no other reason than to earn an *Ole Miss* degree in my name. I wanted my college degree framed in beautiful mahogany wood and hanging on my wall as a proof I didn't fail as Koreans back home expected of me. Of course, becoming a die-hard Rebel fan, chomping on a fabulous gourmet presentation at infamous *Zebra Tent* on the Walk of Champion at the Grove, and cheering "*Hotty Toddy!*" with my boys at *Ole Miss* football games would be pure icing on the cake.

I filled out a schedule designed to complete my mission of earning *51 hours* in one-year and turned it in Beth said, "There's no way you can do that.

Did she seriously just tell me that I couldn't do something?

Beth continued, "You know, on all 300 level classes and up, especially courses you are planning to apply toward your minors, you must maintain 3.0 grade point average."

Without a blink of an eye, I nodded, and said, *"I can do it! I* ill be walking on May 10, 2014."

Shocked. Beth stood in disbelief, gathered my files, and reluctantly added me to the preliminary undergraduate candidate list.

I had set myself up for an almost impossible task. I began my 51 hours in one-year challenge in January 2013.

Little did I know that minoring in psychology, sociology, and history came with seven feet tall stacks of books to read and theses written in perfect English. In perfect English…I had never written in a single paragraph in perfect English in my whole life nor have I even spoken perfectly. There were hardly any multiple choice tests, especially in the history and sociology classes. I had been consumed with learning life skills to survive and had only read one book, John Grisham's A Time to Kill since I had been in *Meegook.*

I couldn't write an errorless paragraph, and I had to write a 1,500 words to 2,000-word book thesis in perfect English format. The odds were against me. What kept me going was Carmen's *"you can't do that!"* ringing in my ears.

I studied twelve to fifteen hours a day, seven days a week. Many nights I didn't' sleep at all. I had to plan carefully because every hour counted. I spent hour upon hour at the library getting extra help with English on every thesis I had written... I was afraid, I misunderstood key words during lectures, so I recorded every lecture and listened to them over and over...., making notes on what I missed from lectures, making additional notes on every single class. I barely was able to squeeze in my daily run from my condo to the Grove and back. Other than that, I would study, eat quickly between classes and, study some more.... I was able to squeezes in visits to see my husband back in Jackson, once every two weeks or once a month. During the six hours from Oxford to Jackson and back, I would listen to the recorded lecture over and over on my iPhone. There was no time to be wasted. That was my one year I spent in Oxford, Mississippi.

At last my day of redemption arrived.

On May 10, 2014, exactly thirty years to the date after I had graduated from Rose State Junior College in Midwest, Oklahoma, I was about to graduate from the University of Mississippi in Oxford, Mississippi.

My husband, Cecil, Jason, his wife Ash, and Ahmad, along with my two precious grand babies, Hartley and Stella stood proudly to witness my childhood dream come true.

My heart was singing as I proudly walked up to receive my degree in my silky graduation gown. As I received my degree, my five-year-old granddaughter Hartley shouted out loud to the audience, "That's my Grandma!"

How time flies. I was Hartley's age when I first dreamt of stealing Dam Keeper's high school education to make it my own.

May 10, 2014

Chapter 36

I Surrender

JAMIE WOODS, MY NEW FRIEND, and I met at an annual leukemia fund raising event. We had nothing in common—but somehow, her over friendliness with her perfect smile won over my heart. Soft spoken, and always caring, she reminded me of my long-lost friend, Woojung. Jamie was a few years younger than I, and she had never played tennis or golf, much less run a 5K race, which I love. She walked slowly and I speed walked, she would take a full twenty minutes to eat her dinner while I would cram my meal in in less than five minutes. She was like Woojung in so many ways. Thinking I was still hungry, she would always ask if I wanted to finish her meal, and she would say that she was on diet so I wouldn't feel embarrassed. Also like Woojung I don't think she had ever been hungry. For a long time, I kept my trials in life secret because I didn't think she would understand.

Despite having nothing in common, we became inseparable. We were almost always together. All my other friends were married, and I couldn't' quite tag along while I was single.

The moment she asked me where I went to church, I knew we

would be friends for life. In Mississippi, the state I fell in love with, the bible-built country, a question like that is for someone you'd like to get to know better.

"I used to a long time ago."

"Really? When?" Jamie asked

I got her attention. "It has been... Eighteen years since I last went to church, since 1994." I decided to tell her. "I attended Family Life Church on Old Fannin Road a long time ago," I said. "For about three years. And then I quit. I left God when my son died. I got angry at Him for taking my boy from me."

Jamie's beautiful blue eyes quickly brimmed with tears, "I am so sorry, Jeanhee. I didn't know. I would like to hear more about your son." Somehow her quick tearful eyes melted my hardened heart aches I kept quiet for so long.

I said, "Okay, we will someday."

"Okay, Jeanhee, when you feel like you can...."

We usually met for dinner at our favorite places where our circle of friends usually hung out, restaurants called Amerigo's or Char.

"Dessert anyone?" our server asked on this particular night at Amerigo's.

"Yes, please. Tiramisu," I said before turning to Jamie. "Would you like to share it with me?"

"Yes," she said.

"Two spoons, then?" the server asked.

I nodded in response.

"Hey, Jeanhee, let's talk," Jamie said once the man walked away.

I met her eyes. "Sure. Go ahead. I'm listening."

"I'll buy dessert tonight," she said, "if you'll go somewhere with me on Sunday."

I balked because I knew what was coming. She was about to ask me the same question she had asked a few times in the past. I always answered with, "Maybe one day."

This was the night, she had me pinned to the wall. "Come to Pinelake Church with me," she said, plunging ahead despite the look I knew had to be on my face. "I want you to hear Chip Henderson preach."

I opened my mouth to tell her no, but she cut me off with her sweet smile.

"You have to say yes because Chip is really awesome." She leaned forward in her chair. "He's a young pastor, and his sermons make sense. He's never boring. He preaches in a way that relates to our lives."

"Jamie, I walked away from church after Josh died." I didn't tell her why.

Her face fell because I had disappointed her.

"Jamie, tell me this," I said. "Has Chip ever told you he could lay hands on dead people and promise to bring them back to life?"

"Of course not. No, Jeanhee." She shook her head. "He doesn't do that. Please come and just listen to his sermon, just once? You might like it. I'll save you a seat next to me. I usually sit in the second row in the center of the church. Please come, for me—but most of all, come for yourself."

I reluctantly agreed.

"You promise?" she said, with that girlish lilt to her voice. The server walked over and set the dish of Tiramisu on the table between us.

I sighed and picked up my spoon to take a bite of Amerigo's famous Tiramisu. "Yes, I promise."

The following Sunday I found myself digging in my closet for a perfect church dress I hadn't worn one for what seemed like a hundred years. Then, I started searching for the Bible I hadn't touched since the day I walked out of Family Life Church. I dug it out of a stack of old books and blew the dust off the cover.

As I was flipping through it, I remembered a vivid dream I had the night before... What a beautiful dream that was. I was standing on a green grassy field in early evening hours, rays of light still beaming in the field after sunset. No one was there, I was alone. I have no idea how I got there. Green is my favorite color, and thick field of grass was emerald green, uncut about four to five inches tall. I'm not sure it had ever been cut and I felt like the grassy rolling meadows has been there for decades unattended. It was spread out as far as I could see. In the far distance to my left, deep forests full of trees were divided by the green grassy field. Suddenly, a large brilliant white tent with the number 333 written on the center of tent, with strings of beautiful lights hung all around, came swooshing down from heaven through where I stood, and landed perfectly in the center of the green grassy field. I physically felt the whip of soft wind on my left cheek as the tent passed down to the field. I waited for a celebration to take place. There were no hands or laborer needed, the tent was already prepared ready to be set up without any interference. It was truly amazing to witness it as the tent landed perfectly. Aww… Wow! I looked around to see who could do that, but I didn't see anyone, not a soul. How was it possible that such a large tent could land so perfectly?

I stumbled into the 11:00 a.m. service at Pinelake Church. Still remembering the swooshing wind's soft touch on my left cheek from my dream, I was met with a jumbo-sized screen in the center of the sanctuary, surrounded by stadium seats. The phrase *The Way Home* in large bold print in blood red and a picture of a large red chair underneath was projected on the screen. I liked the title, *The Way Home*, instantly I began missing my home I once called home before I ran away.

My nerves were on edge as I lowered myself into a chair next to Jamie, wondering why she had to sit all the way down front. If I'd had to choose, I would have chosen the nosebleed seats in the back so nobody would know I was there.

Several friends I knew waved hello and gave me welcoming smiles.

Pastor Chip began his sermon. He said, "Today, I am going to talk about a runaway. It's about a runaway teen ager who rebelled against his father's wishes, demanded his share of inheritance, packed up and ran away from home. He traveled around the world having fun while his money lasted. Once he squandered his inheritance, dead broke, starving, he ended up living with pigs, eating what pigs ate. He was homeless, dead broke, and hungry. At last, when he had nowhere to go, then, he remembered his father and wondered if it was too late to go back home, wondered if he would be accepted back as his son again. He decided to go back home to his father to ask for his forgiveness. His father took him back with open arms, ordered his servants to bathe him, clothe him with finest garments, and prepare for a welcome home party. The father said, "Son, Welcome Home!"

I was in tears through Pastor Chip's sermon, every word landed in my heart.

I knew it was Jesus speaking to me. I remembered His question, *"Why aren't you going to church?"* exactly thirty years earlier. His words came to life as I surrendered myself to his hands. I had no reason to bargain this time. I surrendered all to Jesus Christ! God had already given me everything I wanted in life. He was with me all along, to make sure I could live out my childhood dream. All He wanted in return from me was priceless...one phrase... I asked God, "God! Live with me forever."

I got to watch a movie of my life in my dream that night, a dream sent to me by *God.* The title of the movie was *"Number 40."*. Forty words appeared in my dream and each of those words represented a part of my past, both good and bad. I realized what was in front of me, that I was watching the threads of my life set in exquisite wooden pieces seemingly placed in their perfect spot by an unseen hand. *Redemption, Salvation, Forgiveness, Holy Spirit, Dreams, God's face, White Tent, 333, Angel, Yellow Pencil, Baby Boy...* I couldn't read all of the words. Amazingly, when all forty words found their home perfectly, they created the most beautiful wood floor I have ever seen in my home, but all the words disappeared.

Around the corner to my right, I saw a seven feet tall palm tree in healthy plumage of dark green leaves. I noticed that it was firmly rooted to the ground as if it was never going perish. The Holy Spirit was telling me that was my tree. One leaf on the bottom left was yellow, and I was looking for a silver scissor to cut it off when I woke up.

Back in November 1982, God's angel said to me, *"You should live to see your childhood dreams."*

And, I have lived...

Oh, boy, have I ever... Lived... to see my childhood dreams.

Epilogue

LOOKING BACK TO MY CHILDHOOD—to God's face carved into the rock, the starvation, the shame, and the hurt that sent me fleeing from South Korea. I can only imagine what my life would be like today if I didn't believe my childhood dreams were valid.

It has been raining non stop since yesterday–It was a perfect day to stay home alone enjoying peace and quietness, listening to my favorite song, *"I will survive"* while watching the rain drops hitting on the beautiful golf course. Suddenly, I heard a little voice whispering…, *"Climb up the ladder to the attic,"* and I did. I am a packrat. I had hardly thrown away anything. Over the years, I had accumulated so many things. My clothes from the 80s were all stacked, hung as a reminder of when I didn't' have any along with stacks of shoe boxes and picture albums.

Out of the corner of my eyes, I noticed Josh's treasure chest. I had avoided going through his old belongings for years. All his dreams were captured in that large wooden box. I carefully lifted it open and laid his treasures on the floor one by one. His football, favorite 49er's blanket, his smelly football jersey, his shoulder pads, Nike football cleats, his favorite black gym shorts, football and baseball card collections in mint condition. On the bottom I found his black planner—where he had religiously kept track of his daily squats, pushups, his weightlifting rituals as well as all of the wide receiver routes he had drawn himself. There were also several prayers he had written to God. I picked up his barely-worn 49er's jacket. He was so afraid he would damage it, he wouldn't let neither Jason nor me touch it. Underneath his jacket, there was my own beat up treasure box.

I thought I had lost it for the longest time after moving so many times. I opened the box and came face to face with memories of my childhood.

Inside was the only picture ever taken of me and my dad, a photo in Namsung in my school uniform when I was twelve years old, the notebook, and a yellow pencil. They all brought back vivid memories of the night of Baby Jesus's birthday celebration. For the first time ever, I found myself staring at the pencil as a *pencil,* instead of a as symbol of missing out on the sweet rice cake I had been promised for going to church on that cold snowy night when I was seven years old.

I held the pencil in my right hand as if I was still seven years old. Struck by the sudden urge to write, I opened the fifty-year-old notebook I had won in my first race.

I don't write well nor have I ever written anything other than book thesis.

I sat back down anyway in the attic listening to fifty years old rain drops... Meegook—Dry Bones

The story began as a Run Away story, it ended as His story.
"Thank you!"
"God of Almighty for relentlessly chasing me to come home to you!"
"Amen!"

"Oh, by the way, I am no longer hungry!"

Jeanhee Kang's favorite Bible verses

Isaiah 49:16

I have written your name in the palms of my hands.

Isaiah 139:16

I knew you before you were ever born…

Isaiah 40:13

For I, the LORD your God,

Will hold your right hand,

Saying to you,

'Fear Not,

I will help you.

&

Ezekiel 37:4

Prophesy to these bones and say to them,

"O dry bones, *hear the word of the LORD!

About Author

Jeanhee Kang came to America at age eighteen to fulfill her childhood dreams from South Korea. Kang is an active advocate for high school students' education. She mentors high school scholarship recipients at Rotary International District #6820 and disadvantaged high school teen mothers at Global Learning Center in Jackson, Mississippi. She holds a Bachelor of Arts from the University of Mississippi. She is a motivational speaker, a real estate broker with Berkshire Hathaway HomeServices and the author of Meegook—Dry Bones.

CPSIA information can be obtained
at www.ICGtesting.com
Printed in the USA
FFOW02n0641260218
45246760-45851FF

9 780998 475011